Holy Conversations

Holy Conversations

Strategic Planning as a Spiritual Practice for Congregations

Gil Rendle and Alice Mann

THE ALBAN INSTITUTE

Scripture quotations, unless otherwise noted, are from the New Revised Standard Version of the bible, copyright © 1989, Division of Christian Education of the National Council of the Churches of Christ in the United States of American and are used by permission.

"Power Analysis of a Congregation" is adapted and excerpted from *Power Analysis of a Congregation* by Roy M. Oswald, copyright © 1981, 2001, 2002 (revised and updated edition) by the Alban Institute, Inc. Used by permission.

"Finding Our Biblical Story" and "Generational Watershed" are adapted from chapters 3 and 4 respectively of *The Multigenerational Congregation: Meeting the Leadership Challenge* by Gil Rendle, copyright © 2001 by the Alban Institute, Inc. Used by permission.

"Understanding Your Church's Life Cycle" is excerpted and adapted from chapter 1 of *Can Our Church Live? Redeveloping Churches in Decline* by Alice Mann, copyright © 1999 by the Alban Institute, Inc. Used by permission.

"Healthy vs. Unhealthy Conflict Index" is adapted from *Mediation: The Book: A Step-by-Step Guide for Dispute Resolvers* by Sam Leonard (Evanston, Ill.: Evanston Publishing, 1994), copyright © 1994 by Sam Leonard and excerpted from *Behavioral Covenants in Congregations: A Handbook for Honoring Differences* by Gil Rendle, copyright © 1999 by the Alban Institute, Inc. Used by permission.

"Excavating the Religious Cultures of the Congregation" is excerpted and adapted from chapter 3, and "History Grid" and "Community Leader Interviews" is excerpted and adapted from chapter 4 of *Raising the Roof: The Pastoral to Program Size Transition* by Alice Mann, copyright © 2001 by the Alban Institute, Inc. Used by permission.

"Network Maps" is excerpted from *Studying Congregations: A New Handbook* by Nancy T. Ammerman, Jackson Carroll, Carl S. Dudley, and William McKinney, copyright © 1998 by Abingdon Press. Used by permission.

"Snapshot Page, Ministry Area Profile" is copyright © 1998–99 by Percept Group, Inc., 29889 Santa Margarita Pkwy, Rancho Santa Margarita, CA 92688, and is used by permission.

"The Abilene Paradox Goes to Church" by Jerald L. Kirkpatrick is excerpted from Congregations (May-June 2000), copyright © 2002 by the Alban Institute, Inc. Used by permission.

"A Short Guide to *Lectio Divina*" is excerpted from *Discover Your Spiritual Type: A Guide to Individual and Congregational Growth* by Corinne Ware, copyright © 1995 by the Alban Institute, Inc. Used by permission.

"An Oral Tradition Approach to Bible Study" is excerpted from *In Dialogue with Scripture: An Episcopal Guide to Studying the Bible*, Linda L. Grenz, ed., Adult Education and Leadership Development (New York: Episcopal Church Center, 1993), pp. 88–89. Used by permission, courtesy of The Domestic and Foreign Missionary Society of the Protestant Episcopal Church USA.

Library of Congress Control Number: 2003114298

ISBN 1-56699-286-9

09   VG   7 8 9 10

In memory of Andy Kreider,
who taught appropriate leadership with his life.
—G.R.

For Edward Mann, Senior,
who loved his brief stint as a teacher of management;
and for Mary McCahan Mann,
who thought I should be a writer.
—A.M.

Contents

Introduction

This is a book about planning. A primary responsibility of leaders is to help the congregation understand where it is going, why such a direction is important, and how to get there. By leaders, we mean not only pastors or rabbis, but also congregational members who hold formal and informal positions of leadership. Leaders need to help people find worthy goals. They need to have a plan to structure work and maximize the resources of the congregation. They need to build agreement in the congregation about the plan, so that people are willing to move together toward the goal.

Planning can be challenging in the contemporary congregation, where people share a common faith and values but may have very different preferences and needs. Some leaders want to reach out to potential members of the congregation, while others would prefer to direct resources to support current members. Some desire help for their own spiritual growth, while others would like a congregational initiative to address community issues that might shape or support other people. Some want to emphasize ministry with youth while others hope for help in developing small sharing groups for adults. Some want change. Some want stability. The conversation about what a congregation is to do and where it will direct its resources can be quite complex.

The Central Task of Leadership

What is a leader to do? How do you negotiate all of the preferences and opinions in order to come up with a plan that all agree with and are willing to support and work on?

Leaders can be misled by such questions, because these questions imply that there is *a* plan that will address everyone's interests and meet the congregation's spiritual and organizational needs. This dependence upon *a* plan assumes that the leader is the chief problem solver and that planning is all about finding a "solution" that will satisfy the various voices in the congregation while simultaneously addressing significant faith questions about the purpose of the congregation.

We need to state clearly at the beginning of this handbook that we do not believe that planning centers on problem solving. The leader is not responsible for discovering the perfect solution or for creating a perfect planning process to get people to arrive at a perfect plan. Instead, the task of the leader is *to help the people have a purposeful and meaningful conversation about who they are and what they believe is important to do.* It is a conversation that can, and often does, result in a written plan.

> The leader is not responsible for discovering the perfect solution or for creating a perfect planning process to get people to arrive at a perfect plan.

Planning Is More than Technical Work

We've looked at two false assumptions, that plans solve problems and that good problem solvers need plans. At the heart of these false assumptions is the idea that planning is a technical process. We commonly think of planning as identifying a particular path that we must follow to come up with the right answer. If you do A, it will lead to B, which will take you to C, all of which form a path to arrive at and get agreement on the final answer, which will tell you what you are to "do." In this technical process, we know we need information—data collected from congregational members by surveys, interviews, or group meetings as well as data about the demographic makeup of shifts in the surrounding community. We believe that we must include in the process time for biblical study and discernment, so that we do not forget that this is about the will of God for our congregation. The whole process can feel pretty technical and is often expressed in technical ways. For example, Calvin Pava of the Harvard Business School calls this form of planning "normative systems redesign," which he describes as "beginning with an extensive reformulation of the initial problem using widespread participation to involve diverse interests to focus on the redesign of the system of interrelated factors."[1] His work and understanding of planning is masterful. But the approach, as well as the language, feels heavily technical and formulaic.

We (Alice and Gil) have been clergy leaders in congregations for years (Gil as a United Methodist minister for 31 years; Alice as an Episcopal priest for 19 years), and in addition we've worked as consultants to churches for years (Gil has consulted full time for 16 years; Alice for 29 years, often alongside parish responsibilities). We have each worked with individual congregations on planning, and we have coached leaders and denominational executives on developing and implementing plans. As authors writing about planning, and as trainers who have regularly led an Alban Institute four-day education event to train leaders in strategic planning, we appreciate the technical tools and paths that have been developed. We use them—in part. We even help to develop strategies and tools to contribute to the technical stockpile. But we do not believe that there is a path, a process, a strategy that, if followed by all congregations, will lead to a perfect plan. There is no specific program or style of planning that is not marked by the assumptions or preferences of the one(s) who developed the program. This dilemma was expressed by consultant and coach George Bullard when talking about the path to prepare those who would help congregations:

> Just like consulting thirty years ago, few formal programs in coaching are process driven. Some formal programs that do exist are training coaches to carry out a specific program, project, or process. When this is the approach the focus is not on coaching a congregation to be re-imaged in God's image, *but to be re-imaged in the image of the system's creator* [emphasis added].[2]

To approach planning as a technical, preset process of following necessary steps is to arrive at the destination predetermined by the creator, the one who designed the steps.

Planning as Holy Conversation

We would like to present planning in a different light. We want to talk about the opportunity of planning as discernment. We want to talk about helping the congregation participate in holy conversation.

Planning is *conversation* because it truly is dialogue. People explore their differences and their perceptions. People risk saying what they believe to be important. The talk is full of stories, memories, and hopes—the kind of conversation that strengthens and transforms people.

It is conversation because it will follow its own unpredictable path. Different from problem solving and decision making that focuses and limits, conversation wanders and explores. It can be structured to have purpose. But conversation cannot be predicted or controlled.

Conversation is *holy* because, at its best, it is about a people's understanding of their identity as a faith community, their sense of purpose, and their relationship with God. Though the holy conversation may take a multitude of shapes and directions, at its heart that conversation centers around three critical formation questions:

- Who are we?
- What has God called us to do or be?
- Who is our neighbor?

This handbook will offer lots of technical information and tools. These are the ideas, tools, and processes we use when we work with congregations. However, we hold no expectation that leaders will follow a particular path or use specific tools and processes in predetermined ways to come up with "the plan." Instead, we hope to offer ideas, pathways, processes, and tools to equip leaders to work with a congregation in shaping their needed holy conversation. We want this handbook to be a rich resource of possibilities for ways leaders can support congregations into and through planning conversations. But we do not recommend, nor do we ourselves attempt to use, all of these ideas, steps, and tools in any one congregation. The first task of leaders is to be aware of the many opportunities and tools available to help the congregation to have its holy conversation. The second task is to choose judiciously the methods, tools, and paths to enable this conversation to happen. We hope this book will support you both in expanding your repertoire of tools for holy conversation and in deciding which tools will work best in your congregation.

> We do not recommend, nor do we ourselves attempt to use, all of these ideas, steps, and tools in any one congregation.

How to Read This Book

We have written this book to be read in a particular way. We do not recommend reading the book with an eye to developing a full-blown planning process for your congregation. There are few congregations that need—and are capable of—an extended and exhaustive planning process. Few congregations need to end up with highly specific, measurable goals assigned to accountable people or committees. Congregations do need structured ways to talk about their identity, purpose, and future, and they need a path to develop consensus and a commitment to act.

> Congregations need structured ways to talk about their identity, purpose, and future, and they need a path to develop consensus and a commitment to act.

You are invited, then, to read this book with attention to several focusing questions that will help you to discover the appropriate planning needs of your congregation. We suggest that the reader keep the following questions in mind while reading. They will aid you in deciding which of the ideas, models, and tools will be important to your congregation. (See also Resource A, page 207.)

1. What holy conversation about the congregation's future do I believe we need to have at this moment in history?
2. When I consider the full planning process, what part is most important and appropriate for us to work on at this moment?
3. What strategies can I develop and use to involve people in a structured, open, and positive way?
4. What tools or information will we need to have this holy conversation?

This book was written to introduce the stages, strategies, tools, and information needed and used in a full-blown congregational strategic plan. The reader will also find tools for assessing what is most needed and most appropriate in a specific congregation. We will offer examples and designs used by other congregations. We do not, however, hold the assumption that a given congregation will necessarily follow a full-blown planning process.

Why, then, is it helpful to read the whole book? Clearly, in order for the leader to diagnose the specific planning need of the congregation and respond with appropriate strategies and tools, the leader needs to have an overview of what is possible and helpful through planning. We will be sharing a wide array of ideas, models, tools, and techniques in this handbook. Although we never use them all in one place, we do approach each congregation with all of these ideas, models, tools, and techniques "in our back pocket" so that we are equipped to ask the focusing questions identified above and to respond appropriately. In this sense, we are inviting readers to the double task of reading not only the text of this handbook, but also the more specific needs of their own congregation.

We believe that to take this more open approach to planning is to take the risk of spiritual discernment. When a congregation follows a predetermined planning program, it will begin at the beginning, work through the steps, exercises, and information in the middle, and end up with a plan. Focusing on a preset planning program, however, limits the congregation's opportunity to allow space and time for the intrusion of the hand of God or the movement of the Spirit that might operate outside of the path of the program or work on a different timetable.

One of the intriguing stories in Hebrew Scripture refers to "pitching tent" in the book of Exodus. When the Israelites wandered in the desert, they moved when the pillars of cloud and fire moved; that is, when they had a clear sense of direction. When they were not sure about their next step, they "pitched tent" and waited to discern the next steps of their journey. This suggests that discernment does not operate on a knowable timetable. Instead, the plan and the path were developed within a discerning relationship with God. They were not able to rush ahead directly to the Promised Land. Their lingering in the desert demanded a high level of trust in God, both that their journey had purpose and that manna would be provided each morning to sustain them on the way.

In fact, the story of the Exodus can be instructive for a congregation's planning. In the wandering in the desert, it is clear that it was the journey much more than the destination that shaped the people. Had Moses been a better planner and pathfinder and discovered a straight route to make the trip to the Promised Land in a matter of months instead of wandering for years in the desert, the people may

Allow planning and discernment to take the needed amount of time.

not have been changed when they arrived. They might have arrived much the same as they left Egypt—as a slave people. It was the journey, when they had to ask questions of how they would form community and what was important about their relationship to God, that shaped them into a nation.

Allow planning and discernment to take the needed amount of time. An axiom of general systems theory is that a congregation (or any system) cannot learn faster that it can learn. Don't rush ahead, despite the reality that there will be those in the congregation or on the board—including yourself—who will be anxious to get to the "answer" and know what to "do."

The story of the Exodus also reminds us that leadership is a dance in which we seek a more distant future that is both meaningful and faithful while simultaneously managing the specific day-to-day realities of the trip. A friend who is a rabbi once shared a more contemporary midrash about the relationship between Moses and Aaron in the desert that points to this dance of equal necessities. Moses' task, of course, was to envision the future. It was Moses who went off alone to encounter God face to face. He would return with new energy, a sense of direction, and a visible radiance from the encounter. Aaron, on the other hand, was the voice of management. He structured the trip from day to day, organizing tasks, assigning responsibilities, and making decisions.

In this midrash, the teller focused on the part of the story of the delivery of the commandments. It was visionary Moses who, alone on the mountain with God, received the commandments. It was Aaron who waited below with the people, organizing daily life and trying to address the needs and anxieties of the people. The irony of this story was that just as Moses was receiving the commandment not to make graven images, Aaron was working below with the people who were busy creating these very same images in an effort to offer a visible leader ("gods . . . who shall go before us") on their journey. (See Exodus 32:1-35, especially v. 1.)

The lesson of the midrash is that both Moses and Aaron were needed for the journey. Leadership needs to search for vision and ask the big questions of purpose and identity. Management needs to take care of the travel—determining the steps to take, giving people appropriate tasks, and making clear decisions. The only risk is to let Moses and Aaron get too far apart. It was when Moses and Aaron, vision and management, got disconnected that things fell apart. A planning process cannot be all vision without structure and direction. Neither can the planning process simply be a list of tasks or exercises that will magically lead somewhere. The leader and the planning team must be willing to

> A planning process cannot be all vision without structure and direction. Neither can the planning process simply be a list of tasks or exercises.

dance between Moses and Aaron—to slow down enough to allow vision to take shape while also structuring a plan that will assist the people to move toward a future. Being flexible about the planning process, instead of rigidly following a set process, allows the congregation to be open to discernment. Structuring the planning conversation with appropriate questions and tasks allows the congregation to move ahead and make progress on the journey.

Our Assumptions

The approach to planning proposed here is based on a number of assumptions. Some can already be seen in these introductory pages. Every theory, program, or practice of planning is based on a set of assumptions about what is needed by the congregation. Planning based on the assumption that the goal of the church is membership growth will direct attention to membership and attendance data. Planning based on the assumption that the purpose of a congregation is outreach and evangelism will direct attention to community demographics. Given the importance of such underlying assumptions, it will be helpful to name some of our own assumptions that rest behind our commitment to holy conversation.

Change happens through conversation.
It is not the plan that will change people and give direction to the congregation. It is *the conversation* of the people with one another and with God—that is a part of the planning process—that changes people. In writing about the simplicity of human conversation as a force in creating global change, scientist and author Margaret Wheatley states: "There is no power equal to a community discovering what it cares about." She then goes on to say that "it is always like this. Real change begins with the simple action of people talking about what they care about."[3]

It is not the graph of attendance figures for the past 15 years that will tell you what to do. It is *the conversation about* that graph and those numbers, when people wrestle with the tension between their intent and their reality, as evidenced by the graph, that will provide direction and meaning.

The task of the leader is simply *to structure* the conversation. Indeed, our operational definition of visioning is *"a structured conversation by a group of people about what they believe God calls them to be or to do."*

A planning process provides direction and structure for conversation. The product of a planning process is not necessarily a written plan. The important product of a planning process is a conversation that changes a congregation, whether it results in a written document or a less formal set of agreements. The planning process is a way to provide the direction and the structure necessary for the conversation. As such, a plan is much more than an answer to a problem or question. It is a tool by which people have a necessary conversation about what is important.

Planning is about making decisions.
Discernment does not magically bring us to a destination without our own effort. There will be choice points along the way and we will need to decide what to pursue and what to leave behind.

There is a wonderful piece of dialogue in the movie "Wonder Boys," starring Michael Douglas and Tobey Maguire. The movie tells the story of a college professor of literature who once wrote a prize-winning first novel. He now struggles to complete a second novel, with the reputation of the first resting heavily on his shoulders. In one scene he is pictured as still writing, even though he already has more than 2,000 pages and obviously can't end the novel. When one of his prize students reads the novel, he asks her opinion. She responds, "You know how in class you are always telling us that writers make choices? You didn't really make any choices."[4]

When we neglect or refuse to make choices, the journey has no shape and the end is never in sight. Planning is about helping people make choices. It is about helping people say "this is us" or "that is not a priority for us." The structured conversation of planning helps people make decisions and choices that are authentic and faithful to their belief.

Congregations have short attention spans.
We will return to this point again in this book. There is a limit to the resources that a congregation can give to planning. To begin with, the

Pareto principle suggests that about 20 percent of the people in a congregation will do 80 percent of the work, including administration.[5] In large and very large congregations, the percentage of people engaged in the work is even smaller. Most people do not participate to help "run" the congregation. The people who are available to do the work of the congregation also have limited resources. Congregations are voluntary associations. Moreover, people commonly have to attend to family, work, health, and recreation as well as their service in the church. There is a limit to the people and energy available to work on planning.

The reality of limited resources means that leaders must honor the short attention span of the congregation. Because time and commitment are limited resources, the leaders and the planning team can only direct a limited amount of attention to the planning conversation. Few congregations, except the largest, are able to sustain a full planning cycle over an extended period. (In contrast, very large congregations commonly need a standing planning committee to plan continuously and make ongoing adjustments to congregational life.) Leaders need to ask what part of planning is needed at a particular moment. Is learning about new ideas needed now to get people ready to vision? Do the people need to dream and shape a vision for themselves right now? Do they need help now in being realistic about their current situation by looking at internal or external data? Are specific goals and programs needed now? The operative word is *now*. The planning leader or team must ask what would be the most helpful part of a structured conversation for the congregation at this moment.

The concept of successive approximations may be a helpful way to think about staging a planning process and asking what part a congregation needs to give attention to at a given moment. In behavioral psychology, many experiments involve teaching laboratory rats how to feed themselves using a Skinner box (named after behavioral psychologist B. F. Skinner). The object is to teach the rat to reward itself with food by pressing a bar located on one wall of the box that, when pressed, delivers a food pellet to a small tray located by the lever. Although easily described, that task is, nonetheless, too complex for a rat to intuit, and so the rat is helped to learn when the researcher rewards smaller progressive steps toward the final goal. At the beginning of the experiment, the food pellet delivery is also controlled by the researcher, who begins by delivering pellets to the tray whenever the rat wanders near the bar it needs to learn how to push. Being so rewarded, the rat begins to linger at the wall near the bar and ignores the rest of the box. The researcher now rewards only an accidental brush against the bar to call the rat's attention to it—and then, eventually, rewards the rat only when the bar is accidentally depressed. Soon the rat discerns the bar, learns the connection between pushing the bar and the delivery of pellets, and performs eagerly without the help or direction of the researcher.

Are congregations like laboratory rats to be put through their paces by an all knowing researcher, planning genius, or divine intervener? Of course not. The lesson of successive approximations is that when the learning task is too great, beyond ability or available resources, the leader must work on steps the congregation *is* ready to take that will move it toward the goal. To lead a focused and structured conversation, appropriate to both the congregation and its current concerns, will honor the congregation's learning process. This conversation might not lead the congregation to complete agreement and action. It will, however, offer direction for the next stage of the journey.

To switch images, leaders' willingness to do what is most needed brings the congregation much closer to a process of discernment. In a favorite description of Gil's, discernment is said to function like the headlights of an automobile on a dark evening. They don't show you were you will eventually end up. But they will illuminate the next part of the road.[6]

Planning, when well done, will bring people to points of disagreement and competing preferences.

Too often we think of planning as a way to get to quick consensus and clear goals. It is more helpful to understand that planning gives people a safe and structured place to explore what is important to them and their vision for their congregation. What is important will naturally be different for each participant.

The fact that this structured conversation leads to disagreements (not necessarily fights) is not a failure of planning but rather the object of planning. Arguing over important things is the way congregations come to agreement, not only about their own future, but also about how they, in fact, shape and reshape their faith tradition to be passed on to successive generations. With powerful insight, teacher, researcher, and author Dorothy Bass identifies "bearing the tradition" as a fundamental

task of the congregation.[7] The tradition gets shaped and delivered to
the next generation of believers using two tools: argument and accom-
modation. People argue over what they believe is most important for
their future (e.g., the style of worship or music used, programs or events
most attractive to newcomers, the basic curriculum or body of information needed by a believer, or the most effective models of evangelism
and outreach). People accommodate each other by finally making decisions about their shared future. As they do so, the next stage of the journey
gets shaped. The practice of the congregation is shifted, and the faith is
modified to speak more clearly to its present context and time.

Leaders routinely feel uncomfortable leading people into conversations of disagreement. Our innate discomfort with conflict and our
desire to please people does not make this a natural trip for many of us.
It is important, however, that leaders be aware of and acknowledge
that their role in planning is not to avoid differences and arguments on
the way to consensus or call, but to provide the structure and safety
necessary for people to have the conversation and disagreements needed
to discern their future with God.

Planning is about finding more than agreement.
There is a difference between a consensus that allows us to move ahead
and a clarity of purpose that compels us to move ahead. In many Christian
traditions, that sense of compelling purpose is spoken of as call. A person
or a people feel called to do something, not because they agree to do
something, but because they would feel unfaithful if they did not do it.

The pursuit of simple consensus, an agreement that represents the
greatest portion of the congregation, may result in congregations limiting themselves to a lowest common denominator, an idea or plan that
almost everyone agrees on, so that the congregation can remain "one
big happy family." The holy conversation of planning risks more than
the lowest common denominator. Planning helps people to risk making a commitment to a purpose that is sufficiently compelling to bring
faithful change.

The call or purpose that allows a congregation to move beyond
simple agreement helps to distinguish between issues that represent
competing preferences and issues central to the identity and purpose of
the congregation. Many of the questions that frustrate and divide people
in congregations today, in a culture of individualism, are based on com-

peting preferences—"I like this more than I like that." Ours is a culture that teaches individuals to be sensitive to their own preferences. One needs to know oneself in a new way in a time of individualism. If there are 35 brands of cereal on the shelves of a market, one does not need to know more about the cereal in order to make a choice. Rather, the shopper needs to know more about himself or herself. (Do I need more vitamins or fiber at this time of my life? Am I watching my calories, my cholesterol, or carbohydrates? Or do I just want something colorful and fun to get me going in the morning?) Similar to the choices that we make about cereals or automobiles, congregational conversations and disagreements are often driven by the competing preferences of the people, not absolutes about the faith or the faith tradition. Planning allows us to go beyond our personal preferences and to consider a call that surpasses our differences.

Planning depends upon structure.

Planning is a not a free-form, unstructured conversation. Although we will approach effective planning as more than a prescribed program of identified steps and specified data, we do not assume that a planning process happens in free-form conversations, as people gather to talk about whatever is on their minds or how to solve the most recent problem. Planning is a structured conversation. It needs direction and it needs resources. It needs to be shaped.

A good part of the work of planning must be done by the leader or leaders, outside of the planning meetings, as they continually step back and diagnose the needs of the planning process itself. (This leader might be the pastor or rabbi; a planning chairperson; or both together, sometimes in combination with a planning consultant.) What do we need to talk about? How can we help people enter into that conversation respectfully and safely? What tools, exercises, or resources are available to help? How do we take this next step?

Although not free-form, the planning must be flexible. As we consult with congregations, we have a general conversational path in mind. The beginning of this path is determined by what we have learned from the history of the congregation, its current practice, and its pressing questions. But when entering into each stage of the planning conversation, we cannot anticipate how people will respond and what direction they will take. So each step of the planning conversation is a dialogue between the leader and the process: Now that we've come this far, what do we believe will be the appropriate next step? This is not making it up as we go along. It is being willing to shape the planning process continuously in order to keep people focused on the central questions and concerns that they need to address in their holy conversation.

Can this be frightening at times when the leader is not sure about what has just happened or when the leader is not sure about next steps? Can it be humbling when the leaders must say, "I don't know. Let's talk about what we need to do"? You bet. But the truth is that this is where the fun is. As leaders, we have been called not to try to avoid this uncertainty but to walk willingly into, and lead others into, this rich and rewarding confusion. As Moredecai said to cautious and frightened Esther, "Perhaps you have come to royal dignity for just such a time as this" (Esther 4:14).

There is more than one way to plan, and it is important to be authentic. Planning must be appropriate to the needs and ability of the congregation. It must also be authentic to the leader or leaders. Individual leaders have their own styles and preferences. There are sets of skills that leaders must master. But, after mastering those skills, leaders need to be their authentic selves in order to be effective. Research continues to support the observation that effective leaders evidence a broad range of personal characteristics and traits.[8] Introverts lead as well as extraverts. Visionaries and pragmatists can lead equally well, as can women and men. Since leadership is a relationship between the leader and those who are led, the key to effectiveness is the authenticity of the relationship. Is the leader being himself or herself? Is the leader attending to the needs and capabilities of the congregation by leading people into an appropriate conversation about their future?

As mentioned above, we have, for a number of years, co-led Alban Institute four-day training events for leaders who want to increase their skills in strategic planning. Those who know us will attest that we are very different people—opposites in many ways. During one training event, one of us led a session on theory-based data gathering that had a structured progression of work designed to provide planning teams with key information. At the end of that session, the other of us commented, "Well, that was very interesting. But why in the world would anyone actually want to do that?"

The path that makes the most sense to one leader may not be helpful to another, because it cannot be followed authentically. Our differences continue to help the two of us learn from each other. Those same differences, at times, amuse and frustrate us. But at no point is it necessary for one of us to try to behave like the other in order to be an effective leader. Participants continue to say that they are encouraged and helped as they observe our differences, because the differences are evidence that these leaders also can be themselves in the planning process.

Planning is a holy and structured conversation among multiple partners—the congregation, the leader (or planning team), the tradition and texts of the faith (something that we will take up later in the book), and the discerned will of God. The leader seeks a way to ask important questions appropriate to the congregation in a way that allows all parties to the conversation to be as natural and authentic as possible.

A Final Note

This introduction to our book on planning sets the stage for the leaders to understand their role as the people who help to structure the holy conversation. To help structure the conversation, leaders need to stay in touch with a few basic diagnostic questions. Keeping such questions in mind allows leaders to reflect on how the conversation is going (i.e., the process of the conversation) as well as what the conversation is helping people to discover (i.e., the content of the conversation). Resources A and B (pages 207 and 208) offer a basic summary of diagnostic questions for leaders to use when preparing to plan as well as throughout the planning process. You may want to copy these resources to keep as a handy and constant reminder to focus your work authentically and appropriately at each step.

Notes

1. Calvin Pava, "New Strategies of Systems Change: Reclaiming Non-synoptic Methods," *Human Relations* 39, no. 7 (1986): 615–633.
2. George Bullard, "Coaching Congregational Leadership," *NETResults* 23, no. 8 (September 2002): 29.
3. Margaret Wheatley, *Turning to One Another: Simple Conversations to Restore Hope to the Future* (San Francisco: Berrett-Koehler Publishers, 2002), 22.

4. *Wonder Boys*, directed by Curtis Hanson (Hollywood: Paramount Pictures, 2000).
5. Michael Brassard and Diane Ritter, *The Memory Jogger II: A Pocket Guide of Tools for Continuous Improvement and Effective Planning* (Methuen, Mass.: GOAL/QPC, 1994), 95–104.
6. Suzanne Farnham, Joseph Gill, R. Taylor McLean, and Susan Ward, *Listening Hearts: Discerning Call in Community* (Harrisburg, Pa.: Morehouse Publishing, 1991), 27.
7. Dorothy Bass, "Congregations and the Bearing of Traditions," in *American Congregations: Vol. 2, New Perspectives in the Study of Congregations*, ed. James P. Wind and James W. Lewis (Chicago: University of Chicago Press, 1994), 169–191.
8. Ralph M. Stogdill, *Of Leadership: A Survey of Theory and Research* (New York: The Free Press, 1974).

PART ONE

What Is Strategic Planning?

Planning, and especially strategic planning, is a term used to describe a rather wide range of activities in congregations. People use the term *planning* for many events. A family-sized congregation that meets over a potluck dinner to discuss the coming year is *planning*. A finance committee setting priorities for spending is *planning*. Members of a governing board, on a weekend retreat, brainstorming possible programmatic steps are *planning*. A formally appointed planning team charged with listening to the membership, collecting community data, and developing recommendations for new directions is *planning*. In fact, these are all legitimate forms of planning if they are appropriate to the needs and skills of the congregation. It is not particularly important for a congregation to use planning terminology correctly if the direction they are following is a healthy path of discernment. It is, however, important for a congregation to have an understanding of what they realistically hope to accomplish through planning.

Part 1 of this book will address a series of questions to help leaders think through their goals for and expected outcomes from planning. It is particularly important for leaders to have a clear and appropriate set of expectations about the planning that will be done. It is, at times, equally important for leaders to be able to communicate with others what is intended by the planning effort and what can be expected as a result. The following questions and responses are offered to help clarify such intentions and expectations.

CHAPTER ONE

The Basics

What is planning? In part, this question has already been addressed in the introduction. Our operational definition of strategic planning is *a structured conversation about what a group of people believe God calls them to be or to do.* The goal of the planning process is to structure the conversation people need in order to shape agreement and enthusiasm to pursue what they believe God calls them to be or do.

Three Questions of Congregational Formation

There are three fundamental questions of congregational formation that rest at the heart of congregational planning.

Who Are We?

This is the *identity question.* Congregations are like people, or indeed, like fingerprints. There is a great deal of similarity among all, but each is curiously and wonderfully particular and unique. It makes a difference whether we are 150 years old with firmly established traditions or a new congregational start with little history. It makes a difference whether over the past years we have given most of our attention to educational programming for children or used our resources to advocate for hurting people in our neighborhood.

Like people, congregations cannot approach a future that is not connected realistically to the past. It is not enough to find programs or resources for congregational growth if we have regularly lost members for the last 10 years. The question of identity in this case means we need to become more clear and honest about who we are and why we are not retaining the members that we already had. It is not enough to plan new directions for the next year if we cannot honestly describe who we currently are and who we have been in the past.

When an individual clearly and honestly knows himself or herself, decision making—everything from choosing the next car to choosing a career path or a life partner—becomes much easier and more authentic. Clear and honest self-knowledge is a mark of personal maturity. For congregations as well, honest self-knowledge reflects a maturity that allows for clear and purposeful decisions to navigate the future. Who are we? Who are we *now*? Can we be honest with ourselves in order to be appropriate to our call for the future?

What Has God Called Us to Do?

This is the *purpose question*. Based on what we know about ourselves and our situation, what do we believe we are to do? How are we to develop or mature?

Every faith tradition involves certain disciplines—disciplines of observing holy days and liturgical seasons, disciplines of personal prayer and corporate worship, disciplines of hospitality and forgiveness to guide our relationships, disciplines of daily life to guide our participation in the larger community. By definition, these disciplines invite us to be more authentic and more fully whole than we currently are. Such disciplines are the continuous reminder that God sees in us more than we see in ourselves. A much more modest statement of our larger potential completeness was expressed by a standup comedian: "Someday I hope to be the person my dog thinks I am." To submit to the discipline of the faith means to open ourselves to change and maturity in order to move into a fuller life—to follow a path drawing us closer to what God thinks we are capable of. Is this the time when we need to reach inside to address our fears and mature our spirits? Is this the moment when we need to reach out and serve others? To what are we now called?

Two Canadian congregations in the same village in Ontario were involved in strategic-planning efforts. The two congregations were the by-products of an angry schism that divided the original congregation some 30 years earlier. Independently, as each congregation explored the scriptural base for its current planning, they came to the realization that it was time to heal the competitive relationship that had developed between the two congregations over the years. Independently, each congregation came to the realization that it was time to practice the Christian discipline of forgiveness as a way of redirecting the energy that they had invested in competing with one another. The planning process provided an honest assessment of who they were, which clarified their purpose for the next few years. It was time to heal their own spirits as a way of inviting new energy, new members, and new participation in the larger community life of the village as healthy congregations. Healing the history that kept them from full participation in the community would not be their task for all time. However, their planning clearly showed them that living as healthy, respectful, and noncompeting congregations was their purposeful call for their immediate future.

Who Is Our Neighbor?

This is the *contextual question*. Where do we live in time and space?

It has been said that the secret of life is knowing what time it is. Is what we are doing, at either the personal or congregational level, appropriate for this historical moment or this personal moment? For example, congregations wrestle with this issue of time when they ask whether singing hymns from an old hymnal provides music understandable to a new generation. It is more common for younger people to have grown up in homes with stereos instead of pianos; for this generation, sing-a-long means lip-syncing the music of a pop star instead of singing hymns with a group.

The issue of space is, in part, about where we are located, but it is also about the area of influence that we have developed. Are we connected, are we called to be connected, to the people who geographically surround our congregation or to another describable audience not defined by geography? To be a people of faith is both to search within ourselves for growth and also to reach out to others in service and invitation. Christian congregations may use the word *evangelism* to describe the work of invitation. Synagogues may speak of outreach to Jews without a congregational connection. Who are those others? How do we recognize and know them? How do we speak and relate to them in ways that can be heard and understood?

While these three very basic and simple questions of congregational formation may be universal in application, the responses need to be honest and unique to the individual congregation. Planning provides an excellent means to structure conversations around these three formation questions to help congregations discern the responses that uniquely belong to them.

Different Forms of Planning

The language of strategic planning is popular now, and it is commonly used to describe a broad array of planning processes. There are, however, different forms of planning with different goals. It is the responsibility of leaders to assess the which form of planning is appropriate and to establish a planning process or direction that addresses the current need.

There are essentially three forms of planning and each tries to answer a different set of questions. Resource C, "Types of Planning," in the resource section (page 209) provides an overview of these forms of planning for the leader's review or for use as a handout to help a governing board or planning team clarify its goals and identify the kind of work they are setting out to do.

Problem Planning

The first type of planning is *problem planning*. It is essentially the problem-solving method applied to a clear need. The problem-solving method includes these steps: (1) identifying and clarifying the problem; (2) brainstorming the available options to address the problem given the available resources; (3) choosing one or prioritizing several options; (4) implementing a plan to fix the problem. Problem planning answers the question, How do we fix something to get us back to where we were before the problem? An example would be repairing a broken heating system. The problem is clear and it is appropriate to move directly to a solution. The planning process moves quickly through the problem-solving steps.

Problem planning is short-term work that is designed to fix things. As such, this is not a form of planning that moves a congregation significantly ahead. Instead, it returns the congregation to the level of stability or the path of ministry established prior to the disruption caused by the problem. The timetable for this planning process is immediate. Since it taps into problem solving, the most familiar form of leadership, it tends to happen naturally and quickly as people see a problem and move directly to action.

This form of planning is common and natural; therefore it is not easily thought of as planning. It is, however, included in this description of forms of planning because it can be misused. Problem planning works best when the congregation is actually faced by a problem— something that, by definition, is fixable. Yet, increasingly congregations are faced not by problems but by changing conditions over which they have limited or no control. Since these changing conditions require the leaders and congregation to learn something new, it is not helpful to use problem-planning strategies to move directly to action. Changing demographics in the community surrounding a congregation

Problem planning is short-term work that is designed to fix things.

is an example of a condition that cannot easily be addressed by problem planning, even though the consequences of the changing demographics may create problems for the congregation. Because changing demographics are well beyond the control of the congregation, these demographics cannot be fixed. Instead of trying to control the changing demographics, leaders must help their congregations understand the changes surrounding them in order to respond appropriately. Similarly, the decision to relocate or to build new facilities is not most helpfully addressed through problem planning. These are not problems but decisions about opportunities influencing the development of the congregation in which the congregation has to learn new things about itself. In this case, the leader is trying to move the congregation to a new understanding of life and ministry, and not return it to an earlier time of stability.

Problem planning depends on a very well known and commonly used methodology of problem solving. In many cases this is a reversion to known skills for leaders. One of the realities of systems under pressure is that when we don't know what to do, we do what we know. Doing what we know often means that we fall back to common and familiar problem-solving procedures that are not helpful or appropriate when addressing uncontrollable conditions or new challenges. To move inappropriately to problem solving is to short-circuit the purposeful structured conversation needed to discern a new path into the future.

Developmental Planning

The second type of planning is *developmental*. This is often referred to as long-range planning. Problem planning, as noted above, asks how do we fix something and return to the way things were. Developmental planning asks the question, "What's next?" Now that we have come this far, what are the next steps?

Developmental planning is based on a fundamental assumption that things are good, that what we are currently doing is faithful and authentic. It assumes that the congregation has a clear sense of its identity and purpose and has been actively at work living out that identity and purpose. The primary goal of developmental planning is to determine the next steps, building on what is presently being done.

This kind of planning cannot be addressed with the same expectations of immediate results as problem planning. Developmental planning depends upon some level of assessment or at least a common remembering of what one has been doing and why. Developmental planning requires some level of diagnostic or evaluative work to describe

> **Developmental planning asks the question, "What's next?"**

where the congregation is currently located on its path of ministry in order to plan the next steps or phase of the journey. Because of the need to assess the congregation's current place in its life cycle or program, there is a need for some basic descriptive data gathering and structured conversation. This may be simply remembering why the congregation set out on its current path and what has been accomplished so far. Developmental planning connects the future to the present so that an authentic identity and sense of purpose for the congregation can be appropriately moved ahead to that future.

Note that both problem and developmental planning are forms of planning in which the future can be directly inferred from the shape of the immediate past. As such, they are examples of planning using gap theory, which looks at the gap between present reality and a preferred future. The basic path of gap theory planning progresses through the following logical steps:

- Here's where we are now.
- Here's where we want or feel called to be in the future.
- Here's a description of the gap between where we are and where we want to be.
- Here's what we have to learn or do in order to get there.
- Here are our options for making the changes to get there.

As you can see, the last steps in gap theory planning are very much like problem solving. However, the primary difference between the two is that in gap theory planning, an accurate and honest description of the present and future situation needs to be much more intentionally developed. And, in gap theory planning, the goal is for the congregation to be different from the way it was before the planning.

Frame-Bending Planning

In the third type of planning, *frame-bending planning*, we move beyond the form of continuous thinking found in developmental planning, in which the future steps are directly tied to past and present performance. It is this third type of planning, frame-bending planning, which is most appropriately described as strategic. Here, the guiding assumption is quite different from developmental planning, in which a congregation assumes that they are currently involved with faithful and appropriate ministry. Instead, the guiding assumption in frame-bending planning is that things are not working and are not faithful and appropriate to the present setting of ministry.

We might use an analogy from the world of art to highlight the difference between frame-bending planning and the other two types we have just discussed. Think of an oil painting. Problem planning resembles the work of a restorer: repairing damage and returning the canvas to its original state. Developmental planning resembles a landscape painter's current work in progress, emerging on the canvas day by day in successive approximations of an inner vision. Both the restorer and the landscape painter operate within known rules of the art world. Frame-bending planning is more like the radical artistic innovator who bends the frame on a painting in order to disturb the viewer's expectation about what constitutes art. Frame-bending planning, in a similar way, is a process designed to highlight and disturb expectations in order to make space for the possibility of an unseen or unconsidered future.

There is a little art gallery near one of our offices that shows paintings in which the artist has literally bent the frames on which the canvas is stretched. The wooden frame is not simply cut to form a shape different than the expected rectangle; it is actually curved to give depth to the work as one section reaches out to the viewer while other parts of the frame hug the wall in an expected way. The paintings are not particularly attractive on their own. However, the unique frame captures attention and provides a sense of energy that leaves the viewer wondering about the nature of art.

A Philadelphia-area congregation was confronted with the need for frame-bending planning. The congregation was founded in 1776 and was proud of its start at such an important moment in American history. Their history and their preferences led them to preserve their sanctuary and other parts of their facility in a style authentic to their beginnings. The floors were uncarpeted hardwood, they still used pew boxes with swinging doors, and there was poor lighting throughout. It was difficult for this congregation to understand that they were maintaining a facility that was uninviting to the many young families with children that increasingly surrounded them in the community. Out of respect for their history, they shushed children whose voices carried in the hard-surfaced space and they glared at children who swung on the pew box doors and whose feet clattered on the wooded floors. This congregation needed to confront the reality that their commitment to preserving history did not serve their purpose as a congregation located in a community of young families. They needed to do deep frame-bending thinking to capture a sense of who they were called to be in their next chapter of life.

When the purpose and ministry of a congregation are clearly out of sync with the location and time—when established practices are clearly not working—the congregation must become more strategic in its planning and ask more than developmental questions about what to do next. A strategic situation requires the leaders to back up and revisit the formation questions: Who are we? What are we called to do? Who is our neighbor?

Revisiting formation questions is not easy work. This is the essential task when redeveloping or transforming a congregation and is widely recognized as some of the most difficult work for leaders to do. It is similar to the task of reforming our own personal identities when we have outgrown a former identity. For example, such reformation might include stretching to become responsible adults just as we were learning how to be adolescents; becoming a partner in marriage after understanding ourselves as single adults; or becoming parents having just accustomed ourselves to being a couple. Each change in our life situation carries a threat to the way we presently see ourselves. Such identity changes quite naturally involve discomfort and resistance.

Frame-bending planning is more difficult for a congregation than problem or developmental planning. Frame-bending planning takes more time. It engenders more resistance. Indeed, frame-bending planning carries some risk to the leader, who can easily be sabotaged as she leads the congregation into the disruption that comes from addressing formation questions.[1] Structured strategic-planning conversations require more careful shaping, because the level of learning to be managed is dramatically increased. Because established congregations with a comfortable, although inappropriate, identity will feel threatened, it is often helpful to visit the formation questions over a longer period of time. Such frame-bending work can be done while also working on developmental questions about what's next in areas where developmental program planning may be appropriate. In fact, it is helpful to have one or more developmental questions to work on while doing the more difficult work of visiting the strategic formation questions. Deciding what to do next in some area of the congregation's life that is going well and moving this part of the congregation's work ahead gives members a sense of accomplishment. The feeling of making progress in some area helps the congregational leaders to be more patient and persistent as they work on the harder tasks of frame-bending planning. When members have a sense that the congregation is moving ahead in some areas, they will sustain the exploration of the deeper questions of frame-bending planning.

> When the purpose and ministry of a congregation are clearly out of sync with the location and time, the congregation must become more strategic in its planning.

What Is Appropriate Planning?

The word *appropriate* will be used repeatedly in this handbook. It means that leaders need to go beyond generic responses and address the specific situation facing the particular congregation. Appropriate leaders say what people are able to hear, to help people accomplish what they are able to do. Appropriate planning needs to be connected to an accurate description of the history, capacity, and context of the individual congregation.

For years researchers have been trying to figure out what makes a good leader. Over recent decades they have focused on three streams of inquiry.[2] The first is a focus on the person of the leader and is known as *trait theory*. While this research has not produced conclusive evidence

> **Appropriate leaders say what people are able to hear and help people accomplish what they are able to do.**

of the effectiveness or necessity of any set of traits, it nonetheless pursues the interesting question of what personal or personality traits best describe a leader. The results of this research support the current understanding that no one personality type or set of traits is the best or preferred for leaders. However, this research continues to document the wonderful and varied ways in which people have put their own personal and professional traits to good use as leaders.

The second stream of inquiry is *situational theory*, which suggests that the characteristics leading to effective leadership depend on the leader's situation. While Martin Luther King, Jr., was a skilled preacher and pastor, situational theory suggests that he became a national leader because the situation needed his voice. Similarly, this stream of inquiry might explore the geographic or cultural setting that would call or move a skilled pastor to found and develop a megachurch rather than a more traditional congregation.

Transactional theory, the third stream of inquiry, looks at the relationship between the leader and the people or system being led. It is here that questions of appropriateness are most important. Transactional theory suggests that leadership is effectively practiced when the leader learns who the congregation presently is, what it naturally does, and with what gifts for ministry it is equipped. The leader then must learn the context or environment in which the congregation lives and assess the future potential or possibility for this particular congregation. The leader then invites the people into a conversational relationship to explore what is important, what is meaningful, and what lies within their capacity. Appropriate transactional leadership requires a relationship and a dialogue about important things.

Appropriate, or transactional leadership, requires diagnostic work by the leader. The leader must make some informed decisions about what questions must be faced and what hope or possibility can be offered. Such diagnostic work must be appropriate to the specific congregation. For example, much, if not most, of the literature on congregational effectiveness is currently being written by and about our largest congregations. These congregations most easily fit the broader culture, because they offer options: the opportunity to affiliate with a variety of small groups and, at the same time, a sense of anonymity. These advantages do not easily belong to small and midsize congregations, which have their own mission, skills, and capacities. Appropriate leadership means the leader must diagnose the setting of the particular congregation and then ask what information from the current literature the congregation needs to, and is able to, address. The practice of one congregation, or one kind of congregation, does not necessarily fit other congregations. The leader works with others to determine both what is needed as well as what actions are appropriate for them in their own setting.

Diagnostic work is not necessarily done in isolation. For example, it is helpful for leaders to invite the congregation's governing board into conversation about their goals and the expectations they have for a planning process. (Resource C, "Types of Planning," on page 209 is a handy way to begin that conversation.) If the goals for planning are developmental, the board can celebrate and affirm the present faithful ministry being done and then point to the particular programs or administrative areas that need developmental attention. Focusing the task and the questions to be addressed by a planning team or a planning process in this way is diagnostic and appropriately helpful. When the planning needs are frame bending, it is even more important to have the board and other key leaders involved in a shared diagnosis. The leaders would together identify and acknowledge their need for deep work right at the beginning of the planning process. Acknowledging the need to ask deeper formation questions at the beginning of a planning process helps to reduce the resistance to the more difficult work along the way.

When a governing board or leadership group does this diagnostic work, it is common for individuals to have different expectations, some developmental and some frame bending. When leaders engage in conversation about the types of planning and the specific needs to be addressed by a planning process, they naturally identify areas of strength and faithfulness that need developmental attention; at the same time, they often encourage exploration of the deeper formation questions if this is needed. Perhaps the children's education program is a current strength. Because it is already faithful and vital, it may need only developmental attention. At the same time, planning worship may be a frame-bending task requiring leaders to revisit the formation questions of identity, purpose, and context to ask, not if worship is still comfortable and pleasing for people who currently participate, but if worship is supporting participants' spiritual development and addressing the needs of the people in the community who do not yet participate.

How Much Time Will Planning Take?

Again we need to look at the various forms of planning and their attendant goals. Problem planning is *immediate*. It often can be accomplished in one or two meetings. The problem is identified and then either worked on by the group or delegated to the appropriate person or group.

Developmental planning commonly takes *three to six months* to complete. Time is needed to build consensus about what part of the congregation's life will need developmental attention. Data needs to be gathered to remind people of what has already been done and with what results. Data is also gathered about the potential for the future, which will guide the developmental steps. Because developmental planning will require some, if not many, people to change their current practices, time is required for people to learn about, adjust to, and accept the changes identified.

Frame-bending planning is deeper and more difficult, often requiring *12 to 18 months* (or more) for a congregation to complete the planning. Time is needed prior to beginning a planning process to educate leaders and interested members even about the need for and the potential of such planning. It is not uncommon for this preplanning alone to take from three to nine months, since it builds the interest and commitment necessary for the people to face into the deeper questions of spiritual identity. (In part 2 of this book, we will look at the full outline of a complete planning process that will include this preliminary work of congregational training for planning.) A significant amount of time is also needed for the leaders to make the necessary adjustment in their roles, practice, and alignment of resources as they uncover new needs and opportunities through their planning.

This preparatory work in frame-bending planning is often critical to help people learn about themselves, their current reality, and their

need for change. As mentioned in the assumptions listed in the introduction, one of the common realities in planning is that congregations
have a short attention span. Volunteer organizations, such as congregations, are dependent on the commitment of busy leaders. Because of
this, congregations cannot give uninterrupted time and attention to a
planning process. They can only face difficult questions of discernment
in intermittent segments of conversation. The time committed to frame-
bending planning must be longer because the amount of learning to be
done by already busy people is great and must be paced over time.

Notes
1. For a fuller understanding of this risk, see *Leadership Without
   Easy Answers* (Cambridge, Mass.: The Belknap Press, 1994)
   by Ronald Heifetz and *Leadership on the Line: Staying Alive
   Through the Dangers of Leading* (Boston: Harvard Business
   School Press, 2002) by Martin Lansky and Ronald A. Heifetz.
   Their attention to safe space and the need for a holding environment is evidence of the critical need for leaders to make this
   difficult work possible while managing or preparing for the
   resistance that it will engender.
2. Rodney W. Napier and Matti K. Gershenfeld, *Groups: Theory
   and Experience* (Boston: Houghton Mifflin, 1973), 135–145.

CHAPTER TWO

Questions to Ask Before Planning

Expectations determine results. To expect too much is to produce dis-appointing results. Expecting too little can lead to producing less than is possible. Like other situations in our life and our leadership, appro-priate expectations at the beginning produce realistic results.

In this chapter we will be looking at expectations. Begin with your-self. Then involve others in the conversation about what is hoped for. What is it that you hope to accomplish with *this* planning cycle? (There will be other planning cycles. How much can you hope to accomplish this time?) What resources do you have? What will limit your results? Of course, the act of planning itself will give you a much more accurate assessment of such questions. But, as you set out, what do you expect?

Will Strategic Planning Fix Our Congregation?

The process of planning is not a search for the perfect congregation. By human nature, it is common for all of us to look at our lives, our work, or the organizations we belong to, and to see the problems and limita-tions rather than the strengths and blessings. Given the choice between half empty and half full, one must choose to see the cup as half full. Without an intentional choice, we will default to a problem orientation and look only at what is wrong with our situation. In times of great change and challenge, it seems easier for congregational leaders to re-cite the congregation's problems, and to note what is missing, rather than to see the gifts of the congregation. Under stress, congregations commonly turn to planning as a way out—a way to solve problems, a way to direct or redirect the pastor (with whom they may be wres-tling), or a way to talk about what is wrong with the congregation and correct it. In other words, planning is seen as a way to fix the congrega-tion, to perfect it.

The Bible and Perfection

Curtiss DeYoung, a theologian and mediator of racial differences, reminds us that the search for perfection is not the point of the biblical story. Quoting the work of theologian Justo González, DeYoung notes, "We are comforted when we read the genealogy of Jesus. . . . The Gospel writer did not hide the skeletons in Jesus' closet, but listed them, so that we may know that the Savior has really come to be one of us—not just one of the high and mighty, the aristocrat with impeccable blood lines, but one of us."[1] The message of the Hebrew Scriptures is similarly rooted in stories that include heroes and leaders with severely flawed histories. And in the early Christian community, Paul encouraged individuals both to deal faithfully with their differences and to honor one another. Paul did not suggest that the people needed to become a perfect congregation. Consider Paul's admonitions to the Corinthian church about their divisions. (See 1 Corinthians 3.) He asked individuals to refresh their memory of what they had received and what was expected of them. He did not describe a perfect community.

The planning process is about discernment, not perfection. To be authentic is to know and accept the self, to use our identified strengths and to acknowledge those parts of us that are limited and incomplete. The process of planning encourages the congregation to discern: What are the congregation's strengths? What incompleteness does the congregation need to accept?

The SWOT Step

The natural reaction or response is to fix problems, to correct and compensate for weaknesses. Biblically, we are challenged to be authentic and to use the strengths and gifts we have been given. Planning offers the same encouragement. Fundamentally, either in practice or in theory, the basic idea that rests at the heart of most planning processes is the SWOT. SWOT is a description of the Strengths, Weaknesses, Opportunities, and Threats that face the congregation. These are the internal and external conditions that influence the congregation's change over time. The process of planning allows leaders to describe these conditions in order to discern a faithful future. The SWOT analysis is most commonly graphed in the following way.

Internal Inside the Congregation	STRENGTHS	WEAKNESSES
External Outside the Congregation	OPPORTUNITIES	THREATS

SWOT Analysis

The task of the planners is to offer an honest and complete description of the congregation's setting in each of the four quadrants of the model. Importantly, leaders need to distinguish between internal and external measures—what is it like inside the congregation, and what is it like in the community or the culture outside the congregation? When looking at *strengths* and *weaknesses*, the leaders look *inside* the congregation—to explore what is and what is not done well in terms of programs and congregational care. Leaders often explore the history of the congregation to identify the commitments that were made or not made over the years. This step includes an acknowledgment of the congregation's strengths and weaknesses, including financial and physical resources.

When looking at *opportunities* and *threats* the leaders are looking *outside* of the congregation, to describe the congregation's setting or context, both local and global. The leaders look at the community, to see what changes offer the congregation opportunities for, or threats against, their life and ministry. The leaders look at the larger culture, to assess how changes over time enhance or limit the congregation's ability to live out its goals and purpose.

Planning processes offer a multitude of ways to create a full and balanced description—to look inside and outside the congregation—so that discernment of the present is reality based and plans for the future realistically hopeful. The more honest, thoughtful, and revealing the description, the richer the opportunity for discerning a faithful and hopeful future becomes. Although planning can take a variety of forms, the essential analysis is the same: When you look inside the congregation, what do you see? When you look outside the congregation, what do you see? In what ways do these observations help you to understand yourself, your purpose, and your mission in the next few years?

Leaders and planning teams face a most critical juncture when they complete their SWOT analysis. We have often noticed, over the years of working with congregations, that when the analysis is complete, the attention of the leaders turns naturally and powerfully to one or two of the four quadrants. Interrupt your reading for a moment to guess which two quadrants leaders most often focus on after the descriptive analysis is done.

If you pointed to the negative descriptions of the situation, both internal and external, you are right. *Leaders most naturally zero in on the weaknesses* of the congregation as their focal point for planning. In addition, *they mistakenly fixate on the threats* that loom both in their community and in the wider culture. Such a focus may derive from the false search for the perfect congregation. The presence of any weakness seems to demand a correction, even if it means paying less attention to the strengths and gifts available to the congregation. It is these strengths and gifts that will support movement into the future. Focusing on weaknesses alone often leads congregations to miss their real potential for ministry.

Planning is best used to describe our real gifts honestly. It allows us to understand the limits we face, so that we can authentically use our gifts to address our purpose. Planning—other than problem planning—is not effective if it primarily describes what is wrong with us that needs to be fixed. We have worked with congregations in which the members describe themselves as elderly and note that they do not have a youth group. These congregations automatically conclude that they need to redirect their attention and resources to develop one or more youth groups in the next few years. We have worked with congregations that have exceptional programs in education but worry that they do not have multiple worship settings like the successful congre-

gations trumpeted in their denominational literature. We know congregations that effectively use small groups but that are concerned they
do not have the pastoral-care visitation teams, which have been identified as important to growing congregations. Without regard to the gifts
and graces that do belong to their congregations, these leaders set out
to reinvent themselves in new, and often unfitting, ways.

The Philadelphia-area congregation mentioned earlier, founded in
1776, provides an excellent example of a faith community misdirected
by their attention to weaknesses. This congregation discovered that
the average age of membership was in the high
60s, and that they had few children involved in
their programs. Looking around them in the
community, they saw a growing number of
young families with children, so they set about
fixing themselves. They told their pastor to

> The presence of any weakness seems to demand a correction, even if it means paying less attention to the strengths and gifts of the congregation.

make connections with the community and invite the families and children to church. In an anxiety to fix, the congregation did not examine
their strengths and weaknesses. They were surprised and distraught to
realize that they did not have many gifts for working with children.
They had even fewer gifts for developing a more inviting worship style
in a facility fully designed to reflect their history. The congregation's
unwillingness to look at the strengths they could develop and use in
their changed setting greatly limited their future. This congregation
tried to become something that they were not.

Planning does not fix a congregation. Planning does not make it
something that it is not. As leaders invite the congregation into a planning process, it is important that the participants understand that the
structured conversation at the heart of planning is not meant to make
the congregation look like some other successful congregation. Rather,
the structured conversation is meant to help the congregation be the
people that they most effectively can be, given their history, their resources, and their call.

Is Planning Complicated?

It need not be. In fact, in most congregations, simplicity serves the
planning purpose better than complexity, as long as the goals of the
planning are met. Whether developmental or frame bending, the planning

process is trying to answer a question, address a need, or discern a direction. The work outlined in the planning process needs to be focused on producing structured conversations that will, in fact, directly contribute to addressing that question, need, or direction.

Nonetheless, the preference in planning is simplicity—the more direct path with fewer steps. In the sciences, simplicity is known as elegance. When given the choice among multiple research methodologies or multiple explanations, scientists prefer the methodology or explanation that is simpler and more direct. Living systems can only count on a limited economy of resources in an environment that carries multiple demands for survival. Simpler, more elegant solutions and strategies honor the limits of that economy. This is equally true for voluntary associations, such as congregations, that organize around the economy of attention, time, and interest available to its people.

> **Simplicity requires the leader to ask: how much can we do, how far can we get at this time, and what is the most direct path that we can manage?**

Simplest does not necessarily mean fastest. The leader may need to slow down the work and pace the learning over a longer period of time. This is especially true in frame-bending planning, where people need time to think about new questions and behave in new ways. Certainly such challenges cannot be moved through quickly. But neither can they be complicated or overly demanding. Simplicity requires the leader to ask: How much can we do, how far can we get at this time, and what is the most direct path that we can manage?

Many planning programs are less than helpful to congregations because they lack appropriate elegance. In some cases, the planning program is oversimplified because it follows a predetermined planning path. This path is usually based upon the assumptions of the plan's author or program designer, who has a vision about what a vital congregation is supposed to look like or do. The planning steps of such a predetermined program raise questions, surface data, or direct conversation that will quickly move the congregation to behave like the model church, whether this image fits the call of the particular congregation or not. In other cases, the planning program is overcomplicated and overwhelming. Gathering too much data or addressing too many questions in search of the perfect congregation can sink a planning team into a swamp of information that overwhelms rather than providing helpful focus.

Once again we return to the importance of *appropriateness*. A primary task of the leaders is to step back continuously to ask: What is actually needed? What question, resource, or activity will best help the congregation take a next step? The hard work of leadership is not to discover how many steps are in a planning process or how many resources or kinds of data are available to a planning team. The hard work of leadership is to determine which steps or resources will best help the congregation move forward.

This handbook is, in fact, designed around these central principles of elegance and appropriateness. In part 2, the multiple steps, stages, and processes of planning will be outlined. We do not, however, intend for a congregation to follow all of the steps from beginning to end. Whether designing a unique planning process for one's congregation, or evaluating how to use any parts of an established planning program, the leader has the responsibility to ask what part of this larger process needs to be done now. When planning is understood as discernment, it becomes a means to a much longer and more faithful process of questioning, in which leaders and members are continuously engaged in conversation with one another and with God.

> The hard work of leadership is to determine which steps or resources will best help the congregation move forward. The leader has the responsibility to ask what part of this larger process needs to be done now.

As in all significant relationships, we do not need to have every conversation immediately. Rather, conversations occur over time. Conversations change in order to focus appropriately on the question at hand. When congregations understand planning inappropriately, as a discrete management tool or organizational task, they conclude that the planning process needs to have a clear beginning and needs to produce a formal planning report to direct everyone's effort.

The standard of appropriateness sets people free by continuously asking what would be most helpful, how much can the congregation do, and how much time and resources can the leader and congregation give to this work now. Elegance occurs when we find the simpler path that both keeps us connected to the planning questions and helps us find a way forward.

What Are the Benefits of Planning?

Leaders commonly think that both the benefit and the outcome of planning is a written plan. More formal congregations often like to create a multilevel outline with multiple goals, strategies, activities, needed resources, and the person or group responsible for each step.

Such clearly outlined plans can be very helpful to a congregation that has charted a path and wants to move ahead in an organized fashion. In less formal congregations, or in congregations driven more by vision than plans, such a detailed outline is not required and may even be distracting. To focus only on a formal written plan as the product of a planning process may miss or discount a number of other clear benefits and gifts of planning.

One of the critical benefits of planning is that it gets people talking and thinking about their identity and purpose. Even if little needs to change, the conversation enables people to identify and claim who they are and what they are to do as a faith community.

Another benefit of planning is that it allows a congregation to identify and claim its own story within the biblical story. It is not sufficient for a faith community only to say who they are. The faith community also needs to know and say how they connect to and reflect some part of the larger faith story in which they live. Helping a congregation locate itself in the message and images of their biblical tradition can be very powerful.

Here are two examples. A congregation that Gil worked with developed an image and even a logo of themselves as a flying chicken. An urban congregation with a long history of community involvement,

> Helping a congregation locate itself in the message and images of their biblical tradition can be very powerful.

they explored their biblical center through planning and believed that they were called to "mount up with wings like eagles" (Isaiah 40:31). However, the congregation also recognized a number of times in their recent history when they had the opportunity or challenge to soar as an eagle in addressing neighborhood issues but had "chickened out." Their conclusion was that they were called to be flying chickens. Their challenge was to face their fears and mount up with wings nonetheless. As you might imagine, their perceived relation to the biblical story provided clarity and direction for their decision making over the next several years. As they faced difficult decisions, they reminded each other that it was in just such a situation that they were called to mount up and fly.

Similarly, in another congregation, the leaders were challenged to find their connection to the biblical story. After some conversation, members reported with conviction that they had found five stories, two of which they wished they were living and three of which they wished they were not. Such stunning clarity is hard to come by, but can be the benefit of the structured planning conversation.

Gil has included additional information about connecting congregations to the biblical story in his book *The Multigenerational Congregation*.[2] You will find a brief introduction to this process, along with information on where to find additional examples, in Resource D in the resource section of this handbook.

The power of the planning conversation is that it also offers the benefit of new perspectives. One of the currently popular definitions of insanity is doing the same thing one has always done and expecting different results. In a changing world, people of faith need to find new paths and practice new behaviors to make a difference. Faithfulness is a matter of shaping and changing the way we live out our own faith, so that we can share it with a new generation in a fast-shifting culture. Such rapid change is discontinuous. That is, it does not follow a straight, unbroken path that allows us simply to extend what we already do and know. We are more often required to jump ahead or to radically shift in ways that sometimes seem less than logical and feel less than comfortable.

In a presentation on discerning the path of God in our lives, psychologist and popular author M. Scott Peck suggested that one criterion for knowing that you are responding to God is sensing, even to a small extent, that what you are proposing is crazy. Were it not crazy and unusual, Peck suggested, we would have figured the question or challenge out ourselves and we would be discerning our own logic rather than the movement of God. It is God who breaks through with unusual and unexpected demands. Such discernment takes time, thought, and prayer. It takes the conversation of the community to perceive a different path or even the need for a different path. Will entering the planning process guarantee such breakthroughs? Of course not. But planning does offer an opportunity for this discernment by providing new topics for people to talk about and suggesting that they hear in fresh ways. This is a clear benefit of the planning process.

A final core benefit of planning in a congregation is that it offers a very diverse group of people a way to negotiate their racial, ethnic, cultural, and multigenerational differences. These differences need to

be negotiated in a healthy congregation, or else they become a battle-
ground as portions of the congregation seek control. Planning provides a means of identifying and negotiating these differences in a
structured way.

What Should We Ask Before We Begin?

There are reasons to be careful and cautious about leading a congregation into planning. Leaders need to consider six limiting conditions.

Where Is the Congregation in Its Life Cycle?

Like all living organisms, congregations are at a particular stage of life. We
understand this easily when we think of a human life cycle, which follows
through stages of infancy, youth, adolescence, young adulthood, and so
on. We know from experience that these different stages of life each
present unique challenges that have to be addressed. Maturity is related to being able to be appropriate to where one is in this life cycle
and addressing the necessary tasks and challenges at the right time.

Congregations also have a life cycle that can be thought of in se-
quential phases. In Alice's book on redevelopment, *Can Our Church
Live?*, she has described this life cycle (reproduced as Resource E on
page 217).

It is often helpful for the leader to locate the congregation in the
life cycle. For example, after giving each member of the governing board

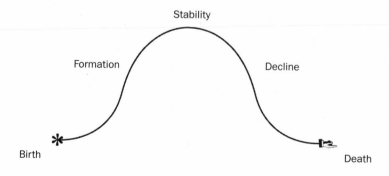

Life Cycle of a Congregation

a handout on the life cycle of a congregation, explain the idea. Then, invite each board member to place an X on the handout, indicating where in the life cycle he or she thinks the congregation currently lives. It is common for people to use more than one X as they realize that different groups within the congregation have, in fact, different perceptions of which stage of life their congregation is involved in. After the members have placed their X or Xs, it is interesting to explore why—and with what evidence—people located their marks as they did.

Although there are certainly no hard and fast guides about congregational life cycles, there are several rules of thumb that you might want to keep in mind in preparing your congregation for planning:

- Congregations experiencing the upside of the cycle, or formation, are often best served by developmental planning. These congregations tend to still be close enough to their most recent driving vision that their worship, programs, and congregational life appropriately reflect their understanding of the formative questions of identity, purpose, and context. The developmental question—"What do we do next?"—is the question commonly asked on this side of the life cycle.
- At the top of the life cycle, the period of stability, the congregation tends to be at its most satisfied and comfortable position. They have worked hard to fulfill their vision. They are enjoying the product of their efforts to be faithful. They have done what they set out to do. Planning, indeed leadership of any type, is most difficult at this stage of the life cycle. Having come to this point of satisfaction, why ask how things might or should be different? Preplanning study and discussion is perhaps most critical at this stage, where people need to be a bit discomforted about their satisfaction. It is unnatural for congregations to leave the stage of satisfaction and move back to formation (congregational renewal, revitalization, or redevelopment). Beginning the planning conversation goes against the congregation's tendency to hold on to the period of stability for as long as possible. Frame-bending methods are especially appropriate at this stage of stability and into the subtle beginnings of decline (which we might call stagnation).

- As congregations enter into a noticeable decline, frame-bending methods are once again an effective means of structuring conversations about why change is needed and why just working harder at the same tasks is insufficient. As in any personal or organizational life cycle, the sooner we face the reality of decline, the better we will be able to adapt.
- The further down the decline side that a congregation goes, the less likely it is that developmental planning alone will turn things around—though developmental planning elements are certainly employed as part of a larger redevelopment or revitalization process. The process will need to be increasingly frame bending.

What Is the Level of Trust?

Planning can seem like a safe way to take on difficult topics. Frequently, the consultants at the Alban Institute are asked to work with a congregation on planning. But behind this request to plan is a hope to resolve an argument between parties of the congregation. Embarking on a planning process might also be a veiled effort to get the pastor to do something that he or she is not willing or able to do. Planning in such situations is conceived as a strategy to change someone else. Planning can also seem like a safe way to try to influence change, without having to admit that there is a disagreement among people or between groups.

Planning actually requires a fairly high level of trust in a congregation. The leaders, or an identified planning group, are going to look intentionally at the state of the congregation, collect information, offer a diagnosis or description of what is needed, and suggest changes. This cannot be done in an atmosphere of conflict or distrust.

The issue is not whether there is disagreement in the congregation. In fact, disagreement—the ability to hold more than one idea at a time—is a sign of systemic health. (A congregation that is fully happy and satisfied—that can only hold one idea—is a congregation that can only do what it has always done. Such stability in an environment of rapid change is a formula for death.) The ability to hold multiple ideas, while people disagree with one another, requires trust.

The presence of differences is healthy and needed. The decision to enter planning depends upon whether the disagreement about differences is healthy or unhealthy. Resource F on page 228 summarizes characteristics of healthy and unhealthy conflict identified by consultant and author Sam Leonard, who is a practiced dispute resolution specialist. A review of these characteristics by an individual leader may elicit evidence to suggest whether it is wise to proceed with planning. Inviting board members or others into such conversations about the congregation's health is even more helpful. Being able to talk about differences using the characteristics of healthy conflict actually builds trust within the congregation. The Alban Institute's experience in working with congregations suggests that the healthier the congregation, the higher the level of conflict the congregation can manage while still maintaining trust.

Another way to measure the trust and level of conflict in a congregation is to ask if there are subgroups in the congregation that have hardened into closed groups, such as oppositional camps, with competing identities and agendas. Most congregations do have natural subgroups—the old guard and the new guard, the youth and the adults, those who give priority to mission and those who give priority to member care, those who appreciate the pastor and those who feel less close to him or her. These subgroups are not only natural, their differences are the occasion of maintaining a necessary and healthy dialogue about what is important. The critical issue is whether these subgroups have hardened into oppositional camps. Do these subgroups talk and work against each other? Do groups hoard information, so that others seem not to know basic things? Do members and the pastor feel pressure to identify with one of the groups, so that there is little or no neutral middle territory for people to live in? When people discuss their differences, do they talk about the issue itself or do they talk about the people who take a different position from them?

In the midst of unhealthy conflict, or when subgroups have hardened into opposing camps, planning tends to become a pawn in the battle. It is necessary to postpone planning and to work instead on conflict management or behavioral covenants.[3]

What Are the Memories or Results of Previous Planning Efforts?

Past experience tends to set the expectations for present efforts. On the one hand, if the congregation has planned well in the past, a review of the previous efforts and previous planning reports honors the past and lends credibility to the present planning effort. If past efforts went well, folks will probably have a lot of energy and enthusiasm for a new effort.

On the other hand, the congregation may have had difficulty planning in the past—perhaps it never agreed on a direction, or perhaps the plan was not acted upon and people remember, "We planned but did nothing." In such a situation, people may feel cynical about entering into planning once again. A review of past planning and the memory of those efforts will at least let others know that the planners are aware of past experiences and, at best, may help to reveal that more was done to fulfill the former plan than people realize. A review of past planning also offers insight about the present planning process being developed. In either case, people's past experience with planning will to some degree affect how it is received—either hampering or supporting new efforts.

How Much Energy and Leadership Is Available for Planning?

Planning in an institution or large corporation may be a formal part of developing a business plan or realigning the work. As such, planning becomes a priority that demands the attention of the leaders as a central part of their work. It becomes a recognized part of employees' daily or weekly work agenda for which they are held accountable. In a congregation led by volunteers, planning coexists with the management of ongoing congregational life, the design and implementation of current programs, and the individual spiritual needs that leaders bring with them to the congregation. Planning must share attention and resources, including available time and energy, with a larger constellation of activities and efforts.

In part 2 of this book, we will discuss who is most helpful to include on a planning team. The leader needs to consider both the people who will be planning and the congregation's current projects, in order to assess realistically how much planning is possible without overwhelming the system.

A related question is whether the congregation has sufficient energy and resources to enter into planning at all. Planning assumes that the congregation is willing and able to change. Change takes effort. There are some congregations that do not have the resources to change. Perhaps members have diminished interest and energy to mount new efforts. The members may be older. They may be parents, overwhelmed by raising young children. Perhaps the congregation is small, and there is no available margin of energy or interest to work at something new in addition to what is already being done. There may also be external reasons a congregation would not have enough energy or resources for planning. For example, when a major employer in town lays off hundreds of folks, many members will need to direct their energy toward providing for their families. Perhaps the church building is in disrepair from deferred maintenance and requires all available resources. Or, the community surrounding the church may have shrunk, limiting the possibility of finding additional people—or additional resources, energy, and commitment to do something new.

There is no objective measure of the amount of change that can routinely be managed by congregations. However, the leader is advised to take a guess. It is not helpful, and may be dispiriting and damaging, to lead people into a change that they have no hope of accomplishing.

Is There a Common Faith Tradition?

Some congregations have clear ways of accessing their resources of faith (for example, Bible or text study, disciplines of prayer, and practices of hospitality). When present, these practices should be built into the planning process. They form a common language and experience that will keep the planning close to the faith tradition and allow it to be more than an organizational activity.

Other congregations are more vague about how they engage their faith tradition. In past decades, when many faith traditions could assume that they had a central role to play in the American culture, it was sufficient to invite people into membership as a way of participating in the faith. It was not as common for people to explore individually why and how they might most meaningfully participate in the faith. Leaders rarely asked whether new members might best deepen their faith through action, by sharing key ideas and beliefs, or by personal and perhaps private devotions and disciplines. Today, these questions are vital.

Planning can be hampered by a limited self-awareness of how the people of a congregation naturally engage their faith. In such a case, the preplanning or preparation phase might involve some spiritual exploration. This exploration will provide a language and a shared set of understandings that will support a later planning effort. For example, leaders and members in the congregation may be helped by exploring the four spiritual patterns identified by seminary professor and family therapist Corinne Ware in *Discover Your Spiritual Type*.[4] This exercise will provide the congregation with a framework for placing itself in the spiritual landscape.

What Are the Gifts and Limits of the Planning Leader?

As mentioned above, part 2 of this book includes a discussion of the traits and skills of people who will be most helpful with the planning process of the congregation. The personal skills people can contribute to congregational planning need to be considered. Do the people most available to plan have the temperament and experience needed, or does a lack of available skill suggest a more cautious approach to planning?

Do you and other potential planning team members have the temperament to work with ideas and experience a bit of discomfort? Can you see new potential without needing to immediately act? Can you and the group see the whole without being driven to fix the parts? Can planners work inclusively, making room for the ideas of others and listening deeply to those in the congregation? Are planners comfortable with repetitive communication, so they will be willing to teach others, continuously, what they have found and remind others what they are doing?

Do you and others have experience planning? In the contemporary workplace people are increasingly responsible for planning. The experience is invaluable and can be used in the congregation—with some necessary translation to a faith-based volunteer organization that is not strong on quantifying results. People with planning skills and experience deepen the potential for successful planning in the congregation. They tend to have a better grasp of the goals and process of planning and maintain a helpful perspective. It can be limiting to work with people with no prior planning experience. The planning goals may need to be more modest and the time given to the planning process may need to be extended.

Seasons-of-life questions also need to be considered. Clergy near retirement have different issues and ask different questions about the future than do clergy who are early or midlife in their serving role. Clergy in the last year or two of service to a particular congregation may have difficulty looking too deeply into the future of that congregation, or may want to imprint their leadership inappropriately and control the life of the congregation beyond their actual tenure. Similarly, the age and tenure of the laity leading the planning process can influence or limit what can be hoped for.

The Journey Continues

There is no perfect plan. There is no perfect planning process. In fact, congregations mature, develop vitality, and become faithful not because they have a plan, but because they have risked asking and answering the formation questions: Who are we? What has God called us to do? Who is our neighbor? Planning is simply a wonderful and structured way to help a congregation risk such a conversation.

It is important for leaders to shape the general path of planning. But the leader need not, and perhaps should not, know every step to be taken along the planning path or the destination at which the congregation is to arrive. To know every step and to prescribe the destination is to not allow any room or opportunity for the involvement of the Spirit. God's intention also needs to be a part of the conversation. Planning has been connected with discernment several times in this handbook. Planning, like discernment, is not about knowing the final destination. It is about illuminating and committing to the next part of the journey with the conviction that it will lead to a faithful destination.

This section of the handbook is intended to help leaders be more clear about the purpose of planning and to consider variables that will influence the planning. In the next section, we will identify the components of strategic planning that provide specific direction, tasks, and processes upon which a structured conversation of discernment can be based.

Notes
1. Curtiss Paul DeYoung, *Coming Together: The Bible's Message in an Age of Diversity* (Valley Forge, Pa.: Judson Press, 1995), 51–52.
2. Gil Rendle, *The Multigenerational Congregation: Meeting the Leadership Challenge* (Bethesda, Md.: Alban Institute, 2002).
3. See Gil Rendle, *Behavioral Covenants in Congregations: A Handbook for Honoring Differences* (Bethesda, Md.: Alban Institute,

1999). The question in congregations is not whether people will disagree. Disagreement should be expected as natural and healthy. The more important question is how people will treat each other when they do disagree. This handbook offers ways for congregation to develop clear behavioral agreements about how people will be expected to live together when they disagree.

4. Corinne Ware, *Discover Your Spiritual Type: A Guide to Individual and Congregational Growth* (Bethesda, Md.: Alban Institute, 1995).

CHAPTER THREE

The Full Planning Process

We turn now to an overview of a full planning process. Seeing the full model, and its component parts, allows leaders to think about what is already in place in the congregation and what may be most helpful to work on in a planning cycle.

An Overview of the Planning Process

See the next page for a full-blown planning process. As we walk through this outline of a planning process, remember that the limitation of a graphic representation is that the process quite naturally appears to be linear. The outline suggests that if the leader helps the congregation start with congregational training for planning, then works through the various stages of planning, and attends to appropriate feedback and Bible or text study, the congregation will end up with an action plan. Life is not that orderly. Rather than indicating a start and an end, the graph can be used by leaders to assess where in a planning conversation the congregation is at the moment, what work would be most helpful for this holy conversation (that is, where on the graph we should be giving most of our attention at this time).

As discussed earlier, developmental planning may require only some external and internal data gathering, a brief review of the mission statement or vision to affirm previous assumptions and agreements, and more attention to the goals and objectives or the action plans. This planning work can often be done quickly. Frame-bending planning needs to go much deeper, and requires increased energy and motivation from the leaders. In an initial planning effort for frame-bending work, a reasonable goal might be to address only the congregational training stage. As will be noted below, this congregational training stage is the place to shape the questions that will make others want to plan. It may take months to work through this initial training stage, before people are

A Road Map to the Full Planning Process

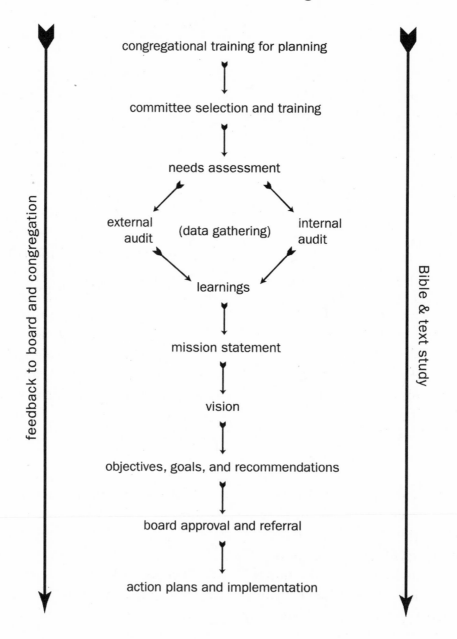

willing to move on to select a committee. The committee might require another significant period to do only the needs assessment and data gathering.

The leaders also need to consider where the appropriate and available entry point into planning process presents itself. While the planning process looks very linear when presented on paper, there is not a prescribed starting place that will lead to a known end. Leaders need to look for what type of structured conversation the people are willing and ready to have and then, if appropriate, use that conversation to enter into the other parts of planning. The beginning of planning might be Bible or text study, which raises questions about purpose and identity, which, in turn, motivates people to prepare to plan. It may take an initial round of data gathering and a brief SWOT analysis to inspire people to plan. (SWOT is discussed in chapter 2.) Or perhaps an initial process of seeking feedback from the congregation, through small group discussion, will shape initial questions that, in turn, will prompt further steps in the planning process. While the full outline of the planning process suggests step-by-step, linear planning, leaders can and must choose a process that is appropriate to the individual congregation.

> While the planning process looks very linear when presented on paper, there is not a prescribed starting place that will lead to a known end.

Phases and Tasks of the Planning Model

Keeping in mind the need to be creative about the planning process, the model noted above will be broken into three phases:

- *Getting Ready*—preparing the people to plan
- *Collecting Data*—gathering relevant information
- *Shaping the Future*—wrestling with, "So what?" What does the information mean?

There are also two continuous tasks that must be followed throughout the planning process:

- *Giving Feedback to the Board and Congregation*
- *Engaging in Bible or Text Study*

Let's begin with the two continuous tasks. We will later devote separate chapters to each of the three phases of the planning process: chapter 4 (Getting Ready), chapter 5 (Collecting Data), and chapter 6 (Shaping the Future).

Giving Feedback to the Congregation

This may seem to be a peculiar place to start the discussion about planning, since there is nothing yet to feed back to the congregation. It is addressed first because it is a practice that should run throughout the planning process. Planning changes the rules by which the congregation lives, and it is not helpful to surprise people with the changes. One of Gil's favorite maxims is, "Surprised people behave badly." Failing to be in continuous dialogue with the board and congregation can surprise people and will invite resistance to implementing the plan.

Following is a picture of the basic dynamic created by establishing a planning team:

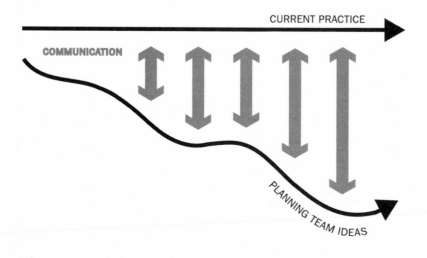

The top steady line is the current practice of the congregation. It is the known path that has been established in the congregation—the way it worships, the people it seeks to include, the programs it offers, indeed, the very way in which the people think about their congregation. Governing boards, in fact, have a responsibility to protect and preserve that known path. Standing committees, such as governing boards, protect organizations by not allowing them to stray too far off a known path, thereby reducing the risk of jeopardizing the future by walking into unknown territory. The common starting position for most standing committees is to begin by saying no to new ideas. Standing committees often evaluate this year's vacation Bible school by asking how much it looks like

Surprised people behave badly.

last year's, or evaluate this year's Christmas Eve worship service by considering whether it carried forward the traditions from last year.

The descending line represents the work of the planning team. Planning teams are initiated because of a need to learn something more or different about the congregation. (Looked at in this way, a search committee is a type of planning team, because its task is to describe the congregation and its future, in order to communicate this information with potential clergy candidates.) By definition, the planning team is asked to see new things, read new books, talk to people, look about the community, and, in fact, to begin thinking about the congregation in a new way. The graph indicates that the longer the planning team does its work, the more it will differ and be distanced from the established way of thinking about the congregation. The planning team will be freer to think about and suggest new actions. It is to be expected that the planning team will come out at a different spot from the governing board. It is not only to be expected, it is to be hoped.

As appropriate as these different organizational roles are for the board and the planning team, the real dilemma comes at the point when the planning team shares its new insights, its new way of thinking, and its recommendations for the new future to the governing board and congregation, which has an established way of thinking and the responsibility to protect the established practice of the congregation from too much risk. For the planning team to go about its work in silence and to present only its results to the board and congregation is a recipe for a guaranteed and quite natural "no."

What is missing is the ongoing communication throughout the process—the connections, indicated by the vertical arrows, created by dialogue between the established path of the congregation and the new learnings of the planning team.

Extraverting the Planning

The communication between the planning team and the congregation needs to be intentional and ongoing. Using the difference in preferences found in the Myers-Briggs Type Indicator may be helpful here.

The Myers-Briggs Type Indicator instrument identifies and measures our individual preferences by exploring two functions and two attitudes that guide people's behavior. Each person has a preferred way of living in the world and will use their preferred style whenever the situation does not require a change. Our preferences can be deeply set and will typically guide the way we make it through the day.[1]

One of the attitudes measured by this instrument is "direction of energy flow." It is the difference between *extraversion* and *introversion*. These terms describe how we like to communicate with the world (they do not measure or indicate shyness). An extravert is a person that is oriented to the outer world and typically thinks out loud. Extraverts are public people who are energized by contact with others. In most situations, extraverts prefer to talk, and can find themselves saying too quickly what they are thinking, giving them the reputation of shooting from the lips. When talking with extraverts, you hear what they are thinking, and it is clear how they arrived at their decisions.

Introverts, by contrast, are inner directed and typically think before speaking. They are more private persons who gain energy by being alone, where they can think things through. Introverts often speak in conclusions since they have done most of their thinking internally, where it is hidden from others. When working with introverts, the decision they propose may be quite clear, since it is offered as a conclusion. However, you may not be aware of the process or information that determined the decision.

In the United States, approximately 60 percent of females and only 40 percent of males are extraverts—a gender difference that has helped to establish the stereotype of the chattering woman and the uncommunicative man. Recognizing that it is a stereotype, let us use it for a moment: When asked how her day was, an extraverted woman might begin by sharing what time she got to work, who was there already, what people were wearing, whether anyone had started the coffee or refilled the empty pot, how many meetings she attended, and so forth. At the end of the extraverted answer to the question, the listener will have a fair idea of how the speaker's day unfolded. By contrast, the introverted man, when asked the same question about his day, might pause for a moment and say, "Fine." For the introvert, that answer would seem sufficient and informative. It is important to recognize that both responses, extraverted and introverted, are accurate and appropriate. The extraverted woman thought out loud about her day. The introverted man thought privately about the day and then announced the conclusion. In both cases, each spoke about his or her experience.

The extraverted response was full of information that helped the listener understand the conclusion, and to which the listener could respond. While the introvert's response was accurate, it was much more difficult to understand and engage. A similar principle applies to the planning process. The task of the planning team is to *extravert* its work! A planning team that works in an intro-

> A task of the planning team is to extravert its work—to work out loud.

verted manner—disconnected from the board and congregation—may produce accurate and insightful recommendations. But, since the team will offer conclusions or recommendations that are difficult to trace or engage, the introverted planning team may invite normal, natural, and healthy resistance.

A task of the planning team is to extravert its work—to work out loud. This is done through continued conversation and reporting about the planning work, its insights, questions, and dilemmas along the way. This planning extraversion can be done in many ways of which the following are only examples:

- Planning teams can creatively look for natural ways, such as newsletters or printed announcements, to give and receive feedback about what they are doing and learning.
- Planning teams usually report to the governing board at regular intervals. It is helpful to move beyond reporting how many times the team met and what they did, and instead to use the time with the board to share new insights and learnings. Although the information comes without conclusions or recommendations in the earlier stages of planning, continuous sharing of the insights and information helps to prepare the way by offering the board members clues about why the planning team might want to finally recommend a particular path.
- Planning teams can report and dialogue with intact groups within the congregation: adult education classes, committees, choirs, and other groups.
- Some planning teams prepare an occasional "state of the congregation" report or call for a town meeting. A full congregational

meeting can be used to talk about what the team is doing and learning.

- A common practice is to organize small group meetings at the church and in people's homes, and to invite all members and participants of the congregation to talk with the planning team for an hour.

In every conversation, it is important for the planning team members to remember that feedback means talking *and* listening. Information must freely travel both ways. The planning team has a responsibility for sharing what they have learned in their work. The team also has responsibility to listen to the responses of others in the congregation and treat the responses as additional information needed to help shape their planning work.

Engaging in Bible or Text Study

Planning in a congregation must be more than an organizational exercise driven by logic and problem-solving skills. It must also be faithful to the purpose of the congregation. The difference between organizational planning in a business and congregational planning and discernment is the need to make room for the presence and the movement of the Spirit of God.

In order to make room for the Spirit of God, the planning team must also help themselves and the congregation engage in dialogue with the traditions and texts of its faith. As we identified in chapter 2, we often ask the planning team (by themselves or in dialogue with the board and other members) to identify the biblical story or stories that they are currently living. Once found, the story is then studied by the planning team. *Studied* means that the story is explored, conversation is structured to learn how this story represents or does not represent the current experience of the congregation, questions are asked about the hopes and concerns that get raised by the story, and insights from the conversations about the story are collected. Gil has written in greater detail about using the congregation's story in

> In order to make room for the Spirit of God, the planning team must also help themselves and the congregation engage in dialogue with the traditions and texts of its faith.

his work on multigenerational congregations. A portion of Gil's description of the importance of story and the use of biblical stories in the planning and leadership work of the congregation is included in Resource D on page 211.

Hopefully the planning team will approach its biblical or textual work as exploration, not as a classroom exchange where the teacher tells and the students receive. In this biblical study as exploration, the congregational members can play with the story or text. It can be returned to when needed. Individuals, in their own private mediation and prayer time, can ponder the text. The story can generate lively discussion or argument within the planning team. The story can be part of a governing board meeting. It can be used wherever and whenever there is need to pry loose the too-tight logic and organizational good sense, which can be both accurate and distracting from the freedom and challenge that is a part of faith.

Recognizing that the two continuous tasks of communicating feedback and Bible or text study must be woven into the ongoing work of the planning team, let us now turn our attention to the phases of the planning process.

Notes

1. For more information on the Myers-Briggs Type Indicator, see David Keirsey, *Please Understand Me II: Temperament, Character, Intelligence* (Del Mar, Calif.: Prometheus Nemesis Book Company, 1998).

PART TWO

Taking the Process Apart

In order to know what part of the planning process is most helpful and appropriate for a congregation at any given time, the leader must have an awareness of the full planning process. This section of the book will outline a complete process, with the expectation that the leader will continuously ask what part of the planning process and what structured conversation will serve the congregation best. We have already acknowledged that few congregations can do it all. As volunteer organizations with limited resources, including people's time and attention, the planning process serves the congregation best when it is appropriate to the questions that need to be addressed. One of the most helpful insights for parents as they raise their children is that it does not help to provide answers to questions that their child is not asking. The better parenting strategy is to recognize, look for, or help one's child find a natural moment in which a driving question is shaped, and then provide just the information that the child needs. The first strategy, providing answers for unasked questions, often forces information on the child and engenders resistance. In the second strategy, looking for or helping to frame questions, the parent waits for a time when the information is wanted. If the information given is helpful, the child will return for more information as his or her questions change. Leaders, like parents, must resist doing too much. Leaders, like parents, need to be appropriate to the questions being asked and exercise good timing with their responses.

> The planning process serves the congregation best when it is appropriate to the questions that need to be addressed.

Following is the outline of a full planning process, which can be adapted for use with either developmental or frame-bending planning. It has been broken into its component stages and parts to allow us to discuss ideas and offer suggestions to help guide your planning. Instead of being a checklist of planning activities, this description of the component parts of planning is much more like a road map. Like most road maps it offers both direction and choices. In this part of the handbook, we will uncover the parts of planning to help you plan your planning trip.

CHAPTER FOUR

Phase One: Getting Ready

The phase of getting a congregation ready for planning typically involves three stages from the full-blown road map presented in the last chapter.

congregational training for planning

committee selection and training

needs assessment

Congregational Training for Planning

In many ways, this is the most critical phase of planning. Planning requires getting the congregation—the board, the leaders, and the full congregation—ready for planning, usually by giving people a reason to plan.

The primary goals of this planning-to-plan stage, which must be addressed on their own time line, include helping people to

- be aware of their actual situation, with some sense of what they can and cannot control;
- become motivated by framing their hope or identifying their discomfort;
- engage new ideas;
- be open to the greater purpose (the call of God, the movement of the Spirit, the congregation's vision);
- feel somewhat uncomfortable or incomplete about limiting themselves to what they currently do or who they currently are.

The First Signals

It is common for the clergy and staff of a congregation to be the ones who first sense a need for planning. These are the people in the congregation most responsible for the health, life, and mission of the congregation. The clergy and the staff are the people who read most of the books about congregations. These are the people who lie awake at night wondering, dreaming, and worrying about the congregation. These are the people who have position descriptions specifying what is to happen in a congregation that is to be different or better than it is now and the ones held accountable to make it happen. It is no wonder that the first signals for the need to plan come from this corner of the congregation. The clergy and staff, who are most aware of the need to dream bigger, often begin a planning process by simply announcing that it is time to plan. This creates tension. In a sense, this announcement can be received as pressure to move toward a new answer about congregational life, long before there is a shared question.

The Happiness Trap

When clergy and key leaders in congregations sense a need for change, they are in a difficult position. On the one hand, many members give lip service to the need for bold visions. On the other hand, members judge their leaders based on how satisfied everyone is perceived to be. Leaders are rewarded for their leadership in worship when people are satisfied that the liturgy, music, and preaching serve well the largest number of people in the congregation. Youth leaders are rewarded when both parents and youth are satisfied with the programming and the relationship between leaders and youth. Leaders are rewarded for their pastoral care when the people in the hospital are satisfied with the visits of the clergy and staff, when shuts-ins are visited, and when clergy respond quickly and appropriately to those in crisis. Because of this reward system, which is so directly based on keeping people happy, the clergy and staff of congregations work long and hard at making things right for people. This is an increasingly difficult task in the current American culture, where individual preferences are honored. In our present cultural context, multiple and competing preferences live side by side in a congregation. Multiple and competing preferences in a congregation make the task of keeping people satisfied complex and difficult, and clergy, staff, and key lay leaders often find themselves over-working to make things right for people. Even with extraordinary efforts, many clergy and staff members find themselves caught in a double bind, as they cannot satisfy two or more people who hold opposing preferences. Nonetheless, most clergy and leaders of congregations respond by working hard to help people feel satisfied about their congregation.[1]

Clergy and other leaders then are rewarded for making and keeping people satisfied with their congregation. However, satisfied people—by definition—do not seek to change. When teaching or consulting with leaders, Gil often asks them, "When was the last time you woke in the morning, looked into the mirror, concluded that just about everything in your life was good and going well, and then asked yourself, 'Then what should I change today about my life?'" Having everything the way we like does not prompt questions about changing things. The more natural movement is to act to preserve what is going well.

> Congregations do not easily enter into conversations about having bigger dreams, doing more faithful ministry, or addressing threats when they are satisfied with the way things are going.

Similarly, congregations do not easily enter into conversations about having bigger dreams, doing more faithful ministry, or addressing threats when they are satisfied with the way things are going. They need, in fact, some sense of dissatisfaction about the way things are in order to think about making things different. People need to have a question in order to want to search for a new answer. People need to sense pain in order to search for relief. People need to have a new and greater hope for being faithful and vital in order to risk letting go of the known.

Clergy, staff, and key lay leaders, then, are caught in a difficult position. It is no surprise that when clergy and other leaders announce that it is time to plan, the planning process is often greeted with passivity, disinterest, resistance, or even hostility. When not motivated or directed by a good question or a healthy sense of dissatisfaction, people have little reason to talk about things being different. The congregational-training stage is the opportunity to help others want to be different, want to be more than they currently are.

It is usually preferable to do the congregational-training work with a larger rather than a smaller group of people. The audience for the initial planning stage needs to be large enough to embed sufficiently motivating questions or discomforts in the congregation and the larger group of leaders. Later, the actual planning work will be done best by a smaller planning team of five to seven members—enough person power to accomplish the work, but not so many people that the work will bog down with competing voices and opinions. (The size and makeup of the planning team will be addressed below in the committee selection and training stage.)

The congregational-training stage is a time of teaching and learning that allows people to

- *See what is possible.*
- *See what is controllable and not controllable.* (It is commonly estimated that 60 to 70 percent of the variables facing a congregation—such as surrounding demographics—are beyond the congregation's control.) To help people see what is and is not controllable has the effect of empowering people, since it allows them to stop blaming themselves or their leaders for not fixing what is unfixable.
- *Become appropriately dissatisfied.* A statisfied congregation is one of the hardest congregations to lead, since it doesn't want to go anyplace. But an overly dissatisfied congregation, one that has become angry and blaming, is equally hard to lead. Members have personalized the congregation's difficulties and blame the leader(s) in an effort to avoid the work of changing themselves.

Moving to the Balcony

The congregational training stage is most effective when conducted from balcony space. *Balcony space* is a term used by Ronald Heifetz in his role as director of the Leadership Education Project at the John F. Kennedy School of Government, Harvard University.[2] Balcony space describes taking a position sufficiently distant from day-to-day operations and worry in order to see the larger picture. The opposite of balcony space is *reactive space,* in which the leader must constantly deal with the immediate person or problem that confronts him or her. If you are a person who typically makes a "to do" list, to remind yourself of the tasks that need to be done, consider what it would be like to make your list for the day as usual. Then, soon after getting to work, you realize that you might as well throw your list away because of the un-expected people or problems that meet your arrival. Working in an environment where you must constantly respond to what confronts you is reactive space. The dilemma is that the tasks present in that reactive space may not be the most important and may not allow the leader to work most effectively.[3]

Moving to the balcony allows leaders the necessary space and distance to learn and to diagnose the situation. This is where leaders read books together, where they talk about what they think is happening in or to their congregation. Balcony space is where there is room for prayers and discernment for the congregation. Like excellent leaders of any complex organization or business, clergy and staff know that they must get at least one foot out of the congregation to think deeply about what is happening within the congregation and to dream of the future. Clergy and staff commonly use personal retreat days, continuing education events, and staff retreats to create balcony space. Balcony space is critical to the congregational-training stage of strategic planning as well. The clergy and staff need to get other leaders and interested members up on the balcony with them to provide both the motivation and the information needed to help people want to plan.

An initial question is who to take to the balcony. Who do you want to take onto the balcony with you to learn something new, to think differently about the congregation, to begin to build energy and interest in what might be different and what might be more faithful? Starting with the right people can make a dramatic difference in a planning process.

There will, no doubt, be some times when the leaders will want to do some balcony work with the full congregation—or at least as many people as respond to the invitation. Teaching and sharing moments for the whole congregation around the issues behind planning are critical. More will be said about this later. But, for the moment, we will consider the people to invite first onto the balcony.

The Invitation List: Who to Invite to the Balcony

Imagine a congregation in which agreement and disagreement on a critical issue is dispersed across the membership in a normal distribution. A normal frequency distribution produces the familiar bell-shaped curve and the congregation would look something like this:

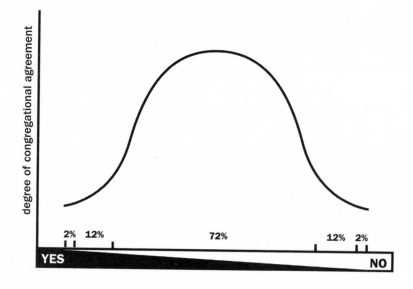

At the outer edges of the curve, the two tails of the curve on the ends are *the positional 4 percent*. These people are *positional*, meaning they have taken a position that they won't change. They have already made up their mind about the congregation, the leaders, or the question at hand. In a normal frequency distribution, about 2 percent of the congregation will say no to any issue, no matter what it is. If the leaders in a Christian church say that Sunday morning is the preferred time to worship, this 2 percent will say, "No, that won't work here." They are simply oppositional people. These are the folk that clergy, staff, and key lay leaders worry about the most. Leaders spend time trying to convince, placate, or befriend them. The work is often laborious, time-consuming, and unproductive. These negative positional people do not change, and they leave the leaders feeling critical of themselves for not succeeding.

Commonly, when leaders are exhausted or sufficiently frustrated from dealing with the negative 2 percent, they like to go to the positive 2 percent, who tell them that everything they do is good, is to be appreciated, and that they are right, no matter what the issue. These agreeable people are positional as well. If the clergy or leader were to say to this group that the facilities are never heavily used except on the Sabbath and that the congregation ought to consider using the program space to open a Taco Bell franchise, these positive positional people might well answer, "Great idea, Pastor! Great idea!"

This *positional 4 percent* (2 percent negative, 2 percent positive) of the congregation often gets a good amount of attention. When something new is being planned or a controversial issue is to be negotiated, clergy and others often quickly assume that it would be helpful to include these people in the process. Leaders consider including the "no people" because they think that if these folks serve on the committee and help make the decision they might stop resisting things and acting badly. They are eager to include the "yes people," because the work would go more smoothly and quickly, and everyone would feel better about himself or herself.

The dilemma is that, in reality, this is the only 4 percent of the congregation that *cannot* help in planning, decision making, negotiating, and discerning. These people may, in fact, be fine people who are capable of much good. However, positional people cannot hold more than the one idea that they already have, the idea that represents their position. The positional people cannot help in the balcony work. They are not good candidates to invite to balcony space. They are also not good candidates for the planning team, which we will discuss later.

Returning to the congregational frequency distribution for the moment, the next group to describe is *the central 72 percent* of the congregation, the people who are neither in *the positional 4 percent* nor *the productive 24 percent* (to be described next). This, again, is a portion of the congregation that leaders worry about when making congregational decisions and creating congregational conversations. This large group of members and participants tend not to get involved and are often difficult to engage. Much of the reason for this group's distance from critical decision making is that they tend not to see the decision as critical for them. They do not easily join in the search for new answers, because they tend not to see the questions. These are the people who come to the congregation for more personal reasons. They seek a place of spiritual development, depend on the discipline of regular worship, or see themselves as a member of a smaller group in the congregation that is important to them. Working hard to involve the people from this *central 72 percent* often proves less than helpful, since, in fact, leaders are trying to provide answers to people who have no questions.

This large 72 percent segment of the congregation cannot be ignored or dismissed, however. Although they are reluctant to get actively involved in discernment, planning, and decision making, they must, nonetheless, be listened to. While they may not come to the table to help, they need to be heard in the learning and planning process. Eventually the planning team will need to structure a way to listen to these people and to demonstrate that they have been heard. In the meantime this 72 percent is, again, not the helpful group to think about for invitations to the balcony.

In between the *central 72 percent* and the *positional 4 percent* is the *productive 24 percent* that is evenly distributed in equal 12 percent segments on the two sides of the distribution. About 12 percent of the congregation in a normal distribution will be inclined to say no to a proposal, and about 12 percent in a normal distribution will be inclined to say yes. What is different about these people is that, unlike the 4 percent, they are not positional; they are thoughtful. These are the people who are in agreement or disagreement because they are listening, they are considering, they are praying. Very importantly, they are interested. Like all thoughtful people, they may be in agreement on this issue but in disagreement on the next issue. No matter. They are working with the leaders and the others to discern what is best, are willing to get involved, and believe the work of addressing questions to be important.

The Pareto Principle in organizations suggests a ratio of 80/20 for problems and solutions. This is commonly expressed by saying that 20 percent of the people will do 80 percent of the work. It also suggests that 20 percent of the people will give 80 percent of the resources needed. It is an organizational principle, because it seems to express a typical pattern across organizations. These 12 percent segments of the congregation that make up *the productive 24 percent* are parallel to the Pareto Principle. These are the people who will be more involved, more thoughtful, and more helpful. As one would expect, since they are the more helpful segment of the congregation, they will easily be found on the boards and committees, as program leaders, and as regular participants in the programs.

However, while the productive 24 (or 20) percent are often found in these conspicuous organizational spots, we recommend that the leader think beyond the normal organizational pattern of the members of the governing board and the committee chairs. While this is where the *productive 24 percent* tends to live in the congregation, the same is true of the *positional 4 percent*. These unhelpful folks show up on governing boards and committees to say their nos and yeses. Another reason to look beyond the board and the committees is that some of the productive 24 percent may have dominant voices and high credibility in the congregation but not serve on the board or in the committee leadership circle. This may be because of age, longevity of service, or large commitments in their personal lives that do not allow regular elected or appointed leadership in the congregation. Or these individuals may simply be people who do not care for committees.

Many clergy and lay leaders intuitively know to look for the productive 24 percent. Interestingly, it seems that the key leaders in congregations do not have a similar intuitive understanding about how to deal with the positional 4 percent and the central 72 percent. Perhaps out of a desire for inclusivity, a need to care for everyone, or a need to try to keep everyone happy, leaders often expend unnecessary energy trying to be too inclusive of the 4 percent and 72 percent when simple listening is enough. In the congregational training stage, it is important to get the productive people to the balcony and look for the teaching moments through which they can see their congregation in a new way, frame new questions about what the congregation should do, or become appropriately uncomfortable with what the congregation is currently doing.

> Leaders often expend unnecessary energy trying to be too inclusive when simple listening is enough.

Extending the Invitation

This conversation leads to the question, "If we know who we want to get to the balcony, how do we get them there?" What invitation would fit these people best? Here, once again, we are framing the work in terms of appropriateness—what is appropriate to the group you are leading? What would make the opportunity attractive to them?

- Will the potential participants give a day or a day and half for a spring or fall retreat? Then the appropriate response of the leader is to program a retreat with a balcony agenda that invites people to talk about the most important things, without pushing (perhaps, without allowing) them to search for answers.
- Do the potential participants hate retreats and prefer to give balcony work only 20 minutes at board meetings? Then the

appropriate response of the leader might be to barter to set aside that 20 minutes at each board meeting over a period of months, call it an open discussion, include some non-board members for that brief portion, and share balcony ideas and discussion to get people thinking.

- Do the productive 24 percent like to read? Great, give them books.
- Are they better listeners? Fine, tell them what you have been reading.
- Do they learn best from experience? That's OK. Take them on a trip to another congregation that is very different from yours.
- Do the leaders pay more attention to experts? Then get a presenter from outside to tell them what they wouldn't really hear if you said it.
- Will they give a special time outside of the regular programs and meetings of the congregation to learn? Then plan an event or a series of meetings in someone's home.
- Will they only show up for conversation within the normal structured life of the congregation? No problem. Offer an alternative adult education class during the regular teaching cycle of your congregation, and make sure that some of your productive 24 percent are attending or co-leading.

The congregational-training stage can be approached in many ways. What is most critical is to have something important for the right people to talk about. It is not the process that you design that will get the people ready and motivated to plan. It is not the right book or the right question, and particularly not the right answer that will prepare people for the important discernment of planning. What changes people and gets them ready and motivated for something new is the structured, holy conversation. This conversation will make them want to dream bigger than they currently do.

> What changes people and gets them ready and motivated for something new is the structured, holy conversation.

The leaders of the congregational-training stage do not need to be certain about what to teach people or what might be learned. The leaders' role is to structure the conversation, to ask the conversation partners continuously what would be helpful next, and to keep the process open to God and to the actual setting and context of the people.

Do not rush the congregational-training stage. As noted in Part One, different forms of planning require different time lines. The congregational-training stage in developmental planning might only take one or two gatherings to help people focus their goals and set the next steps for the planning to be done. In frame-bending planning, however, it may take a good bit longer—maybe longer, in fact, than the formal planning steps that will later be pursued by a planning team.

Committee Selection and Training

Participants in the planning process need both an interest in the process and skills for it. Skills and gifts needed for planning include those that are spiritual, organizational, and personal. To recognize planning interests and skills as personal gifts helps us to acknowledge that when it comes to planning, some people have the skills and some people do not, some people can help with a planning process and some people cannot. Yet, the people asked to work on a planning team and to lead a congregation in planning can easily make the difference between a healthy holy structured conversation and a repetition of old ideas, stories, and problems.

Commonly, when there is a conviction by the governing board or key leaders that planning is necessary, the initial instinct is to move quickly to naming the planning team. The first impulse is often to turn to the people who have been most faithful and helpful in the past—the tried-and-true, the people who are a part of the productive 24 percent. These are the folks who show up first for volunteer duty and leadership, and these are the first people the board tends to think about when additional energy or expertise is needed to get something done. These folks have already demonstrated a deep concern for their congregation and a willingness to do what is necessary to make things happen. They tend to be key leaders, both formal and informal, who care most about the congregation and who know most about the congregation.

However, before moving quickly to name these people as the new planning team, it is important to reflect on why these might *not be the best and most helpful* people for the team. The fact that these people care the most suggests that they also have the deepest investment in this congregation and may well be the ones who have the most difficulty letting go of things as they are. The fact that these people know the most suggests that these people have deeply internalized the norms by which the congregation currently lives. These people may well be the ones who have the most difficulty thinking new thoughts because they are so convinced that long-standing practices are best. The board, clergy, and staff must be very careful at this point to remember that this commitment to the way things are does not suggest that there is anything wrong with these tried-and-true folk. It simply means that these people commonly do not have the interests and skills that you will find most helpful and most freeing in a planning process.

Please note that when we at the Alban Institute do planning with congregations, we nonetheless look for one or two of these higher profile leaders to serve on the planning team because of their valuable insight and expertise in the congregation. To invite none of the tried-and-true may serve to disconnect the planning from the congregation and undermine trust. If the only people invited are people who can only think new thoughts because they don't know past history and practices of the congregation, the planning process risks becoming detached from the history that brought the congregation to the present. Planning does not represent a detachment from the past but rather a connection to that past which offers new development or new direction for the future. Including one or two of the tried-and-true leaders invites greater congregational trust in the planning process. People will feel more assured that the planning process will care for the congregation since these tried-and-true people have demonstrated their care for the congregation in the past. When building the planning team, it is also very helpful to ask one of the tried-and-true to be the chairperson, since the chairperson's voice is usually the one that the congregation hears when team reports, invitations to participate in the planning, and results are offered. People will feel more receptive to the process when the chairperson is someone the congregation naturally listens to and trusts.

If it is not best to turn only to the tried-and-true, then how does a governing board find the best people to ask to serve on a planning team? A very helpful strategy is to encourage the board to begin not by thinking about people but by thinking about skills. The question governing boards most naturally begin with is "Who can we get?" The more helpful step is to think about the skills, attributes, and attitudes that are most helpful to the goals of planning by asking, "What types of skills do we need?"

Assumptions

The four-step process, to be discussed shortly, has proved to be a healthy and vital way to name a planning team and train them for their work. As we continue to remind the reader throughout this book, every congregation is different and requires different approaches, so we continually adapt the following four-step process as appropriate. Let's begin with several important assumptions that underlie the four-step process.

Assumption 1: Board Ownership

It is our strong preference that the governing board name the planning team. The governing board must clearly understand that they are commissioning a planning process that is accountable to them. The planning team will report findings and recommendations to the board. Because we prefer that the planning committee include more than the tried-and-true, the board itself probably should not serve as the planning committee. In fact, governing boards are often one of the more difficult places to encourage new thoughts and do planning, since this is the group to whom the congregation gives responsibility to guard and protect what is.

Although the board does not do the actual planning work, the board needs to own the planning process. Without such ownership, the planning process can be perceived as a set of activities producing recommendations that the leaders do not have to accept or take seriously. If the board does not recognize that they own the planning process and the subsequent recommendations, it will be fairly easy for them to side-step responsibility when it comes time to implement the plan. More than a few congregations have experienced significant disappointment when the planning process came to an end, a report or recommendations were offered, and the board responded by proclaiming to the planning team, "Excellent work. Let us know how it turns out!" If the planning team is also looked upon as the implementation team, then it is fairly guaranteed that the plan will not move the congregation ahead. The board must have interest, agreement, ownership, and some passion for the plan. Responsibilities to make the plan live must be delegated to the right people, committees, or groups, or the congregation will experience only a very short-lived impact while the plan tries to travel on a parallel track alongside the current practices of congregational life. The dominant organizational practice of *business as usual* will overcome the planning recommendations. The planning process is a *process*. A structured conversation is a *conversation*. In both cases, the process or the conversation must come to an end, the planning team must go out of business, and the board must own the results in order to move changes ahead.

Assumption 2: Naming the Group

We have spent time in this book distinguishing between various types of planning: problem, developmental, and frame-bending. We have also discussed conducting a full-blown process versus intuiting the parts of planning that would be most helpful. These distinctions are critical for the leaders of the planning process to understand and to negotiate with the governing board, so that there is shared understanding and agreement about what is to come out of the planning process. The people in the congregation, however, typically have little energy for making such diagnostic distinctions and determining the correct name for what they will be doing. As a leader, you may be clear that you are doing developmental planning but realize that the name "developmental planning team" may not provide the impact needed. We encourage boards and leaders to find the name that sings for them. Some congregations like committees—planning committee or futuring committee. For other congregations the term *committee* already signals an old model, and they prefer *team*—planning team, vision team, or dream team.

The correct name, in a technical sense, commonly turns out to be rather unimportant. The right name, in the sense that it embodies the aspiration of the congregation, is of great importance. When working with the governing board to help these leaders own the process of planning, it is not a distraction but rather supportive of the effort to spend time naming the planning group. Naming represents ownership. Naming focuses expectation and accountability. The best name for the planning group is the one that works.

Assumption 3: The Size of the Planning Team

As noted above, we commonly recommend that the ideal size for a planning team is five to seven people, including the senior pastor. The

maximum size recommended is nine persons, including the senior pastor. A team with fewer than five members often does not provide a
sufficiently rich conversation and may not include enough person power
to do the needed work. To invite more than nine people will slow the
planning process significantly because of the oversupply of voices, ideas,
and preferences.

Assumption 4: The Role of the Pastor and Staff

We recommend that the pastor *not* be the chairperson of the planning
committee. If the pastor chairs the committee, the process can become
pastor driven, and committee members will be inclined either to accept
too easily or to resist too quickly suggestions about both the process
and the outcomes of the work. The preferred chairperson is that person on the planning team who has both process skills and a voice that
is trusted in the congregation.

When there are multiple employees, ordained and lay, on staff in a
congregation, we recommend that the senior clergy be the only staff assigned to the planning team. To have more that the senior clergy is to invite
the planning process to be staff driven, since the staff tends to have more
information about the congregation and more investment in directions
suggested by planning. Staff members do not need to be participants on
the team. They do need to have access to the team, and they do need to
provide the team with their information. Keeping the staff connected to
the planning process and making sure that the appropriate staff information is available to the planning team is one of the responsibilities of the
senior clergy as a planning team member.

Assumption 5: Functional Is Better than Representational

It is not necessary, and often not helpful, for the planning team to be designed as a representational committee in which all of the diverse voices of
the congregation are represented as team members. The problem with
representational committees is that their members *represent*. If someone is
asked to serve on the team as the representative of the women's group, the
youth, the trustees, or the finance committee, that person is invited to be
sure that the interests of their group are clearly understood and accounted
for in any planning recommendations. By their very design, representational committees make it difficult to think about and on behalf of the
whole rather than about the part each member represents. This struggle
wastes energy and reduces the effectiveness of the results.

A planning team does not have to include all of the diverse voices of the congregation in a representational manner. The planning team, however, *does* need to be open to and actively invite information from the diverse voices of the congregation in order to understand and work on behalf of the whole. The planning team needs to listen to the full congregation. Listening is at the heart of the continuous task of offering feedback to the congregation. As discussed earlier, feedback includes both listening and communicating (or extraverting).

The Four-Step Process for Committee Selection and Training

Let's now return to the preferred four-step process again, with the reminder that the four steps need to be modified as appropriate to the particular congregation.

Step 1: Skills, Attributes, and Attitudes

In this first step the governing board is cautioned *not* to begin thinking about names of people to serve on the planning team. Instead, board members will be invited to talk about what skills, attributes, and attitudes will serve their congregation best in a planning or discerning process about the future. It is helpful to have conversation at this point about the natural difficulties for the most involved leaders to think beyond the established norms and practices of the congregation. Acknowledging the importance of the gifts and commitment of the tried-and-true folk, the discussion must move on to talk about the specific skills, attributes, and attitudes needed for planning.

It is helpful to work with the governing board to develop two lists of skills, attributes, and attitudes on a large piece of newsprint. The two lists are: (1) skills, attributes, and attitudes *not* needed, and (2) skills, attitudes, and attributes needed. It is often helpful to begin with the not needed list, since this frees the board members to let go of some assumptions and to think more freely about what is needed. The leaders of this process should keep the following principles in mind as the board creates its lists:

- These lists are to be brainstormed, so the ideas are neither corrected nor discussed while the brainstorm list is developing.
- It is helpful for the person leading the brainstorming exercise to offer an explanation of what the board is being asked to do and why—and then to start with one or two examples on each list.

- The leader of the brainstorming exercise may also want to keep any key skills, attributes, or attitudes that he or she is aware of in mind, to be added in case they don't get named.
- It is helpful to frame responses with the phrase "people who . . . ," so that the board members are reminded that they are thinking about people, but not about names of particular people.

Following are examples of the lists a board might create:

People Not to Invite

- People who are not good at decision making or able to consider consequences
- People unwilling to change themselves or the congregation to accommodate others
- People who move too quickly to decisions
- People who do not like talking about ideas
- People who are the pastor's opponents

People to Invite

- People who are open to what God calls the congregation to be in the future
- People willing to learn new things and think new thoughts
- People comfortable discussing ideas
- People willing to put time, energy, work, and prayer into this effort

More complete brainstorm lists can be found in Resource H, "Building a Planning Committee," on page 230. However, it is important for each board to shape its own list. It is not helpful to present a list developed by another congregation for their use, no matter how accurate it might seem. If the board is to own the planning team and its process, board members need to name for themselves what they understand to be important.

Step 2: Looking and Praying for Nominations

Once the board completes the two brainstorm lists, there should be some general discussion of the lists. Board members should still be cautioned not to jump too quickly to thinking about names. Board members will then be asked to take two to three weeks to think about the lists and consider which individuals in the congregation (both members and participants; that is, active nonmembers) seem to *best* exemplify what is needed, taking account of both lists. Assure everyone that they are not looking for the perfect people, who accurately match all the identified skills, attributes, and attitudes. The search for perfect people is impossible and frustrating. Rather, they are to look for the people who exemplify the gifts needed (based on both lists) in their own lives and way of working. To search for these people the board members can be encouraged to

- Spend time praying for people who can help
- Browse through congregational pictorial directories, if available
- Read through congregational membership lists
- Carefully observe people who attend worship or programs of the congregation over the next few weeks
- Discuss their ideas about helpful people with other board members (caution members that this is not a time to caucus for agreement to nominate particular people)
- Consider to what extent they themselves mirror the skills, attributes, and attitudes identified as helpful

Instruct the board members that when they return after two or three weeks (or at the next board meeting), they will be asked to submit a 3x5 card with the names of the *three* people that they believe best exemplify what is needed. They will not be asked to sign the card, so no one will know who submitted the nominees. Board members will be able to submit their own name as one of the three nominees.

Step 3: Naming the Team Members
When the board members submit their 3x5 cards with names of nominees, a volunteer board member will then quickly develop a rank-order list of nominees, beginning with the person who received the most nominations and ending with those who received just one nomination—until all nominees are listed. The board is invited to look at the full list. With the assumption that the ideal size of a planning team is five to seven people, draw a line under the seventh nominee to separate this top group from other nominations.

The board will then be invited to review the two lists of skills, attributes, and attitudes to discuss whether the top nominees as a group fairly and helpfully reflect these lists. It is common for groups to look at the list of top nominees and conclude that the list includes too many men or women, too many people with finance background, not enough recent members, and so forth. Adjustments to the list that come from open conversation by the board are welcomed.

When the board is satisfied with the list of nominees, someone (the chairperson of the board, a clergy member, or a volunteer) takes responsibility to invite the nominees to serve on the planning team. Beginning at the top of the list, the person offering the invitations will continue to work down the list in descending order until the agreed-upon number of planning team member slots are filled. It will be helpful for the inviter to have a couple of resources in hand: a job description, so that potential members know what they would be getting into; a sentence indicating why each person is being invited; and a time frame for responding.[4]

The job description should indicate what the planning team will be asked to do, how often they will meet, for how long (how many months) the team will be working, to whom the team will report, and how they will be supported in their work. In this invitation stage, it is also important to let people know what gifts they have that the board found appealing. This is a good time to do an initial sharing of the list of skills, attributes, and attitudes developed by the board.

The board will also need to discuss whether they will name the chairperson of the planning team or invite the planning team to choose its own chair. Different congregations seem to have different preferences about this and both practices seem to work well.

Step 4: Forming the Team and Defining Its Task
When the needed number of nominees has accepted the invitation to serve, the pastor or the chairperson of the board leads a first meeting. At this first meeting there are four key agenda items:

1. Update the newly named team members on the conversations about planning that led to their selection for this team.
2. Review carefully the two lists of "People not needed" and "People needed" that were developed by the board. Walking through these two lists slowly has two powerful effects on the team:

   • Reviewing the lists honors the people chosen. When asked how they feel about being identified for this task by the board, which used the two lists as a guide, our consistent experience is that people feel honored and somewhat humbled to consider that their board members think of them in such a way. People often talk openly about wanting to rise to the challenge by being the best they can in the way described.

- Reviewing the lists offers a very powerful training moment for the team by setting the norms by which they will do their work. By rehearsing the items, the team is in fact provided with a set of norms and practices to follow that are clearer than most other groups. They know what skills, attributes, and attitudes to practice and *not* to practice. By sharing the list in the first meeting, the team is offered powerful training on how to pursue their task.

3. Help the team organize its work. The leader may want to have a discussion about the goals of the planning. It may be helpful to share the full-blown planning process described in this book and talk about what is most important to accomplish. It is helpful to offer a description of the anticipated overall process of planning, with recognition that it will have to be adapted along the way.

4. Turn over the chairing function to the appointed chair, or help the team select its own chairperson.

Needs Assessment

Needs assessment is the third stage of the initial, getting-ready phase in the planning process. In this stage, the planning team wrestles with the reality that there are both too many questions and too many possible answers. The planning process could take the team down innumerable paths, as they try to figure things out. However, not all of the paths are necessary, productive, or faithful. The stage of needs assessment is the time to clarify the questions that the planning team most needs to address in their planning work. What is it that we most need to know about our future? What questions do we most need to answer? About what do we need to learn?

It is both possible and tempting for the team to bypass the needs-assessment conversation and begin immediately to gather data—

information about the congregation, the community, or the culture. However, in today's data-rich environment, there is too much information to take in. It is also too easy for the team to become data driven (a danger that will be addressed in the discussion about the next phase of planning). In order for the team to know what data to gather and talk about, the team first needs a filter by which to select the data. That filter is the needs assessment—what question(s) are we trying to answer?

The needs-assessment stage is an effort to limit the number of possible paths that planning can take. It begins by limiting the planning conversation to key issues that need to be explored. Of course, the beginning paths defined by the needs assessment may later branch out to wider related questions. It is, however, necessary to agree on the initial question to be addressed. To skip the needs-assessment work, to place no limit on the possible lines of inquiry, can undermine the effectiveness of the planning by

- overwhelming the planning team with too many questions, too much information, and too many expectations; or
- underwhelming the planning team by not offering enough guidance to help them move into critical conversations.

Planning can be a confusing time in which the planning team can be unsure about directions of inquiry and conversation. There is a saying that "when we don't know what to do, we do what we know." In other words, if the direction is not set by clear questions produced by a needs assessment, it is quite possible for the planning team to limit itself to exploring what it already knows best, by developing what already is most developed. For example, if the congregation is known for excellent music and liturgy, and no clear question, path, or need has been identified to direct the planning conversation, then the planning team might easily find itself problem solving about how to improve worship. When work is too complex or confusing, there is a natural tendency toward work avoidance—and so we return to what we know we can comfortably do best.

Ways to Do Needs Assessment

There are a number of ways in which the planning team can do its needs assessment:

- The team may be able to do its needs assessment simply by talking about the reasons the board formed a planning team. If there is a consensus on what needs to be investigated, the team might be ready to begin gathering data.

- The team may request an additional meeting with the board to clarify its task. The board and the planning team may want to use the resource in this book about the types of planning to clarify whether they are asked to do developmental planning or frame-bending planning. (See Resource C on page 209.) As the board and team talk, it is helpful to frame the specific questions for the team to begin to work with.

- If the board and team determine the task is to do developmental planning, they can agree on which developmental questions need to be explored. For example, they may want to discuss faith formation programs for youth and young adults or other age-specific ministries. The planning team may, of course, be drawn into other areas of the life of the congregation or community as they do their work. But it is necessary to assess the driving needs of planning and to start with the most important questions.

- If the board and team determine the task is to do frame-bending planning, it is important for the team to understand why the board feels the large formation questions need to be asked and what prompts them to be asked now.

- The team may want to begin their planning with a needs assessment that includes a larger group, such as board members and all other leaders in the congregation, or that allows for initial conversation with and input from a larger circle of members and participants in the congregation. This can easily be done by inviting a larger group to work with the planning team for an initial SWOT analysis (see part 1).

- Conduct the analysis by inviting a group to gather for an evening or afternoon. Break them into small groups to discuss and identify the key items in each of the four SWOT quadrants. Have each group post its work on newsprint on the wall. Lead a conversation that explores each group's work and moves to the development of a shared SWOT in which the key elements in each quadrant are identified. *Being careful to focus most of the attention on quadrants 1 and 3, strengths and opportunities*, help

Internal Inside the Congregation	STRENGTHS	WEAKNESSES
External Outside the Congregation	OPPORTUNITIES	THREATS

SWOT Analysis

the group to shape three to five key questions for the planning team to pursue.

- The planning team may want to do this initial needs assessment by listening more broadly throughout the congregation using small, informal listening groups. In this case, congregational members are invited to sign up for one-hour conversations in a number of small group meetings that might be held at the congregation's facility or in members' homes. Each group is limited to 12 participants. A member of the planning team leads the group. Another member of the planning team attends as a listener and note taker, so that the information from the conversation is not lost. Such listening groups tend to discuss three questions:

1. The positive question: What is most important to me about my congregation?
2. The negative question: What do I worry most about when I think of my congregation?
3. The change question: If I could change one thing about my congregation at the drop of a hat, what would it be?

When using small listening groups to do the initial needs assessment, the planning team has to allow time in its own meeting schedule to review the gathered information and to discuss the key hopes, dreams, and worries that surfaced in the meetings with members. (Other ways of using small group meetings are discussed in chapter 13, in the section entitled "Use of Home Meetings," on page 172.)

When developing the needs assessment for the planning process, the planning team should be willing to talk about what needs to be explored and discovered in *this* planning cycle. The team does not need to assume that it must plan all things for all time. The needs-assessment stage of the work is to determine what is most important to do at this time, to find a starting place with the board's agreement, and to set a path of inquiry that is both clear and also open to the discovery of unanticipated issues and information. Beginning with an agreed-upon question greatly increases the effectiveness of the team and the importance of their conversations. (Some common driving issues are explored in chapter 15 on page 189.)

Notes

1. Gil Rendle, "The Illusion of Congregational 'Happiness,'" in *Conflict Management in Congregations,* Harvesting the Learnings Series, ed. David B. Lott (Bethesda, Md.: Alban Institute, 2001), 83–94.
2. Ronald A. Heifetz and Donald L. Laurie, "The Work of Leadership," *Harvard Business Review*, Reprint #97106 (January-February 1997): 124–134.
3. See the discussion of the Time Management Matrix in Stephen Covey's *The Seven Habits of Highly Effective People* (New York: Simon & Schuster, 1989), 146–162.
4. Jean Morris Trumbauer, *Sharing the Ministry: A Practical Guide to Transforming Volunteers into Ministers* (Minneapolis: Augsburg Fortress, 1999), 105–123.

CHAPTER FIVE

Phase Two: Collecting Data

What Is Data?

The phase of data collection takes the needs assessment as its guide; the team will search for the information needed to answer the primary questions identified in the assessment. The components of the data collection phase are:

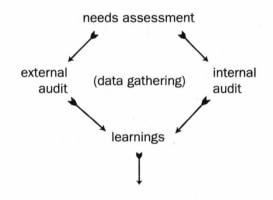

While the getting-ready phase is the most critical phase, since planning without readiness is destined to be ignored or resisted, the phase of collecting data is potentially the most dangerous part of planning. The data-collecting phase is dangerous because we believe data. We like information. There is more and more discussion about our cultural orientation to the scientific worldview that has guided our philosophies and sciences for centuries. We have come to believe that our world and our experience can be measured, understood, and controlled. If we don't believe, we at least hope that there is a clear answer available for each of our questions.

Our orientation toward data and the belief that answers are found in data makes this part of the planning process dangerous, because information in the form of collected data may inhibit, or even stop, the holy conversation of discernment by giving the appearance that the answer has been found. Data often comes in the form of numbers or can be reduced to a set of numbers that suggest clarity and finality. However, data alone—without the conversation to interpret the data—can be misleading. For example, a congregation in a large metropolitan area built its current sanctuary in the early 1950s to seat 550 people in worship. In the late 1950s through the early 1960s, the sanctuary was typically filled to capacity for morning worship and this era, 40 to 50 years ago, is still remembered by members as the highlight of this congregation's life. By the year 2000 average attendance at worship had slipped to 125 people. The data irrefutably said that something was wrong. People within this congregation were so convinced that something was wrong that every Sunday when they came to worship, they could not see a gathering of 125 people;

> Data alone—without the conversation to interpret the data—can be misleading.

they could only see 425 empty seats! The leaders of this congregation were so convinced that something was wrong—and that it was somebody's fault—that they had gone through a series of three short and broken relationships with pastors, each time concluding that the pastor was a poor preacher, a bad administrator, or sufficiently uncaring so that people would not return to the church.

What was missing from this data—which by itself was accurate—was holy conversation. The leaders allowed the data to speak for them, and did not question or try to uncover what was behind it. It was only when the data was questioned that the leaders began to look for more of the story. The quest for the rest of the story helped these leaders look outside of themselves to understand changes in their community. They learned that since the 1950s, a railroad company had built a set of tracks through the middle of their section of the city, greatly reducing travel from one area to the other. They were surprised to find that most of their new members over past years came from their side of the tracks, whereas, prior to the railroad, members came from a much wider area. They were also surprised to discover that in the past 50 years, a rather complete generational migration had occurred around them. Former residents had left the area for suburban homes as their families grew. New residents moved into the neighborhood from areas closer to the center of the city, in order to begin raising their families. The former residents were predominantly Protestant. The new influx of residents was predominantly Roman Catholic. The leaders also began to explore the information available about declining membership in their denomination and saw themselves as a part of a much larger trend. More data, to be sure. But each layer of data was the result of the need to answer new questions that came from *the conversation about data* that is so necessary to planning and discernment.

It was only after this series of conversations that the leaders began to feel some pride in their average attendance of 125 people. They began to make plans to change the way they used their sanctuary, so that the 425 empty seats would not overwhelm them. These empty seats created cavernous holes between people as they scattered themselves all over the huge auditorium for worship. The congregation began to trust and appreciate their pastor's leadership and began conversations about collaborative efforts that used the best of their and their pastor's skills. Had they stuck only with the original data, sure that they had evidence of some truth, they would have cycled on to the next pastoral leader, who would also have disappointed them. It was only in the conversation about data—which led to new questions and new insights, and then to new conversations—that they were able to sense a future! Data does not change people or situations. Conversation about data creates change.

It is often important to help people break through their assumptions about the place of data in planning. One of my favorite exercises with groups is called "real triangles." People are each handed a copy of the triangle below and simply instructed to count the number of real

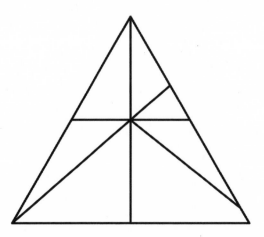

How many triangles do you see?

triangles they see, with no help from their neighbor. The participants are asked to write the number on a piece of paper. Despite group members' pleas to define a real triangle, no other instructions are given.

People are then asked to share their number. The number of triangles counted by people in groups doing this exercise usually ranges from 1 to 21. It is not uncommon to have someone count only 1 real triangle, because their definition of a triangle is equilateral, or count only 2 real triangles because their definition of a triangle is a right-angle triangle. It is not uncommon for participants to count more than 17 or 18, because they continuously look for anything close to a triangle and include it. Other participants will have counts in the middle because they have been more discerning about counting only actual triangles (see the bottom right corner of the large triangle). Variations in numbers are also due to the seriousness with which people take the task and the method they use to count triangles (and avoid double counting). A copy of this triangle can be found as Resource I on page 231. Try it with your planning group and have a discussion about what data is and what it does.

The point of this exercise is to help people see that if data truly provided answers, then everyone in the group would arrive at the same number of triangles on the paper. There are few situations in life that involve such straightforward answers as the number of triangles on a piece of paper. But data—even the simplest information—is contextual and is interpreted differently by all of us because of our experience and definitions of what should be. It is only the conversation that comes from looking at and working with data that produces helpful information.

Don't Start with Data

These cautions about the use of data suggest several strategies for the planning process. First, don't start by collecting data. Too often a board will see the need for planning and name a planning team, which will immediately begin to gather data (even before its first meeting). Such premature collection of data invites the planning process to be data driven. People will look only where the data points and conclusions will be reached quickly, often without conversation and without understanding the context.

It is much more helpful for the team to clarify the questions it has been asked to address (needs-assessment stage) and to gather data primarily related to the driving questions. Conversation about the data collected when addressing the initial driving questions will, no doubt, lead to gathering more data. However, to gather data without clear driving questions allows the data to direct the holy conversation. To gather data without being steered by driving questions invites the planning team on a fishing trip across a broad range of information (helpful or unhelpful) to see what they can catch.

Begin with Internal Data

Second, begin by collecting internal data, information about the congregation and its participants. Who are we? What are our gifts? What are our strengths? Use of a SWOT analysis (see part 1) is very helpful at this point. Here is a list of examples of internal data that planning teams may find useful. Planning teams are cautioned, once again, to collect that data which is most directly related to the question or questions guiding the planning process:

- 10- to 20-year membership statistics and trends
- 10- to 20-year participant statistics and trends
- 10- to 20-year worship attendance trends and ratio of membership to average attendance at worship
- Sunday school membership and attendance trends
- Membership addition and deletion patterns
- Age and gender profiles for members and participants
- Tenure studies (how long, by decade, people have belonged to the congregation)
- Marital status for members and participants
- Geographic location of members in relationship to the congregation's location
- Congregational histories
- Pastoral expectations
- Facilities assessment or overview (including site plan and parking evaluation)
- Financial assessment—trends in giving over 10 to 20 years

- Financial assessment—trends in budget over 10 to 20 years
- Interviews with recent new members
- Interviews with participants who attend but decide not to join

A capturing of less-formal congregational history and information is also important data, since our most authentic future will build in some way upon the values of our most faithful past. The planning team may also wish to consider using some of the suggestions in this handbook for listening to members in small discussion groups.

External Data

Third, move to an external exploration of the community and context for the congregation. Let's begin with a caution. Data is powerful and easily directs attention. Demographic and psychographic information about the community surrounding the congregation is increasingly available, detailed, and accurate. This information can give the team descriptive information (in which individuals and groups are counted according to their similarities) about the community. Examples of demographic information might include:

- How much has the community grown or shrunk?
- How many people of what ages live in the neighborhood?
- What is the racial breakdown of the community?
- How many people live in single-family housing?
- How many men? How many women?

Psychographic information is demographic census information to which economic information is added in order to provide a sketch of lifestyle similarities and differences. Psychographic profiles include lifestyle information such as the following (the phrases in quotation marks indicate psychographic marketing categories indicating lifestyle similarities):

- What are the dominant lifestyles of people in the community?
- How many live in "established country families"?
- How many are "empty nesters"?
- How many are "suburban mid-life families"?
- How many are "new beginning urbanites"?

This information is very important and enormously helpful in planning. But it can easily overwhelm and misdirect. For example, a congregation with an average attendance of 100 persons did a community study to discover that a cluster of empty nesters were located north of the church, a cluster of young urban singles lived to the east, a cluster of young urban families lived to the south, and a cluster of young country families lived to the west. With such clear insight into the subgroups with lifestyle differences living in their community, the planning team immediately began to recommend programs appropriate to each of these groups. The planning failed for a number of reasons. First, the planning team did not discuss the information sufficiently to understand that these different clusters of people do not easily live with each other because they have few common interests and experiences. Second, the planning team overwhelmed the congregation by trying to plan multiple new programs for new people in addition to the traditional programs and functions cared for in the church (overworking the 20 percent of the members willing to get involved with decision making and programming). Third, and most important, the planning team had not paused to ask about the gifts of the congregation. There were still critical conversations that needed to happen inside the congregation, to discern the congregation's real gifts for ministry and to shape the vision of the congregation. This conversation would direct what the congregation could offer to any of these community people. The task of data collection is not to figure out how to be all things to all people but to discern how to be authentically oneself and then offer one's gifts to others in appropriate ways.

> The task of data collection is not to figure out how to be all things to all people but to discern how to be authentically oneself and then offer one's gifts to others in appropriate ways.

Denominational offices and parachurch resource providers often offer affordable demographic and psychographic information, which is so powerful that it can easily drive your planning process. In chapter 10 of this handbook you will find more information about the use of demographics, including ways to locate much of this information on the Web.

Demographic and psychographic studies are often fairly long documents with graphs, map studies, and a good amount of backup information. The studies tend to overwhelm a planning team. One of the most efficient and effective strategies for understanding this rich community data is to have only one or two members of the planning team study the information in depth. They can become familiar with all of the information and present only the most important information to the full team, along with what they believe they have learned from their study. The information selected from these community studies should be related to the driving questions of the congregation as directly as possible.

> The information selected from these community studies should be related to the driving questions of the congregation as directly as possible.

Beyond purchased demographic and psychographic community studies, the planning team can also explore their surrounding external context by taking neighborhood walks (see Resource Q on page 271). The team members may also want to plan interviews or conversations with others in the community whose job it is to track the changes happening: realtors, school board members, municipal planning commissions, and local universities with an urban planning department. The planning team may discover that some of these community people are already members or participants of the congregation.

Learnings

Gil affectionately calls this phase of the work the "So what?" moment of planning. The team may have participated in congregational training and balcony work. They have been named by the governing board to carry out a specific task. They have collected data. They have listened, talked, prayed, and discerned. So what? What is the product of their work?

Collecting the learnings from the planning process is one of the most important stages of the work. Collecting the learnings means identifying important insights or information. The planning team is challenged to focus on their most important new ideas and convictions. Having looked widely, the team now begins to narrow in on what is most important for the future ministry.

Planning teams, like all other groups, tend to have preferences about how to work. Some planning teams are highly structured, and they prefer to collect their learnings meeting by meeting as they go along. In this case, one person might be given the task of being the learning keeper. At the end of each meeting or stage of the planning process, every member of the team is asked to offer at least one key learning they got from that session or stage. The learning keeper maintains a running log of insights and learnings. At the end of the data collecting stage, the learning keeper prepares a

> Collecting the learnings means identifying important insights or information.

summary of all suggested insights for the planning team to review. Critical insights and learnings are then identified in this portion of the team's structured conversation, and will be used in reporting to the board and making recommendations. Some teams are less structured and choose to spend a session or two at the end of their data-collecting process to brainstorm what they remember as key insights and to discuss what is important to share with others.

One of my favorite integrating exercises in a Christian context is to use a passage from the New Testament book of Acts to frame a conversation about learnings for the team (and others). The passage comes from the account of the ascension of Jesus in which Jesus tells his disciples, "You will be my witnesses in Jerusalem, in all Judea and Samaria, and to the ends of the earth" (Acts 1:8).

Four geographic areas are mentioned in the text: Jerusalem, Judea, Samaria, and the ends of the earth. In the diagram on the next page, a ring of concentric circles indicates these areas, with Jerusalem at the center and the ends of the world beyond the final ring.

Each of these four areas can be given descriptors:

- *Jerusalem*: This is us. It is the people who are already here as members and participants of this congregation. These are the people whose names we know, whose faces we recognize. We are comfortable with these people.
- *Judea*: This is the area of sameness. These people are like us, but they are not yet participants or members of the congregation. We do not know their names, and we do not recognize their faces, but when they show up we know that they are like us and we welcome them. It is expected that everyone makes a pilgrimage to Jerusalem at some time, so when these people show up on high holy days or in times of personal change or need, we are comfortable with them.

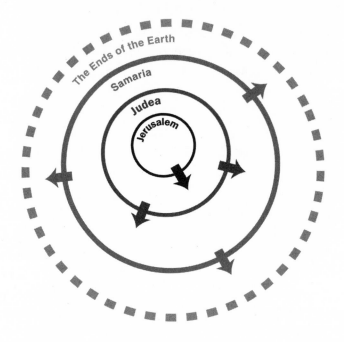

- *Samaria*: This is the area of difference. These people are not like us. We see them as different, and sometimes perceive them as difficult or dangerous. Samaria may be nearby but, given the choice, people would rather walk around it than go through it. When the people of Samaria show up in the congregation we notice they are different and we are not sure what to do with them.
- *The Ends of the Earth*: These people live far beyond our area. (In a dense metropolitan area, "far" may begin just a few miles away.) We will never know their names. We may never see their faces. Nonetheless, we are convinced that we have some responsibility to them or for them.

These descriptions can provide a very effective learning summary if the planning team (and others) uses this construct to respond to a series of questions like those below:

Jerusalem
- How would we most accurately describe ourselves?
- What are our gifts?
- What do we value most?
- What are our hopes?

- Who naturally comes to visit or join us?
- How do we treat others and welcome them?
- How do we deal with differences?

Judea

- Who are these neighbors?
- In what ways are they similar to us?
- Where do we find these similar people in our community?
- How would we invite and welcome them?
- What do we have to offer them? What do they have to offer us?
- How do we treat "Judeans" when they make a pilgrimage to our congregation?

Samaria

- Who are the people of difference in our midst who make us uncomfortable?
- What is our responsibility to and for "Samaritans"?
- How do we treat outsiders? How should we treat them?
- What does our vision for our congregation and our understanding of ourselves suggest for our relationship with Samaritans?

The Ends of the Earth

- Who are the people at the ends of the earth for us?
- How do we reach out to these people?
- What does our faith expect from us in a relationship with these people?

Using simple conversational constructs, such as this biblical exercise, at the learning stage can be very helpful in crystallizing the work of the team. One planning team was surprised to discover that for them, Judea included all of the people who lived in single-family homes in their urban area. Almost all of their members (Jerusalem) were long-tenured residents in the area who lived in their own homes as well. Samaria, on the other hand, was represented by apartment dwellers, who were usually younger and much more transient. It was very telling for this planning team to recognize that immediately adjoining their property was a very large apartment complex, with which the congregation had no relationship and about which members had few good feelings.

CHAPTER SIX

Phase Three: Shaping the Future

This final phase of the planning process is the point at which all of the hard work and holy conversation of planning is shaped into a story about the future.

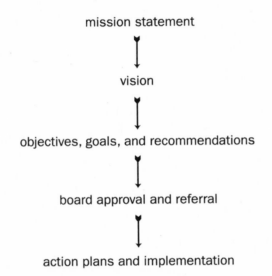

mission statement

↓

vision

↓

objectives, goals, and recommendations

↓

board approval and referral

↓

action plans and implementation

It is important for the planning team to remember that this is often the messiest part of planning, because there are few formulas to help bring focus to the plan. This is the creative moment. It is the time to trust discernment, and risk new thoughts and feelings that might not have been easily accepted before. As mentioned earlier, psychiatrist and author M. Scott Peck suggested that one of the criteria for discernment might be craziness or risking new and previously unconsidered ways. His reasoning was that if God's future were a logical path, we would have figured it out long ago. But, since God's future for us is unknown, we need to move beyond our own logic and welcome a bit of craziness (creativity, newness, risk) in order to find our path. This phase of shaping the future needs to be based on the insights, information, and learnings that come from the work that precedes it. It also needs to be the moment in which we reach for a new future with the knowledge that God has a picture of us that describes what we could be. It is a future that invites us to be more than we currently are.

Mission Statements and Vision Statements

If shaping the future is messy work, clarity comes from our conversations about who we are, what biblical stories shape us, what memories of congregational life we cling to, what values we most want to carry with us, what geographic and human areas we have been called to serve, and what our community needs from us. What makes this work difficult is that the team must now move from the exploration of multiple possibilities to the claiming of a meaningful direction. This is commonly done using two organizational tools known as the mission statement and the vision statement. Let's begin with the classic definitions of each.

Mission Statement
A mission statement is a statement of identity and purpose. It expresses what we believe in unity with other congregations and what we uniquely believe because of who we are, and when and where we live. It defines our ministry in terms of biblical understanding (what we believe), geographical scope (where we minister), the people we have been called to serve (target audience), and what gifts we bring to our unique ministry. Despite carrying so much information, the mission statement is to be brief, concise, and memorable. Obviously, to create a mission statement, we must use heavily coded words that have deep meaning for the members of the congregation.

Vision Statement
A vision statement is a word picture of what our congregation would look like if we were, in fact, able to fulfill our mission statement. It identifies what would be different if we were faithful. It includes hints of the criteria by which we will measure our ministry by describing what will be different about us in three to five years. Vision statements are descriptive and therefore usually not as brief and concise as mission statements. They draw a picture of a future that is sufficiently rich in detail to offer some direction and guidance for the trip.

Much has been said in the planning literature regarding the importance of mission and vision statements, and we agree that they are important. However, throughout this book we have been stressing the need for creativity and appropriateness and believe that these guidelines apply here, too. There are fewer hard-and-fast rules about planning than one might think, and the development of mission and vision statements is another area in which rules do not need to dominate.

> What makes this work difficult is that the team must now move from the exploration of multiple possibilities to the claiming of a meaningful direction.

There are two components to all mission and vision statements: the axiomatic and the unique. The *axiomatic* states what is self-evident for all congregations, or all congregations of a particular denomination. This is the part referred to above as "what we believe in unity with other congregations." An axiomatic statement about a congregation might be: *Third United Methodist Church of Anytown is called to serve both members and the wider community through worship, the administration of the sacraments, Christian education, acts of caring, and outreach.* This statement may be true for Third United Methodist Church, but it is also true of other United Methodist Churches and carries little information beyond a general description or definition of what any congregation within that tradition does.

The *unique* states what is important to the particular congregation because of who it is, where it is located, and the historical moment it is in—all of which separates this particular congregation from other congregations of other locations, gifts, and times. A unique statement about a congregation might be: *Third United Methodist Church of Anytown believes that all people are equal in the eyes of God and deserving of the basics of food, shelter, clothing, and care and is called to*

> The energy that will drive this congregation to seek the fulfillment of its future will come from a unique statement of identity and purpose.

stand with and on behalf of those whose basic needs are not met. The axiomatic still applies to Third Church. The congregation still provides worship, sacraments, education, and caring like other congregations of its tradition. However, the energy that will drive this congregation to seek the fulfillment of its future will be the unique statement of identity and purpose around which members and participants can unite. It is the sense of uniqueness that provides the shared identity and energy to align both hearts and hands.

Given this distinction between the axiomatic and the unique aspects of mission and vision statements, we consistently encourage planning teams and governing boards to shape their future by giving particular attention to unique statements about themselves. It is important to remember that mission and vision statements are tools. They exist to bring focus to the congregation, and are not planning tasks to be completed in and of themselves. When working with a congregation, we will often talk about the importance of a unique mission statement, only to be told by the leaders of the congregation that they already have a mission statement that they like. Upon exploring it, we often discover that the mission statement is highly axiomatic. Rather than suggest that the leaders must correct or give up a statement that helps them, we then suggest that what the leaders now need is a vision statement (knowing that we can urge them to be unique in this next statement). At this point in the conversation, a planning team member might protest that a vision statement is also unnecessary because they have one of those as well. Usually it again turns out that the vision statement is also highly axiomatic. No problem. We will now suggest that they need to provide a purpose statement or an action statement or any appropriate statement of agreement and learning that expresses as sharply as possible the unique gifts, call, and challenge that this congregation claims. The statements themselves and their forms are not sacred. The statements may be played with and adapted. They must, however, claim a very clear and specific future.

Objectives, Goals, and Recommendations

Once the uniqueness of the congregation and its future has been shaped in descriptive statements, the next stage is to move toward workable plans. In planning terminology, the ideas are then translated into objectives and goals. While the terminology is consistent, different planners will use these terms in different ways. The definitions are generally agreed upon; which definition fits which term is not. Following is the form we feel most comfortably using:

- **Objectives** state what the congregation and its leaders must commit themselves to do or to be in order to address the unique future being shaped. Objectives describe the specific areas in which that the congregation will work. Objectives identify who or what will be the object or recipient of the congregation's ministry.

- **Goals** state how the congregation will accomplish those objectives. Goals are often expressed as action plans: *who* will do *what* by *when* and at *what cost*. Goals are specific. At their best they are measurable, achievable, specific, and time limited (MAST). Goals are often expressed as programs, events, or strategies to accomplish a stated objective.

By the time the planning team begins developing objectives and goals, the territory becomes very familiar to leaders trained in problem solving. The mission statement and vision statement describe what is to be in the future. The planning process has involved gathering data and structuring conversations about what is currently happening. Objectives and goals speak directly to the question of how we get from the known present to the hoped-for future. In the discussion of types of planning in Part One of this book, we noted that focusing on this difference between what is and what is hoped for results in gap theory planning. Gap theory planning is heavily dependent upon problem solving. The basic path of gap theory is to follow these steps:

> Objectives and goals speak directly to the question of how we get from the known present to the hoped-for future.

- Here's where we are now.
- Here's where we want or feel called to be in the future.
- Here's a description of the gap between where we are and where we want to be.
- Here's what we have to learn or do in order to get there.
- Here are our options for making the changes to get there.
- Here are our recommendations and action plans to achieve our vision.

Because problem solving is a basic leadership skill, this part of the planning process tends to move quickly. We are trained to move quickly to action plans.

If the planning team reaches this point and still finds it difficult to move to specific recommendations and actions, the team may need to learn more before a clear path presents itself. This would indicate a need for the planning team to take a quick trip back into the data-gathering stage to address the new questions that have surfaced as they tried to complete their work. Something more needs to be learned. The path to the future is not yet clear.

Board Approval, Referral, and Implementation

Once objectives and goals have been identified and recommendations have been shaped, it is important for the planning team to go out of business. This stage of the planning process includes reporting to the governing board with the key learnings and the recommendations that came from the planning team's work. The importance of the governing board naming and owning the planning team by selecting its members and giving the team its charter was addressed above. It is time for the team to complete its work and give it back to the board. To do otherwise will severely short-circuit any changes that might come from planning.

Governing boards are busy groups and the board members often prefer to ask the planning team to implement the plan they developed and presented. If this path is chosen, the dilemma is that the only part of the congregation that owns and believes in the plan is the planning team. This is an open invitation for resistance or apathy. There is an old truism that suggests that the more difficult the decision a congregation must make, the fewer people will come to the meeting. The problem is that when a person comes to the meeting and helps to make the decision, he or she is more bound to the decision and obligated to seeing it though. However, if one was not at the meeting, that person is still free to disagree with the decision since "I didn't help make it." For the board to accept and approve the planning team's results requires the board to be present and make a decision. Having formally adopted the planning team's recommendations, the board is not free to disregard the plan and, in fact, has responsibility to implement the plan. After all, board members were there and said they affirmed the plan.

If the planning team remains intact, and is the primary group responsible to implement the plan, the board and others are free to distance themselves from the planning work, saying to the planning team, "Wonderful plan. Let us know how it turns out!" Certainly members of the planning team, because of their interest and their work on the plan, can help carry out the plan as board or committee members or volunteers. The planning team, however, must come to a formal end in order for the plan to live fully and independently within the congregation.

Once the board has approved the plan and disbanded the planning team with thanks, the board assumes responsibility for implementing the action plans. In small congregations this often means that the board itself will lead the implementation. Board members will themselves begin to shape their actions and decisions at programmatic levels to follow the plan to a new future. In larger congregations, the board will appropriately assign the parts of the plan to staff, committees, teams, or individuals who will be accountable for making the plan come alive.

> The planning team must come to a formal end in order for the plan to live fully and independently within the congregation.

Giving Voice to the Congregation

The planning process is an effort to help the congregation tell its story. The congregation has a past, and the planning team must remember and capture what is important from that history. The congregation has a present, and the planning team is to be unflinchingly honest and accurate about the congregation as it presently is. The congregation has a future, and the planning team must point to an authentic future that is neither disconnected from the past nor ignorant of the present.

Biblical theologian Walter Wink suggests that every congregation has an angel. He notes how the letters in the book of Revelation differ from Paul's letters, which were commonly addressed to the people of a congregation ("To the church of the Thessalonians," "To the church of God that is in Corinth"), the seven letters to the churches in the book of Revelation were all addressed to the angels of the churches (e.g., "To the angel of the church of Ephesus write . . .").[1] Wink suggests that the image of the angel is compelling and that the angel of each congregation has two voices: the voice of personality and the voice of vocation.

> The angel of each congregation has two voices: the voice of personality and the voice of vocation.

The *voice of personality* is the voice of the past. It speaks of the important events in the life of the congregation that have shaped it through challenge or through accomplishment. It speaks of the remarkable people who have left their imprint on the congregation and helped to shape it. It speaks of the commitments made, the risks taken, the bumps and bruises that make the congregation what it is. The *voice of vocation,* however, is the voice of the future. It talks of commitments and values to be lived out, hopes to be realized, and costs to be paid willingly for the greater purpose.

Wink cautions that it is imperative to be sure that the voice of personality is connected to the voice of vocation. If the voice of personality dominates the angel of the congregation, then the congregation cannot be more than it has been in the past. If the voice of vocation dominates the angel of the congregation, disconnected from the voice of personality, then the congregation will live an inauthentic life that cannot be sustained because it has no foundation. The purpose of leadership, guided by the discernment of a planning process, is to hold the two voices of the angel in relationship and in tension with one another, so that the congregation claims its own authentic story connected to the grander story of faith.

> The result of the planning process is naming, claiming, and committing to a vocation.

The result of the planning process is not a clear and guaranteed path into the future. It is naming, claiming, and committing to a vocation. Like all vocations, it is an "impulsion to perform a certain function or enter a certain career."[2] It points to the beginning of a critical and meaningful path to be taken.

Notes

1. Walter Wink, *Unmasking the Powers: The Invisible Forces That Determine Human Existence* (Philadelphia: Fortress Press, 1986), 69.
2. David Guralnik, ed., *Webster's New World Dictionary of the American Language* (U.S.A.: William Collins and World Publishing Co., 1978), 1590.

PART THREE

Issues in Strategic Planning

Now that we have identified possible steps in a full-blown strategic planning model, it is time to return to a set of overarching issues that planning leaders typically encounter. Topics in this section include:

- *Sources of energy in a planning process.* Pain plus possibility can allow a congregation to risk change. (Chapter 7)
- *Where vision comes from.* We will look at congregation, pastor, and denominational connection as possible sources of vision, then offer an understanding of vision as "meaning we make together." (Chapter 8)
- *Ways to read the congregation's culture.* To a large extent, a congregation's culture determines the purposes it can embrace, the populations it can passionately serve, and the kinds of planning conversations in which it can engage most naturally. (Chapter 9)
- *Ways to read the community context.* Planning gains energy when members take a fresh look at the lives of the people around them. As the congregation answers the question, "Who is my neighbor—today?" people may find themselves called to express in new ways their enduring faith. (Chapter 10)
- *How congregations discern God's leading.* Planning requires an attitude of discernment and appropriate practices for listening to self, other, and God. (Chapter 11)
- *How people in different roles contribute to the planning process.* We will review the roles of the planning committee and its

chair; the pastor; the governing board; and, where appropriate, the planning consultant. (Chapter 12)

- *Ways to involve the congregation.* A wider circle of leaders needs to get on board with the planning questions, the learning process, and the key choices before the congregation at this time. Beyond this circle, the entire congregation needs to become aware of the process, feel invited to participate according to their energies and interests, and trust that those more involved in the planning are doing the right work in a thoughtful way. (Chapter 13)

CHAPTER SEVEN

Energy to Plan

Within your congregation, you will find a small subgroup of members for whom planning work is inherently engaging—even fun. This is probably not the attitude of your average member or even your typical core leader. While a sense of duty may bring that person's body to the planning table, it takes more than obligation to elicit energy for the conversation. What generates energy?

Pain as Energy Source

One familiar source of stimulation and motivation is a clear-cut presenting problem within the congregation, an *ouch* that is being experienced and named by enough of the influential people to get a planning conversation launched. We're overcrowded. We're understaffed. Or we're losing an effective long-term staff person.

Paradoxically, the motivation generated by pain may lead directly to one of the key obstacles for strategic planning that we identified in the Introduction to this book: the congregation's impulse to fix the situation quickly and restore things to their previous state. While the fix-it approach is quite desirable when the boiler happens to break down on a Sunday morning in January, it becomes a dead-end path when the congregation

> While a sense of duty may bring a person to the planning table, it takes more than obligation to elicit energy for the conversation.

needs to grapple with bigger questions about its identity, its mission, and its relationship to its neighbors in the community. For example, it is not uncommon for a dying church to spend its energy and financial resources repairing an organ or restoring stained glass—resolving an immediate pain people know how to fix—simply because the leaders don't have a way to channel energy toward the central questions.

Organizational change expert John Kotter[1] notes that the first step in a turnaround may be to intensify, rather than to relieve, the pain. In order to build the necessary feeling of urgency in the system, he says, a leader needs to put the bad news into sharp focus. For a congregation, this might mean:

- *Making a chart to show changes in attendance over 20 or 30 years.* A congregation that has described itself as stable may suddenly see the bigger reality of steady, long-term decline.
- *Charting the number of pledging households rather than total number of dollars given.* The total number of dollars almost always goes up because of inflation; but a drop in the number of supporting households could mean real trouble.
- *Doing a bit of actuarial projection.* A treasurer might use average life-expectancy figures to project how many pledging households are likely to disappear in the next decade—and might make the story even more alarming by noting the difference in the average pledge amount for people in senior years as compared with those in midlife or early adulthood.
- *Illustrating a key demographic trend.* A pastor might choose one aspect of demographic or cultural change that is especially threatening to the congregation's current way of doing ministry. Illustrate that change with photographs or stories that dramatize how the world around the church is different today. Project what will happen if the congregation tries to keep the same programs going in this changed environment.[2]

Since clergy and elected board members usually feel it is their job to reduce anxiety, these tactics will probably seem counterintuitive. The goal is not to overwhelm people but to get them mobilized to face into the challenge with sustained effort. The strategic planning process can serve as a sturdy container—a place where bad news can be held, and beheld, while the larger system gets ready to grapple it.

If the planning team practices a bit of judo, the congregation's immediate presenting issues will provide energy and focus to the strategic planning process. The pressing practical question—about finances, or staffing, or building expansion, for example—is faced and welcomed, just as one would receive a charging opponent on the mat. What makes all the difference is the *way* the incoming energy is received, what leverage is applied, what final destination the judo master has envisioned for the sparring partner's force. An immediate cash-flow problem can be leveraged into an examination of long-term trends in membership, attendance, and giving. A staff expansion debate, initially framed as youth worker vs. associate pastor, could be transformed into a look at the whole staffing pattern and ways the staff team as a unit might best support the congregation's mission at this time. Urgent building issues might provide the opportunity to ask: "What kind of church are we, and how might

> The art of strategic planning lies in the leaders' ability to keep both the pragmatist and the dreamer involved in the work.

our building communicate our identity and mission to our surrounding community?" The art of strategic planning lies in leaders' ability to keep both the pragmatist and the dreamer involved in the work in appropriate ways—and to recognize the moment when the system must see some visible results. In his writing about organizational turnarounds, Kotter points out that clarification of a bold vision must be followed by some early wins, that is, small accomplishments that embody or advance the larger intention.[3] Here are some examples:

- A congregation includes in its planning structure both a task force on long-term space needs and a task force on short-term solutions to relieve overcrowding.
- At the end of every key event in its process, a planning team collects statements of potential goals. Some of the easiest projects are tagged for immediate consideration and implementation and referred to the appropriate committee for action.
- A congregation identifies several peer churches that have addressed their presenting problem in some creative way. They visit these congregations to gain perspective on the problem and to learn about possible long-term approaches. But they also look for ideas the congregation could experiment with right now, to stir up new thinking that will support the vision in the long run.

An early-win objective should relate to a key problem or opportunity the congregation needs to confront; avoid initiating early projects that will divert attention from central issues. Early wins should also tap into existing energy and readiness. Don't choose anything that's a hard sell—you may use up your political capital before you've even presented your primary goals. Early-win objectives should be aimed at visible, immediate, and satisfying results that *do not interfere* with the full exploration of long-term options. For example, renting additional space across the street would be a better short-term move than building a temporary addition; paying rent would actually motivate people to find another solution, while investing in a makeshift addition could cause people to resist a more comprehensive construction proposal later on.

Hope as Energy Source

One reason a dying church may pour its meager resources into ill-considered repair projects is the absence of hope. When the threat is so big that death seems assured, fixing the organ is a palliative measure, a way of passing the remaining time a little more comfortably. It would be hard to challenge such a use of resources unless people started to believe they had a future, that is, the possibility of a different life that would be worth the pain of living.

Renowned organizational consultant Margaret Wheatley[4] suggests that hope is an issue not only for dying churches, but also for people everywhere in the world (including you and me).

> I don't meet many people who are optimistic any more. . . . Almost everyone is experiencing life as more stressful, more disconnected, and less meaningful than just a few years ago. It's not only that there's more change, or that change is now continuous. It's the nature of the change that is upsetting. For example: A small political incident sets off violence that doesn't end. A small computer malfunction disrupts lives for days or weeks. . . . The undetected rage of a person or group suddenly threatens us or someone we love. A disease in one location spreads like wildfire into global contagion. . . . These crises appear suddenly in a life or community. They always feel surprising, out of control, and irrational. . . . It's changing how we act and feel. . . . We're more cynical, impatient, fearful, angry, defensive, anxious; more likely to hurt those we love.
>
> How can we become people we respect, people who are generous, loving, curious, open, energetic? How can we ensure that at the end of our lives, we'll feel that we have done meaningful work, created something that endured, helped other people, and raised healthy children? What can we do now to restore hope to the future?[5]

Wheatley's overview is frightening—as a result, we may refuse to ponder this picture on days when there is no immediate cataclysm that forces us to look. But her proposed antidote is both simple and powerful. Slow down, pay renewed attention to relationships, and engage in real conversations about the things that bother us deep down.

> There is no more powerful way to initiate significant change than to convene a conversation. When a community of people discovers that they share a concern, change begins. There is no power equal to a community discovering what it cares about. . . . Solidarity in Poland began with conversation—less than a dozen workers in Gdansk shipyard speaking to each other about their despair, their need for change, their need for freedom. In less than a month, Solidarity grew to 9.5 million workers. There was no e-mail then, just people talking to each other about their own needs, and finding their needs shared. . . . At the end of that month, all 9.5 million of them acted as one voice for change. They shut down the country.[6]

"It's not easy to begin talking to one another again," says Wheatley.[7] Some of us have never found a voice and cannot imagine speaking from the heart; others are drowning in pointless talk at meetings that make no difference; still others of us feel frightened by voices (sometimes including our own) that quickly turn ugly when we become intense.

When we don't engage in real conversation, the cost is high: the resulting void "is soon filled with poison, drivel, and misrepresentation."[8] But deep, honest exchange about the truth of our own lives generates creative energy. Congregations can draw upon several resources to elicit more authentic conversation among members:

- *Personal Sharing.* To begin at the most basic level, the creation of some "Story Circles for the Soul"[9] in the congregation could strengthen the bonds of trust and respect. A Story Circle is a group that practices respectful listening as members respond in turn to an evocative question by spinning out a part of their own life story. Small-group materials from the Serendipity[10] series can be used for the same purpose. They create similar safety to share about one's own life, in the context of a more explicitly Christian and biblical framework. Such circles of conversation would be most fruitful in a climate-setting stage—beginning at least six months before a formal planning process is launched. Small-group sharing is certainly helpful in the midst of the planning as well, but once the formal planning begins it is much harder to stimulate conversation, for its own sake, about the shape of our own lives. As church innovator Richard Melheim[11] has pointed out so well in his online book, *The Fifth Church,* we move too quickly to the organizational level and attend too little to the individual heart (the first church) as a primary temple of the Holy Spirit.

- *Building Conversational Skills.* To help people gain skill in handling important but stressful conversations—not only in the congregation, but also in their daily lives—you might teach skills for one-to-one dialogue. One excellent resource would be *Crucial Conversations: Tools for Talking When the Stakes Are High*[12] (from which we borrowed the above quotation about "poison, drivel, and misrepresentation"). Another resource with a more specifically Christian orientation would be *Speaking the Truth in Love.*[13] Either book would be an excellent basis for an adult education series or weekend retreat. Working with this material would not only improve parish planning conversations; it would offer people vital skills for family life, work, and civic involvement.

- *Engaging in Difficult Conversations.* To strengthen the congregation's practices in tackling controversial issues, you might use as a guide Katie Day's *Difficult Conversations: Taking Risks, Acting with Integrity.*[14] If you know that the planning process will call attention to a potentially divisive issue (for example: "Will this congregation celebrate services of blessing for gay or lesbian unions?"), study of this book would be excellent preparation for the board and the planning team.

No planning format—or process gimmick—will guarantee that people speak to each other from the heart and listen with respect. These are matters of broad congregational practice and climate. It takes time, leadership, and persistence to build trust and mutual attentiveness, but when congregations practice conscious trust-building every time people gather, the tone begins to change.

Here is how truth telling generated hope and energy in one small congregation located in an old suburb just outside Boston. This church had become a bit of a joke among its neighbors for having the longest-running interim ministry in history—they had been searching for a new pastor for about three years with no success. After attending a workshop on redevelopment strategies, they entered into a more intentional visioning process with

> When congregations practice conscious trust-building every time people gather, the tone begins to change.

the help of a consultant. By clarifying the kind of ministry the *congregation* felt called to do, they hoped to give their search for a *pastor* better focus. But, no matter how many options they identified, they just couldn't get any traction on defining a future. One plausible idea after another seemed to sink into a bog of depression.

Finally, in response to sympathetic questioning by a trusted consultant, the deeper truth came out. About seven key leaders, aged 30-55, felt unbearably burdened. They were trying to keep in place all the familiar ministries—a traditional Sunday service, a choir, and a Sunday school—for about 25 attendees, most of whom were elderly. They could identify very little about the whole experience that fed them spiritually, and they were exhausted.

As each member of this small leadership core owned up to his or her real experience, and discovered that others were having similar feelings, the group was able to endorse a radical proposal with three elements. First, they would look for a new interim pastor who could lead them in spiritual growth activities for an hour each Monday evening. (To their surprise, they readily found a part-time pastor with excellent training in spiritual guidance to lead their "Monday sabbath" and to provide pastoral care to the older members.) Second, they would remain together for another hour each Monday evening to handle board and committee tasks—the same seven people held all the leadership roles anyway—and to continue their discernment about the congregation's future. And finally, instead of struggling to hold Sunday services, they would for a period of time meet each other on Sunday morning in the parking lot, load the rest of the congregants into their cars, and travel as a group to a hospitable neighboring church. They asked this neighbor church to allow them to be sojourners—enjoying the vigorous Sunday worship and participating in ministries like choir

and Sunday school while maintaining membership and group identity
in their original church.

Truth telling about the terrible feeling of burden led to about a
year of refreshment and spiritual growth in the Monday sabbath format. This period of spiritual nourishment enabled them to be patient
and to pray for discernment of God's larger call.
They finally developed the confidence to try out
a partner relationship with a Korean congregation that needed a permanent home. They discerned that it might be a good match, because
the Korean pastor had gifts that could help both groups to grow spiritually and to explore patiently the possibilities for a shared ministry in
that place.

> The energy and courage to risk
> new life started bubbling up when
> seven people started telling
> deeper truths to each other.

For this congregation, the energy and courage to risk new life—spiritual and organizational—started bubbling up at the moment seven people
started telling the deeper truth to each other. Although fear, confusion, and
depression sometimes returned, those feelings did not prevail. Instead, can-
did and caring conversation released energy and inspired innovation. As
they abandoned false optimism—the initial belief that finding the right
pastor would be enough to save a dying church—they discovered, paradoxically, greater hope for God's action among them in the stage of the
journey they were actually experiencing at that time.

Vision as Energy Source

A third source of energy for the planning conversation is vision. As we
have seen in the outline of a full-blown process, articulation of vision
usually comes toward the end of the work, when the planners have
moved from fearless contemplation of what is, to bold imagining of
what might be. Occasionally, however, a pastor or lay leader starts out
with a very clear dream—a dream communicated in such a compelling
way that others join the conversation with excitement. Where a key
leader proposes a particular vision up front, the planning work will
need to focus on questions of participation, teamwork, and investment.
While an individual leader may have sufficient influence to get an innovative program launched, the new venture will only become integrated
into the congregation's core identity if many leaders and members have

the opportunity to take the project into their own hands—to shake it, to shape it, to make it their own.

Notes

1. John Kotter, "Leading Change: Why Transformation Efforts Fail," *Harvard Business Review*, Reprint #95204 (March-April 1995): 59–67.
2. Here are two examples of ways to illustrate demographic trends. First, Gil Rendle's video presentation, *Living into the New World: How Cultural Trends Affect Your Congregation* (Bethesda, Md.: Alban Institute, 2000), illustrates a generational watershed between those born before 1946 and those born after. Second, when Alice worked with a congregation in an old suburb outside Boston, she noticed that the small, older shops on the main avenue—shoe repair, barber shop, pharmacy—were either closing or slipping into disrepair. One whole block of these stores, however, had been purchased and renovated into a first-rate bicycle sales and repair facility. The fate of the shops symbolized broad demographic changes: the population of blue-collar families was declining, while the number of young professionals starting careers was increasing. A simple slide show (with photos snapped over the space of a few weeks) brought the community changes into sharp focus.
3. Kotter, "Leading Change," 65.
4. Margaret Wheatley, *Turning to One Another: Simple Conversations to Restore Hope to the Future* (San Francisco: Berrett-Koehler, 2002).
5. Ibid., 14–17.
6. Ibid., 22.
7. Ibid., 24.
8. A quotation attributed to C. Northcote Parkinson, used by co-authors Kerry Patterson, Joseph Grenny, Ron McMillan, and Al Switzler as the epigraph to chapter 1 of *Crucial Conversations: Tools for Talking When the Stakes Are High* (New York: McGraw Hill, 2002), 1.
9. These groups have been pioneered by an organization called Story Circles International. See www.StoryCirclesInternational.com.

10. For information about a wide variety of resources in the Serendipity series, visit www.serendipityhouse.com.
11. You can download *The Fifth Church* from Richard Melheim's Web site: www.faithinkubators.com.
12. Patterson, et al., *Crucial Conversations*.
13. Ruth Koch and Kenneth Haugk, *Speaking the Truth in Love: How to Be an Assertive Christian* (St. Louis: Stephen Ministries, 1992).
14. Katie Day, *Difficult Conversations: Taking Risks, Acting with Integrity* (Bethesda, Md.: Alban Institute, 2001). Katie Day is associate professor of church and society at the Lutheran Theological Seminary at Philadelphia and a developer of experiential education programs.

CHAPTER EIGHT

Where Does Vision Come From?

Let's go a little further with the question of vision, since so much is being said and written about it these days. We at Alban are often asked where the vision is *supposed* to come from in the life of a congregation. The emergence of vision is not really a technical issue that can be addressed with a correct method. Rather, assumptions about how vision emerges reflect the underlying ecclesiology of a particular faith community. By ecclesiology, we

> The emergence of vision is not really a technical issue that can be addressed with a correct method.

mean one's understanding of the nature of the church, and as a corollary, one's assumptions about religious authority. In practice, we can identify at least three common approaches to the issue of vision—each reflecting a different theory of church. While it would be rare to find the positions stated quite as extremely as we have done here—in our "quotations" of three imaginary church leaders—the sharp contrast may be clarifying.

A Congregational Theory of Vision Formation

Authentic vision for our congregation can only originate in the membership. Members' aspirations may be clarified in several different ways: through a congregation-wide planning process, through the work of ongoing committees, or through informal conversation among members. As any proposal for future direction takes shape, it will be brought to a congregational vote in order to ensure that it truly represents the people of our church—who we are, what we value, how we understand our future calling.

This theory is a common basis for planning in the explicitly congregational traditions (United Church of Christ, Unitarian Universalist, and American Baptist, for example). Even in traditions where pastors, rabbis, or bishops have more formal authority, the behavior of leaders and members in North American congregations is often shaped by congregational assumptions.

A Pastoral Theory of Vision Formation

Our ordained minister is our spiritual leader. As a person of prayer, our pastor spends time discerning God's intentions for this church. Through preaching, teaching, and organizational leadership, our pastor offers the congregation a unifying vision for the future and invites other leaders to participate in bringing that vision to fruition.

This theory of vision formation is often presented in books on leadership by authors from the evangelical tradition; these authors commonly describe the pastor's task as casting the vision. Lay leaders with a business background sometimes advocate a variation on this model, arguing that the top organizational leader in a congregation must set the future agenda—a common, but not universal, view of the executive role. (Where this view is advanced, further questions may arise: Who is the "top organizational leader"? Is it the pastor? Or is it the senior lay official?)

A Connectional Theory of Vision Formation

The primary unit of mission is not the congregation, but rather the wider fellowship of believers in this region. To discover an authentic vision for our congregation, we look to our mutually acknowledged religious authority (bishop or presbytery, for example) for inspiration and guidance. We test our congregation's particular aspirations against that larger vision whenever we engage in discernment about the future.

This approach to vision formation might be found in the Episcopal, Presbyterian, or United Methodist traditions, for example. Goals of the regional unit (diocese, presbytery, conference) are lifted up as benchmarks for congregational mission. The vision of the regional body may be implemented through funding of congregations, clergy placement decisions, and each pastor's self-understanding as one with dual accountability—serving both the congregation and the wider body.

Vision as Meaning We Make Together

The congregation's vision might be seen in another way—as the meaning the congregation makes about its present and its future. Theories that rely on either the visionary leader (whether this is the local pastor or the bishop) or on the conventional machinery of parliamentary self-governance may miss the underlying process by which people make sense of their faith lives—as individuals and as congregations. Writing primarily for corporate executives, leadership theorists Wilfred Drath and Charles Palus[1] argue for a richer view of a leader's work and a subtler account of the way vision emerges. They see the person in formal authority as one participant in an organization-wide process of the meaning-making that is going on all the time. "Meaning-making is all about constructing a sense of what is, what actually exists, and, of that, what is important. . . . When this happens in association with practice (work, activity) in a community, we say that the process of leadership is happening." In this framework, leadership is seen not as a trait or an official role, but rather as a *process* in which people *make meaning together*. (The title of the Drath and Palus monograph— "Making Common Sense"—emphasizes that leadership involves the creation of *shared* meaning). Further, this leadership process may be occurring anywhere in the system, not just at the manager's desk or the board table.[2]

While Drath and Palus's specialized vocabulary can be a bit daunting, they highlight fundamental human longings (meaning, purpose, significance) and competencies (telling a story, making meaning together) that are home territory for a religious congregation. In fact, meaning-making occurs at two levels in a religious system. Just as in any other organization, people need to make sense of their experiences as members or leaders. Why am I part of this congregation? What kind of participation is meaningful for me? What is going on here?

However, religious systems engage in another level of meaning-making not found (at least consciously) in most other organizations. A central function of religion *per se* is to interpret reality, to make sense of the cosmos, to tell the foundational story in which other stories may find their proper context. So, when leaders work together to articulate a vision for the congregation, they are making meaning of an enterprise that itself makes meaning of the universe.

Because of this duality, the leadership process in a religious system is especially complex and demanding. But the process also contains, at least potentially, rich layers of significance, beyond what we might ordinarily expect of routine planning tasks—provided that we invite participants to interact with the deepest source of meaning as they undertake their work. Each faith tradition identifies this source in a particular way—ultimate meaning may be sought in Torah, in the story of Jesus, in Word and Sacrament, or in a founder's writings, for example. When members, gathered for a planning activity, connect their work with a source of meaning they hold sacred, they may suddenly know themselves to be standing on holy ground. Here are some examples of the ways congregations connect planning with deeper sources of meaning:

> When members connect their work with a source of meaning they hold sacred, they may suddenly know themselves to be standing on holy ground.

- As they work on their mission statement, a planning committee in a large Lutheran church struggles to articulate the larger purpose that holds together all the key activities (worship, study, outreach). One member suggests the word *discipleship*, and the whole committee senses it has broken through to an important insight. Over the next few weeks, the pastor helps the planning committee and board study 10 biblical passages that illuminate different aspects of Christian discipleship. When the committee presents its report, it uses the visual image of a flower. Discipleship is shown as the center, with a variety of ministries as petals all around it.

- The key planning question for an interracial Baptist congregation is whether and how to make the transition from pastoral- to program-size congregation. One team within the planning committee studies the church's history and discovers that one of the founding members in 1837 was an African American man; they feel they have discovered a local saint who symbolizes the congregation's long-standing commitment to reach across racial barriers. At the same time, the pastor asks the congregation to study Bruce Wilkinson's best-selling book *The Prayer of Jabez*, and to pray Jabez's prayer: that God might extend their territory. The congregation's biblical grounding and belief in the power of prayer gives them boldness to plan for the next stage of outreach and growth. They are confident that they have heard an authentic call from God.

- At the urging of their half-time director of Christian formation, an Episcopal congregation sets its planning process into the context of a year-long study of the Baptismal Covenant from the *Book of Common Prayer.*[3] They allow the baptismal promises to draw them beyond the question, "What do we want?" to the deeper question, "What kind of life does God call us—and empower us—to live in a broken world?" Toward the end of the study and planning year, when a set of proposed goals has emerged, they hold a prayer vigil from 9 P.M. Saturday through 9 A.M. Sunday, and they sign up members for different hours of the silent vigil. The Eucharist service that Sunday, held at the close of the prayer vigil, is greatly simplified. The Liturgy of the Word consists only of a hymn, a Gospel reading, and a time of silence resembling a Quaker meeting. Members are invited to speak quietly, without discussion, about the way they perceive God to be leading the congregation at this time. After the service, the congregation gathers over breakfast to review the proposed goals and suggest any final revisions. Each member is encouraged to identify one goal to which they would especially like to contribute time and talent in the coming year and to pledge participation in that aspect of the congregation's ministry.

In each case a leader, lay or ordained, has helped the group tap into a deeper source of meaning as it engages in the work of planning.

Sacred meaning is carried through the generations in symbols—words, stories, objects, places, ritual actions. We might use the term *breakout* to describe the moments—like those described above—when a congregation's symbols come alive in the immediate situation, when they work to give profound meaning to what is happening right now among us.[4] To take a secular example, we might think about the damaged flag from the World Trade Center that was carried to many locations in the following year, including the Olympic Games in Salt Lake City. Especially in the era since the war in Vietnam, the American flag—potentially a symbol of patriotism and national unity—had for many people either lost meaning or become associated with negative meanings (bitter division over the rightness of that war, cultural imperialism, commercialism). While those painful associations did not disappear entirely, two historical events intervened to refocus the flag's potential meanings. The first stretched over several years, as our country celebrated a whole set of fiftieth anniversaries related to World War II. And the second was, of course, September 11—a moment when differences and disagreements were largely (though never completely) overshadowed by national trauma. As a result, many people experienced *breakout* moments related to the American flag.

The opposite of *breakout* is symbolic *breakdown*. During the Vietnam era, antiwar protesters burned the flag to dramatize their loss of confidence in American values. The objects and images we had relied upon to connect us with the deeper meanings of our national life often seemed bitterly ironic—or simply irrelevant as consumerism took over as the dominant shared value among us. (One might argue that the Nike swoosh logo replaced the flag as the single most potent emblem of American culture.)

When church leaders work together to articulate a vision for the congregation, they are making meaning of an enterprise that itself makes meaning of the universe. Just as in the case of our national life, it may take an experience of breakdown to reveal the connection between making sense in our organizational decision making and making meaning of the cosmos in a religious sense. Today's most profound example of symbolic breakdown in American religious life revolves around the sexual abuse of children by clergy, and the ways religious institutions (across many faith traditions) have engaged in collusion and cover-up. Here the connection between the two levels of meaning-making is powerfully revealed. If the God-symbol in the God-place abuses me (or my

> **When congregational leaders work together to articulate a vision, they are making meaning of an enterprise that itself makes meaning of the universe.**

child), how can I experience God as trustworthy and life giving? If I reported this behavior to other religious leaders and they betrayed me (by calling me a trouble-maker, by hiding the abuser's history, or by passing the problem on to another congregation), how can I trust the faith community as a meaning-making body? Where symbolic breakdown has occurred, the relationship between the two levels of meaning must be built up anew from the fundamental source. People must tell a new story together that is large enough and powerful enough to incor-porate the betrayal, and to suggest an interpretation of the world that makes sense once again.

Even in the absence of a major symbolic breakdown, however, the connections between the two levels of meaning are constantly under construction. We may say that spiritual leaderhip is occurring wherever members of the faith community are weaving new strands of connection between the source of meaning (as defined by their religious tradi-tion) and their present situation—with all its

> Spiritual leadership occurs when members of the faith community weave new strands of connection between the source of meaning and their present situation.

perils, opportunities, and choices. The act of weaving, no matter who is doing it, *is* spiritual leadership.

The weaving of new connections happens in unpredictable ways. Earlier, in chapter 7, when we explored how energy is gained from truth telling, we considered the story of a dwindling congregation in an old suburb outside of Boston. As that con-gregation sought a vision, many different voices interpreted the deeper significance of the church's situation and its choices—that is to say,

> The act of weaving, no matter who is doing it, *is* spiritual leadership.

many people played a role in the process of spiritual leadership. Here are a few examples of the contributions different people made in the process of making meaning together:

- The neighborhood around the church houses a good many out-patients in care of a nearby psychiatric hospital. One woman, whose life is a constant struggle for emotional balance and eco-nomic survival, wrote simple, powerful poems about the an-choring role that congregation has played in her life; she read these poems at several of the meetings about future options.
- Many 12-step groups have met for a long time in the church's fellowship hall. One of the organizers—aware that the church's future was up in the air—sent a letter of appreciation for the church's long-standing hospitality. He was gently reminding the church that there was more to its life and ministry than might be apparent on Sunday morning.
- The moderator of the congregation wrote thoughtful letters to the members at each step along the way. In one case, he drew on

a passage from a children's Bible—more specifically, from the book he and his wife used in the daily religious formation of their own small children. Citing the story of the house built on rock and the house built on sand, he made the case for an unconventional worship format (Monday sabbath) by reminding the congregation that any worthwhile future must be founded on the rock of spiritual vitality.

All three voices contributed to the leadership process—to the congregation's work of making meaning together. Each voice invited the congregation to honor a deeper source of meaning as they discerned a future direction. The moderator's letter reminded the congregation not only of its scriptural grounding (as a Christian congregation in the Reformed tradition); by quoting from a children's Bible, he also seemed to be invoking powerful congregational memories and values about Christian nurture. Both the poet and the AA organizer implicitly reminded the members of key values embedded in their Congregational heritage: in that faith tradition, the congregation is presumed to have a powerful role in creating the good society and caring for the neighbor in need. The leadership circle of this tiny church took all of these sources of meaning—scripture, the congregation's particular history and values, and their denominational heritage—to heart as they weighed their options.

> Each voice invited the congregation to honor a deeper source of meaning as they discerned a future direction.

This sacred work—weaving new strands of connection between the source of meaning (as defined by a particular religious tradition) and the present situation—can happen within all three of the models of vision formation, provided that members and leaders generally concur that the model applied is appropriate. Each model, in its more extreme expressions, can rob the vision-tapestry of some of its richness by banning the participation of weavers from other parts of the system. Extremely congregationally oriented vision-formation processes tend to block contributions from the pastor or denomination. A highly pastor-centered process tends to limit members and denominational colleagues to the role of responder. A vision-formation process dominated by the denomination may ignore the insights of the clergy and laity closest to the ministry situation. Nevertheless, each of the three basic approaches can be implemented in a way that demonstrates open inquiry and recognizes the interdependence of the parties.

This section began with two broad issues in strategic planning—energy to plan and sources of vision. We will turn now to a core task of the strategic-planning process: reading the congregation's internal and external environment, and, in particular, reading the *culture* of both the congregation and the surrounding community. We will begin with the culture of the congregation.

Notes

1. Wilfred Drath and Charles Palus, *Making Common Sense: Leadership as Meaning-Making in a Community of Practice* (Greensboro, N.C.: Center for Creative Leadership, 1994), 9.

2. Kerry Patterson et al., in *Crucial Conversations: Tools for Talking When the Stakes Are High* (New York: McGraw Hill, 2002), use similar language: "Each of us enters conversations with our own opinions, feelings, theories, and experiences about the topic at hand. This unique combination of thoughts and feelings makes up our personal pool of meaning. . . . People who are skilled at dialogue do their best to make it safe for everyone to add their meaning to the *shared* pool . . . [hence] the Pool of Shared Meaning grows" (p. 21).

3. *Book of Common Prayer* (New York: Church Hymnal Corporation, 1979), 304–305. The baptismal questions include these: "Will you proclaim by word and example the Good News of God in Christ? Will you seek and serve Christ in all persons, loving your neighbor as yourself? Will you strive for justice and peace among all people, and respect the dignity of every human being?"

4. Linda J. Clark, Joanne Swenson, and Mark Stamm, *How We Seek God Together: Exploring Worship Style* (Bethesda, Md.: Alban Institute, 2001), 19 and 35–42.

CHAPTER NINE

Reading the Congregation's Culture

People who have participated in strategic-planning processes in congregations sometimes express disappointment with the results.

- "We proposed bold goals, but the congregation (or board) turned them down."
- "The congregation adopted the plan, then promptly forgot about it and went back to business as usual."
- "As the board started to implement the plan, members became more and more uncomfortable. People felt they were being asked to do things that were foreign to them."

In many cases, these outcomes occur because the planning leaders have not taken time to understand and interpret their congregation's culture.

Let's start with an analogy. Culture is to the congregation what personality is to the individual—a unique pattern of traits, capacities, and propensities that shape how a person responds to the world. Since individual personality is itself shaped (especially in the first few years of life) by a set of genetic and environmental factors, we might say that a person's identity emerges out of the ongoing interaction between inside and outside.

So it is with congregational culture. Founding personalities and early events create a kind of genetic inheritance and determine the way the congregation positions itself within its environment. This legacy becomes embedded in narrative: members begin to tell a characteristic story about what is going on in the world and what the congregation's proper place in that world seems to be. As a result of the way the church positions itself with respect to its neighborhood and its wider faith tradition, certain responses are elicited from that environment and certain kinds of people cross the boundary into membership. Leaders who

> Members begin to tell a characteristic story about what is going on in the world and what the congregation's proper place in that world seems to be.

emerge within the membership pool tend to interpret and react to the world using a shared frame of reference—expressed in an overarching congregational narrative that is both internally consistent (in its basic orientation to the world) and evolving (in the details and nuances of its content).

Culture and Narrative

If congregations express and transmit culture through the basic story they tell about themselves, what do these overarching narratives look like? Sociologists Carl Dudley and Sally Johnson[1] have gleaned, from their study of congregations, five different kinds of story from which the pattern of a church's life and ministry might organically emerge. As they listened to members speak about their congregations, these researchers heard:

- Journey stories of ethnic-cultural congregations
- Crisis stories of churches that struggle for survival
- Rooted stories with a place for spiritual growth
- Service stories of caring for people
- Mission stories of vision for a better world

As an example, we might look at a church whose overarching narrative features service stories of caring for people. A United Methodist congregation on Long Island recently sought to clarify its mission focus and to raise its profile in an adjoining community where many elderly people live. As they recounted favorite stories about the church's past, leaders discovered a common theme—providing care and assistance to people one at a time. They also noticed how much enthusiasm the members had for the church's annual work-camp project in Appalachia. As a result of this reflection, the congregational leaders decided to launch a new domestic work-camp program. They will reach out to elderly members and nonmembers one household at a time, providing teams to do simple home repair and maintenance work. Leaders believe that such a program will illustrate a core strength of the church to the wider community, attract helpful press coverage, encourage visitors to try out the church, and perhaps even draw some nonmembers into the volunteer corps. (Digging into the history of their denomination through its Web site, one planning-team member discovered that the Social Gospel Movement was profoundly influential during the era of the church's founding. This research caused the team to ponder the historical roots and theological implications of their church's ministry preferences today.)

Shortly before his death in 1984, religious scholar James Hopewell[2] had developed his own categorization of congregational narratives and worldviews, based on the work of literary critic and theorist Northrop Frye.[3] Hopewell noted the way Frye had "laid out Western literature in a great imaginary circle" with "four cardinal points much like those of a compass." Starting at the easterly point on the face of compass and moving clockwise, the four points are comedy, romance, tragedy, and irony. *Comic* tales are those that present "positive resolution of difficult situations" through deep and transforming knowledge; they are fundamentally optimistic, even if they are not light or funny. *Romantic* tales revolve around a heroic quest filled with perils; some miraculous power makes the decisive difference, allowing the hero or heroine to attain a deeply desired object. *Tragic* tales show the human person wrestling with, and finally surrendering to, the eternal order of the universe. "The tragic hero is not cured but saved" by his willingness to pay the ultimate cost. *Ironic* tales offer no ultimate purpose or salvation. "Miracles do not happen; patterns lose their design; life is unjust, not justified by transcendent forces." In the absence of any divine salvation or humanistic triumph over adversity, the best a person can do is to "embrace one's brothers and sisters in camaraderie."

Hopewell accepted Frye's hypothesis that any literary work can be placed within this geography—"if not fully within a particular genre, then somewhere between two adjoining types."[4] Hopewell translated this literary compass into a map of four worldviews that might, alone or in combination, guide a faith community (see diagram on next page).[5]

Starting again at "east" on the face of the compass, Hopewell uses the terms *gnostic, charismatic, canonic,* and *empiric* to describe the religious stance associated with each genre. (His book includes the "World View Test," a self-scoring inventory that might be used by an individual or a church group to explore the theological frameworks through which people interpret their lives.) We will use hymns to illustrate differences among these four overarching ways of seeing the world.

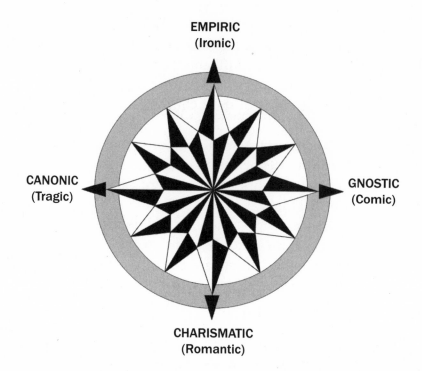

According to Hopewell, a *tragic* orientation in religious narrative translates into a *canonic* worldview, with an emphasis on the motif of sacrifice. Authority derives from "God's revealed word and will," and the most valued behavior is obedience. A congregation where this view dominates might sing with conviction the words of Isaac Watts:

> When I survey the wondrous cross
> where the young prince of glory died,
> my richest gain I count but loss,
> and pour contempt on all my pride
>
> . . . .
>
> Were the whole realm of nature mine,
> that were an offering far too small;
> love so amazing, so divine,
> demands my soul, my life, my all. [6]

In contrast, a *comic* orientation in congregational story generates a *gnostic* worldview, with integration as a central motif. Authority is located in "intuition and esoteric wisdom," and the prized work is interior awareness. This life-stance might lead a congregation to resonate with this verse from a hymn text composed by a Dutch mystic in

1729. This particular verse of the hymn was translated and popularized by renowned preacher Henry Sloane Coffin around 1910:

> Thou pervadest all things; let thy radiant beauty
> light mine eyes to see my duty.
> As the tender flowers eagerly unfold them,
> to the sunlight calmly hold them,
> so let me quietly in thy rays imbue me;
> let thy light shine through me.[7]

Although the term *duty* implies that responsible action will follow, this
verse focuses on inward illumination and transformation of the believer as the source of hope for a better world.

A *romantic* orientation in a faith community's self-understanding
becomes Hopewell's *charismatic* worldview, organized around a core motif
of adventure. "Evidence of God's immanence" is the key source of authority when it is "personally manifested," and the valued behavior is "recognition of God's blessings." Such a view is reflected brilliantly in John
Newton's testimony to the life-changing moment on the high seas, when
God called him to renounce his old life as captain of a slave ship:

> Amazing grace! how sweet the sound,
> that saved a wretch like me!
> I once was lost but now am found,
> was blind but now I see
>
> . . . .
>
> Through many dangers, toils, and snares,
> I have already come;
> 'tis grace that brought me safe thus far,
> and grace will lead me home.[8]

Finally, an *ironic* orientation translates into the *empiric* worldview, revolving around a central motif of testing. Authority arises from objective verification through the senses, and pragmatic behavior is especially
valued. Hymnody is not a natural place for this stance to find expression, and the rare examples, like this one, are almost never sung:

> God, you have given us the power
> to sound depths hitherto unknown,
> to probe earth's hidden mysteries,
> and make their might our own
>
> . . . .

So, for your glory and our good
may we your gifts employ,
lest, maddened by the lust of power,
we shall ourselves destroy.[9]

The empiric approach to life tends to lead in one of two directions: either away from religious language and practice entirely (since the rituals, songs, and doctrines may seem increasingly hollow and false), or toward the embrace of another view. This alternative view may be essentially premodern (note the current attraction in our culture to the literal certainties of the "Left Behind" series of novels) or postmodern (a provisional suspension of disbelief without the full embrace of any particular religious narrative).

A pastor or lay leader might reflect on the congregation's narrative style(s) by using the following steps:

- Identify a few of the important stories that were told to you when you were new to this congregation—stories through which the speaker seemed to be sharing with you the tribal lore.
- Select a story that seems to contain a clue to the "meaning these people make" about their life together and about the world they live in.
- Write down that story. Imagine that you are transcribing—word for word—the story as it was told to you. Recall the facial expressions, the tone of voice, the significant pauses.
- Imagine that a hymn or theme song accompanies the telling of this story. What would that hymn or theme song be?
- Reflect on the four genres presented in this section. Which genre is most intensely reflected in the story *as it was told to you*? Your hymn or theme-song selection might give you a clue. Remember that the historical facts alone do not reveal the genre. Look instead at the way the events are presented, the meanings that are attached to them, the tone and style of the storytelling.
- Think about other aspects of the congregation's life. Does this story and its genre provide you with any clue about the way people in this congregation interpret the world or the way they experience God?

An individual pastor might repeat this reflection process in relation to several different stories that she was told during the search and start-up phase. A planning chair might ask his committee to identify key stories in the oral lore of the congregation. Enlist committee members to act out the telling of these stories, exactly as they heard them the first time, then use the compass diagram to identify the congregation's preferred narrative style(s).

Culture and Size

Size determines a great deal about your congregation's culture. A large congregation is not just an expanded version of a small one. In order to change in scale, congregations (like other organisms) must also change their form. This shape-shift is not limited to the narrow realm of the by-laws or the organizational chart. Size has an influence on many aspects of your congregation's culture.

Take worship as an example. Sociologist of religion Mark Chaves has shown a clear-cut difference in worship style between larger and smaller congregations.[10] (Chaves directs the National Congregations Study; see the section in chapter 10 entitled "Surveys about American religion.") Working with a very broad

> Size has an influence on many aspects of your congregation's culture.

sample of American congregations from all religious traditions, Chaves gathered information about the levels of enthusiasm and ceremony that characterize the main weekly worship occasion. On the enthusiasm scale, the largest and smallest congregations were virtually identical; such elements as spontaneous movement, applause, testifying about religious experience, or the use of piano or drums were just as likely to occur in larger congregations as in smaller ones. But on the ceremony scale, the largest congregations (900 or more regular worshipers) occupied a noticeably different place on the scale than the smallest ones (75 or fewer at worship). Worship in the larger congregation was reported to be more formal, making greater use of elements such as choir music, soloists, organ music, or a printed bulletin. We might summarize this finding by saying that larger congregations tend to have a more ceremonial worship style than smaller ones, even after we correct for regional and denominational differences. Style is "the kind of order we give . . . to the material of our lives"[11] as persons and as communities. Worship style—one significant expression of a congregation's culture—is affected by size.

In what other ways does size affect a congregation's culture? Church growth expert Gary McIntosh[12] describes the organizing principle of a congregation as *relational, programmatic,* or *organizational,* depending on its size. I think of these three words as describing different ways of congregating or ways of being church. Different rules (written and unwritten) govern behavior in each of these three modes of congregational life. Hence, each of the three sizes has a distinctive culture.

According to McIntosh, congregations with up to 200 people attending (often called family and pastoral size[13]) are likely to have a more *relational* orientation. Leadership "resides in key families." The pastor's key role is "lover." Growth happens "through relationships," and change occurs from the "bottom up through key people." McIntosh estimates that 80 percent of American congregations fall into this category. To put it another way, we might say that the great majority of congregations have a relational style or relational culture.

A congregation with 201 to 400 people attending (program size[14]) is likely to have a *programmatic* orientation. Leadership "resides in committees." The pastor's key role is "administrator." Growth usually occurs "through [a] key ministry"—for example, a Sunday school program, an intentional small-group ministry, a multiple-choir music program, or a weekday nursery school. Change moves from the "middle out through committees." According to McIntosh, about 10 percent of congregations operate in this way. Or, to frame the findings in terms of culture, we might say that one congregation in ten does church in a programmatic style. (Remember that style—the order we give to the material of congregational life—is an expression of the congregation's culture.)

Congregations with more than 400 people attending (corporate size or larger[15]) are likely to have an *organizational* orientation. Leadership "resides in select leaders." The pastor's key role is leader. Growth occurs through word of mouth (since this congregation has a high profile in its community), and change works its way down from the top through key leaders. McIntosh suggests that the remaining 10 percent of congregations operate in this way. Again, using words that have to do with culture, we might say that one congregation in ten has an organizational style of church life.

When congregations change size, they undergo significant cultural change. This is one powerful reason a growing congregation usually gets stuck when it hits the boundary between two size categories, even if the community context provides great potential for continued numerical growth. Adding 50 people is one thing; changing our congregation's *culture* is quite another. If numerical growth or decline emerges as a priority question to consider in your planning process, you will want to look carefully at the cultural dimension of size change.

> When congregations change size, they undergo significant cultural change. This is one reason a growing congregation may get stuck when it hits the boundary between two size categories.

Other frameworks besides narrative orientation and size might be used to assess a congregation's culture. Two more examples are included as resources in this book: "Excavating the Religious Culture(s) of the Congregation" by Alice Mann (Resource J on page 232), and "Generational Watershed," by Gil Rendle (Resource K on page 240). Another framework may be found in church sociologist Penny Edgell Becker's study, *Congregations in Conflict: Cultural Models of Local Religious Life.*[16] Becker identifies four models (House of Worship, Family, Community, and Leader congregations), each with a distinctive culture.

Culture as Tool Kit in the Planning Process

The congregation's culture may be seen as the primary tool kit[17] a faith community has at hand to make sense of the world together. As a distinctive collection of "stories, symbols, rituals, worldviews, and patterns of thought,"[18] congregational culture figures into the planning process in at least two ways—as a category of information to be gathered, and as a guide to planning process itself.

Culture as a Category of Information to Gather

The church's particular culture may be a central focus of inquiry and learning during the internal audit phase of the planning work. The "Favorite Hymn" exercise (Resource L on page 231) is one simple and enjoyable way to get members thinking about the different ways people frame the world in language. Looking for the biblical story that belongs to the congregation (see Resource D on page 211) is another. For a more intensive exploration of church culture and style, we would recommend the fascinating book-and-video package, *How We Seek God Together*.[19]

On the basis of its reflection about church culture, a planning team can answer more wisely certain critical planning questions:

- What type of story does our congregation understand itself to be living?
- What purposes can our congregation most deeply own and enact?
- What particular populations and life situations can our congregation respond to "with gladness and singleness of heart"?[20]

Coherent action is certain to suggest itself once a congregation has taken the time to honor its own particularity with culture-based questions like these.

Culture as a Guide to Planning Method

Those who determine the style and shape of the planning process should take careful account of the congregation's culture. While many useful planning methods can be obtained from books, consultants, or workplace experiences, any ready-made planning process has one inherent danger. The rules, rhetoric, and worldview of the designer may ride roughshod over the congregation's distinctive (and often subtle) ways of making meaning together.

> Reflect upon some moments when the congregation has done a good job of talking through an important question together.

In the "congregational training for planning" phase, it is wise to identify and reflect upon some moments when the congregation has done a good job of talking through an important question together. Here are some examples of such reflection:

- Leaders of one large synagogue in the pre-planning phase recalled the success of several town meetings in which the rabbi had facilitated discussion about new gender-inclusive options provided by the book of ritual.

- A midsized Protestant congregation looked back on a painful disclosure of sexual misconduct and realized that the staff, the board, and the staff-parish relations committee had learned a lot from the denominational response team about helping members to speak the truth to each other in love.
- A small congregation in a small town remembered the way people had pulled together at a member's home to plan a response after a fire.

Once several examples of good conversation have been lifted up, the culture question can be posed: *Given the distinctive style and personality of our congregation, what kinds of planning conversation would seem most natural—and most affirming of who we are at our very best?*

Dealing with Culture Clash

In either the "congregational training for planning" or the "internal audit" phases, a congregation may discover that it has two or more cultures competing for dominance. At this particular moment in history, culture clash seems to be the norm rather than the exception. We can identify several reasons congregations are experiencing this clash.

The first common reason for culture clash is generational difference. Research on the typical distribution of member-tenure in congregations reveals a common pattern (see figure on next page).[21]

The longer-tenured group on the right tends to operate by the value system of the "GI generation"—deferred pleasure, group identity, assumptions of sameness, and spirituality of place. The shorter-tenured group on the left tends to operate by the value system of the "consumer generation"—instant gratification, individual orientation, assumptions of difference, spirituality of journey. The in-between group (often people born around 1946), who are potentially a bridge between two worldviews, is often small or missing. Even if the congregation seems to have a rather homogeneous religious culture in other ways, this major difference in perspective between generational cohorts in North America creates an automatic culture clash in a great many congregations.[22]

A second common reason for congregational culture clash is demographic change in the community surrounding the church. To the extent that congregations succeed in drawing members from the newer

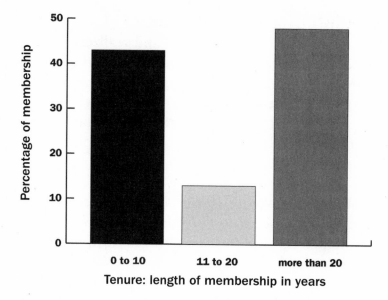

populations around them, they also increase the cultural tension that members experience.

A third reason for culture clash is size transition. Congregations stuck in the plateau zone between sizes usually find themselves in conflict about which is the right style of congregating. Particularly in the transition from being a pastoral- to a program-size congregation, longer-tenured members may feel considerable loss at the prospect that the *relational* mode will no longer dominate. At the same time, newer and younger members often yearn for the quality and variety of organized activities associated with the *programmatic* style.

As a result of generational, demographic, and size-related culture shifts, congregations have more and more difficulty finding an overarching story that lends coherence to the life of the faith community. Whatever immediate issues are motivating your congregation to plan at this time, the planning team's most important work may be to honor important cultural differences and to search for unifying stories and symbols.

By exploring the congregation's story, its culture, and its natural orientation to ministry, leaders generate planning capital—trust, communication, energy, curiosity, self-esteem—that they can draw upon in the next phase of work. Observations about the church's distinctive personality form a template for looking outside; they become the basis for extracting relevant facts and opportunities from the mountain of data typically generated in an external audit.

Notes

1. Carl Dudley and Sally Johnson, "Congregational Self Images for Social Ministry" in *Carriers of Faith: Lessons from Congregational Studies,* eds. Carl Dudley, Jackson Carroll, and James P. Wind (Louisville: Westminster John Knox, 1991). The list here is quoted from Carl Dudley, *Basic Steps toward Community Ministry* (Bethesda, Md.: Alban Institute, 1991), 60.

2. James F. Hopewell, *Congregation: Stories and Structures* (Philadelphia: Fortress Press, 1987); see especially chapters 4 and 5.

3. Northrup Frye, *Anatomy of Criticism* (Princeton: Princeton University Press, 1957), 158–239. Cited from Hopewell's notes to chapter 4. The summary in this paragraph is based on Hopewell's discussion on pp. 58–62.

4. Hopewell, 58.

5. Ibid., 70.

6. Isaac Watts, "When I Survey the Wondrous Cross," cited from *The Hymnal 1982* (New York: The Church Pension Fund, 1985), hymn 474, stanzas 1 and 4.

7. Henry Sloane Coffin, (tr.), "God Himself Is With Us," from *The Hymnal 1982,* hymn 475. Coffin translated the old sixth stanza from the old German version and brought it up front to become stanza two in his *Hymns of the Kingdom of God*—expressing the optimism of the Social Gospel Movement at the turn of the 20th century. In the current Episcopal hymnal (1982), Coffin's translation of the verse appears as stanza 3.

8. John Newton, "Amazing Grace," from *The Hymnal 1982,* hymn 671, stanzas 1 and 4.

9. "God, You Have Given Us the Power," from *The Hymnal 1982,* hymn 584, stanzas 1 and 4.

10. Mark Chaves, *How Do We Worship?* (Bethesda, Md.: Alban Institute, 1999), 40.

11. For an excellent discussion of the religious import of style, see Clark, Swenson, and Stamm, *How We Seek God Together: Exploring Worship Style* (Bethesda, Md.: Alban Institute, 2001), chapter 1, which includes on p. 14 this quotation from "Style and Community," by Salin Kemal. Kemal's article is from *The Question of Style in Philosophy and the Arts,* ed. Carolyn Van

Eck, James McCallister, and Renee van de Vall (Cambridge, England: Cambridge University Press, 1995), 125.

12. Gary McIntosh, *One Size Doesn't Fit All: Bringing Out the Best in Any Size Church* (Grand Rapids, Mich.: Fleming H. Revell, 1999); see especially the summary chart on pp. 143–144.

13. For a summary of the four sizes of congregations, see chapter 1 of Alice Mann's book, *Raising the Roof: The Pastoral to Program Size Transition* (Bethesda, Md.: Alban Institute, 2000). This chapter may be downloaded from the Bookstore section of the Alban Institute Web site, www.alban.org.

14. Ibid.

15. Ibid.

16. Penny Edgell Becker, *Congregations in Conflict: Cultural Models of Local Religious Life* (Cambridge, Mass.: Cambridge University Press, 1999). See tables 1, 9, and 10 for a useful summary of cultural differences among four types—called House of Worship, Family, Community, and Leader congregations.

17. Clark et al., *How We Seek God Together*, 13.

18. Ibid.

19. Ibid.

20. *Book of Common Prayer*, thanksgiving after communion in the Holy Eucharist, Rite II.

21. Gil Rendle, *The Multigenerational Congregation: Meeting the Leadership Challenge* (Bethesda, Md.: Alban Institute, 2002), 40ff.

22. For an examination of differences among specific cohorts on each side of the divide, see Carl Eeman, *Generations of Faith: A Congregational Atlas* (Bethesda, Md.: Alban Institute, 2002).

CHAPTER TEN

Reading the Community Context

Congregations are born from a spark of interaction between a faith tradition and a particular context. If you go back and review the founding story of your church, you will almost certainly find that its emergence was closely linked with the political, economic, social, and religious dynamics of its wider community at a particular moment. In periods of slow cultural change, the niche a church occupied within its community could remain constant for long periods of time. But, especially since World War II, the pace of change has accelerated in even the smallest towns, creating a growing gap between a congregation's earlier identity and present community realities. Periodic rereading of the community context is a vital discipline. Simple approaches—focused in conversation and story—often yield rich results. Here are some examples.[1] You will note that we begin with the congregation's points of closest connection with its context, and then move outward.

Time Line

Your congregation's story is tied in important ways to community changes and world events. These connections can be traced through a time-line exercise, like the "Wall of Wonder" (Resource M on page 262) or the "History Grid" (Resource N on page 263). The "Wall of Wonder" exercise is best for drawing out a continuous narrative of the congregation's life and context; it allows themes and issues to emerge naturally. The "History Grid" design can be used to explore more directly a key issue or focus though snapshots of selected eras. The grid is illustrated in the diagram on the next page.

Note that this example of a History Grid was designed for a congregation whose key planning questions included size and numerical growth. Another focal question could be substituted. For example, a congregation anticipating a pastoral transition in the near future might use the third row of the grid to ask: "What did we see as the right kind

	FOUNDING ERA	GLORY DAYS	NOW
What was going on in our context? • local community • wider culture • wider church			
How did we understand our distinctive "calling" as a congregation? Clues: • Name • Location • building style and size • clergy strengths • primary programs			
What was our definition of the "right size"? How did that definition relate to: • our context • our distinctive calling			

of clergy leadership?" in each era. A congregation seeking to overhaul its outreach ministries might ask: "What was our paradigm for community service in each era?"

Pin Map

Locating member households on a street map of your area is another simple way to explore the relationship between inside and outside. Some planning teams bring the map to coffee hour for several Sundays right at the beginning of the planning process, and ask those present to place their own household on the map. (Be sure a team member is present to check off the person's name on a parish list—the team needs to know whose pins have been placed during coffee hour so that they can eventually add the pins of those who were not present.)

You will note in Resource O ("Membership Pin Maps" on page 269) a suggestion that you highlight the newest members (five years of participation or less) on your pin map by using pins of a special color. Resource P ("Whom Do We Draw?" on page 270) can help you to reflect on the characteristics of your newest members—what they seem to have in common with each other, what clusters they fall into, and how much they may differ as a group from the longer-tenured members of your church.

Walk-Around and Drive-Around Exercises

Much of the information we need about our community context is right in front of us to behold—if only we can enter into a different frame of mind, a different attitude of heart. In a city congregation, a planning committee might send its members two-by-two on a silent, contemplative walk around assigned sections of its ministry area. In a suburban or rural congregation, teams might go on a silent, contemplative drive-around. We use the word *contemplative* here to mean open and receptive to the sacredness of the world around us—just as it is. People

> The information we need about our community context is right in front of us, if only we can enter into a different frame of mind, a different attitude of heart.

begin their journey with a time of prayer that God might open their eyes and warm their hearts to the world around them. The leader of the exercise invites participants to relax, to settle into a few minutes of quiet together, to suspend mental effort (judging, problem solving, predicting), and to trust that God will illuminate whatever the team truly needs to see. As people return, the leader brings them into a quiet space, perhaps into the church, and provides writing materials with which they can create a journal of their impressions. After a time of individual reflection, impressions are shared with other members of the planning team. Further suggestions for structuring a neighborhood walk (with observation suggestions adaptable for a drive-around) are found in Resource Q on page 271.

Exploring Network Maps

Mapping the weekly routine of several members can vividly highlight aspects of the context you might otherwise miss. For each round of this exercise, one member serves as the subject while others in the group observe. Using a cardboard-mounted map, pushpins, and yarn, the subject links his or her home with key destinations—such as work, school, shopping, gym, and church. The resulting map illustrates the way this member (or household) interacts with the community context week by week. Others in the group can then reflect on how their own pattern would be different.

Your planning team could use network mapping to examine differences among key constituencies—long-time residents versus newcomers, people from different ethnic groups, or people of different generational cohorts. Full directions for this exercise may be found in Resource R on page 272.

Interviews with Community Leaders

This approach to exploring the context is especially fruitful because it builds face-to-face relationships with people who are deeply concerned about your local community—such as school superintendent, police chief, director of social services, and town planner. In larger urban areas, you may be approaching neighborhood leaders, agencies that use your building, and your local school principal. It is a mistake to start off by asking them what your church should be doing—they may have an opinion, but this is not the thing you need from them most. Get them talking about what *they* see as they look at your local community—realities, trends, initiatives, problems, cultural changes. More details may be found in Resource S on page 274.

Some congregations that have become involved in community-organizing projects in their city or region have the opportunity to send members for training in the art of the one-on-one. This is a conscious form of conversation in which we encourage people to give voice to the hopes and concerns that are most central to their life. Teams from congregations often practice the one-on-one conversation with fellow members first—both to build relational energy and to get comfortable with the method. Then they are encouraged to talk with neighbors, friends, and co-workers using the same eliciting and listening skills. If connection with a faith-based community organization is (or might be) part of your congregation's ministry, you may want to make extensive use of "one-on-one" conversations—not just with community leaders, but also with all kinds of people you are naturally connected to in your environment.

We would note that community-organizing methods form a parallel track to strategic planning as a means for generating congregational energy and focus. Practices like the one-on-one conversation have their own particular purpose, discipline, and spirit. If your congregation has made a commitment to the community-organizing path, you should probably avoid launching a major strategic-planning effort at the same time.

Demographics and Psychographics

After you have explored your community context using some of the powerful, low-tech methods just described, you may want to consider gathering demographic and psychographic data. Demographic information comes from counting heads—United States Census reports would be the most obvious example. Subcategories are based on relatively objective factors, such as age, gender, or income, as reported by each household. Psychographic information describes attitudes and preferences (usually cross-referenced with demographic factors), and is gathered through a survey. Using

> **Psychographic information describes attitudes and preferences (usually cross-referenced with demographic factors).**

psychographics, a marketing firm may discover that MTV is most popular with the 18-24 age-group, but that fewer of those people are watching this year than last. The most credible psychographic data is gathered from a statistically significant random sample, using questions carefully designed to minimize bias. The least credible survey is the push poll, where a question is carefully constructed to elicit a particular answer, rather than to understand the perspective of the respondent.

Demographic Data from the Web

These days, census information is very easy to get—so easy, in fact, that most users will quickly have more than they know what to do with. One approach is to work through your city, town, or county planning officials (or Web sites) to get their summaries. Another is to go straight to the census bureau Web site: www.census.gov.[2] Here is a suggested path for a first look at census data for your location:

- On the home page, click on "Your Gateway to Census 2000."
- The resulting page will offer a section called, "Access Data By Geography." Click the highlighted phrase, "street address."
- Type in the street address of your church, and click "Go."

- A box will list various geographic units that include the address you submitted: state, county, city, census tract, census block group, census block—plus, if you scroll down, a dozen other options including zip code. To get started, I suggest that you choose "census tract." Click "Map It" to see the exact area included in the tract. The map also shows you the numbers and boundaries of adjoining census tracts.
- Print out this map. If you have already done a pin-map of congregational households, you should be able to identify several census tracts of special relevance to your congregation.
- Click "Close" at the bottom of the map. Click on the "Go" button that is under the "Map It" button.
- On the list of data choices, look for the section titled "Quick Tables and Demographic Profiles." Find a choice labeled "DP-1: Profile of General Demographic Characteristics 2000." (This choice shows up several times on the list in various forms; click the first one you find.) Click this choice and print the profile.
- To get profiles on other census tracts shown on your map, the easiest route is to go back to the beginning and enter any street address located in the desired tract. Profiles from three tracts provide plenty of information for some initial exploration.

Scan the information from one tract at a time, starting with the one where your church is actually located.

For this research exercise, Alice scanned the profile for the census tract where she lives, in a small New England city. The tract is a four-mile strip along the Merrimack River and contains about 1,700 households. From the detailed three-page profile, she picked out the following facts that seemed interesting:

- The area is almost equally split between owned and rented housing units.
- Two-thirds of the units house families that include children under 18.
- One household in ten consists of a senior citizen living alone.

Once you have studied a census-tract profile from this site, stop to identify a handful of facts (similar to the examples given for Alice's home area) that might be useful to your congregation in its ministry exploration. State the facts in sentences, then tuck the statistical profile away for future reference. Focus your discussions in the planning team and in the congregation on the *statements* you have gleaned from the numbers. These sentences express the meaning you are beginning to make together about the context—much more important material than the statistical tables themselves.

Your denomination may produce its own free or low-cost demographic data in a more user-friendly form. In addition, many denominational bodies contract with a company called The Percept Group that combines demographic and psychographic information in a visually integrated presentation. The next section provides some hints about using such material.

> **The *statements* you have gleaned from the numbers are much more important material than the statistics themselves.**

Using a Commercially Prepared Profile

The Percept Group is a California-based company that provides congregations with well-organized demographic information enhanced by two other kinds of data. First, Percept is licensed to adapt the MicroVision[3] system to congregational use. MicroVision combines geographic and demographic information with records of individual consumer behavior from the Equifax Consumer Marketing Database to classify every household in the United States into one of 49 unique subcultures (which Percept calls lifestyle segments). On a Percept profile, these segments have names like "Established Empty-Nesters" and "Struggling Urban Life," and they are comprised of people who share similar interests, purchasing patterns, financial behavior, and needs for products and services. Socioeconomic differences figure heavily into this description of subgroups within the American population. The sourcebook that accompanies your profile provides a brief description of each segment.

Using the MicroVision system and other sources, Percept creates a customized report for an individual congregation called a Ministry Area Profile. From this document, leaders can see at a glance which lifestyle segments are predominant in their vicinity—and even pinpoint where the greatest concentrations of particular subgroups are located. The profile presents a far richer description of local population characteristics than census tables ever could. To this helpful picture, Percept adds another dimension. Because they have undertaken their own survey of religious attitudes and preferences (called the Ethos Survey Series) among a national sample of households in each lifestyle group, they are able to suggest some potential implications for congregational style and programming. It is important to keep in mind, however, that their national survey sample of less than 2,000 households in each segment—though statistically valid—may not have included anyone at all who lives in your particular neighborhood. If you have taken our suggestion and begun with more relational ways to explore your context, you will have a good basis for evaluating the relevance of particular findings in the Ministry Area Profile and Ethos study documents.

When contemplating the use of any location-specific demographic profile, a key question is: "What area will we study?" Possible ways of defining a study area might include county or municipal boundaries, zip codes, or a defined radius around your church. With any of these

> When contemplating the use of any location-specific demographic profile, a key question is: "What area will we study?"

methods, you run the risk of including large chunks of geography that have little relevance to the congregation's current or likely ministries. One advantage of the Ministry Area Profile is that it can be ordered for a "custom polygon," an area defined by any combination of map features. For example, a rural church's ministry area might be bounded by a highway to the north, a county line to the east, and a river that curves around to form the south and west sides of the polygon. Your pin map of congregational households will help you to see clearly the areas from which you currently draw (and do not draw) members. Here are some considerations in choosing ministry-area boundaries for your demographic profile:

- Your map of member households may contain some far-flung pins, representing families who used to live closer to the church. These more distant locations are not really part of your current ministry *area* (even though the people are part of your current *ministry*).
- Some churches can see two distinct ministry areas on their pin map: a neighborhood ministry area around the church where perhaps 50 percent of the members reside, and a wider ministry area representing members who have been drawn from surrounding towns or less densely developed areas. In this case, you might

want to order both a nearer and wider study (which won't cost twice as much). The same advice might apply to an urban congregation whose members no longer live in the neighborhood.

- Some congregations face vital questions about whether they should reframe their ministry area to address different opportunities for ministry. A congregation located close to a cultural or racial boundary line may want to learn about populations they do not currently reach. In that case, you may wish to order side-by-side studies—one showing only the area from which you currently draw, the other showing only the area you feel you may be called to serve. This will highlight the nature of the work that will be required to create ministries that cross the boundary line.
- Even after giving careful thought to the boundaries, you may still discover that your area definition somehow yielded results skewed to the wrong geography or populations. Don't hesitate to phone the provider to see if an adjusted version might be obtained without undue cost.

In any case, the profile you receive will probably contain far more information than most leaders can assimilate. If you order a Ministry Area Profile from Percept, focus considerable attention on the Snapshot page, which summarizes critical information quite succinctly. In Resource T on page 275, you will find a sample of a Percept Snapshot page, followed by a worksheet (Resource U on page 278) that your committee members can use when they study the specific Lifestyle Segments found in your ministry area.

Trends in the Wider Culture

While congregations usually focus on their local community when they seek to understand the context of their ministry, a strategic planning committee will also want to consider wider societal and religious trends. This exploration might be undertaken as *balcony work* right at the beginning of the process—to help frame the driving questions—or as part of the external audit. One resource is the Alban video *Living into the New World.*[4] Here are some further sources that foster understanding of the wider cultural context in which your congregation's ministry is set.

Surveys about American Religion and Religious Attitudes

For decades, Princeton Religion Research Center has done careful polling about religious issues. Their most recent findings were summarized in the 2002 edition of their periodic report "Religion in America,"[5] a potential study document for your committee. Three other research groups have completed major sociological studies of American congregations in the last few years and are making findings available in accessible forms. First, the Hartford Institute for Religion Research offers an "Interactive Workbook."[6] A planning committee or adult study group can select a theme addressed in the research, print some survey questions from the Web site, and compare their answers with responses of similar groups (by denomination, church size, or location, for example) that have taken the survey. Second, the International Congregational Life Survey has produced *A Field Guide to U. S. Congregations*[7] highlighting "who's going where and why." This small, attractive book would help your planning team to see the whole landscape of American congregational life. Finally, the National Congregations Study[8] offers a Web site where users can study the relationship of selected factors to each other. A planning team could find out, for example, how many full time staff a church of their size is likely to have. Findings about worship from this study are available in a small book suitable for study by a planning committee.[9]

Notes

1. The basic categories in this section are drawn from Nancy T. Ammerman, Jackson W. Carroll, Carl S. Dudley, and William McKinney, eds., *Studying Congregations: A New Handbook* (Nashville: Abingdon Press, 1998), 40–62. Examples of exercises come from the sources noted in each case. If not otherwise attributed, the exercise came from the practice of Alice Mann or Gil Rendle.
2. Web references accurate at the time of our writing may have changed. You may need to explore a bit to find the material you are seeking.
3. A product of Claritas.
4. The video, *Living into the New World: How Cultural Trends Affect Congregations* (Bethesda, Md.: Alban Institute, 2000), features a presentation by Gil Rendle on large cultural changes.

5. The report, "Religion in America," is published periodically by Princeton Religious Research Council.
6. Go to www.fact.hartsem.edu and click on "Workbook."
7. Cynthia Woolover and Deborah Bruce, *A Field Guide to U.S. Congregations* (Louisville: Westminster John Knox, 2002).
8. The study is directed by Mark Chaves at the University of Arizona. Go to www.alban.org/NatCongStudy.asp
9. Mark Chaves, *How Do We Worship?* (Bethesda, Md.: Alban Institute, 1999).

CHAPTER ELEVEN

Spiritual Discernment and Planning

Some faith communities have traditionally used the term *discernment* to describe the process by which we notice, ponder, and interpret our experience in the light of faith. In spiritual discernment, we perceive sacred significance in the current moment and in the winding path by which we have arrived. We listen for the still small voice that beckons us onward, quietly revealing what we are here on earth to do and to become.

For a congregation, how is discernment different from planning? We would say that discernment is not usually a separate activity. Rather, it is a *dimension* of our planning, our action, and our rest—a set of attitudes and practices by which we willingly open our hearts to the heart of God, our minds to the mind of God, our intentions to the purposes of God. Since scripture describes a love affair between God and creation, discernment involves attentiveness to the yearnings by which we are drawn to the divine lover. Discernment in a congregational setting usually requires that we attend with care to one set of voices, one set of desires at a time—as illustrated below.

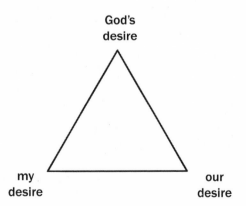

Let's examine each corner of this triangle one at a time.

My Desire

Individual yearnings constitute a starting point for spiritual awareness. When we risk exposing what we really long for deep down, we become more vulnerable, more open to God and to each other. Truthfulness about our desires may reveal painful distortions in our lives. (Addiction is one contemporary word for distorted desire.) But for those who believe that they are made in the image of God, every craving can be traced back to a yearning for something holy—for life, for love, for sacred significance.

Planning processes can offer participants a profound opportunity for spiritual discernment by helping them to reflect more deeply on their own yearnings—not just what they want the congregation to be and do, but what they are longing for in their *lives*. Alice recently spoke to a lay leader who was so frustrated about his experience that he was thinking of changing churches. She asked him the same question several times, "What do you really want most from being part of a congregation?" He identified many desires: to be part of an outreach-oriented church; to hear sermons that would help him live his life better; to be welcomed into leadership without entanglement in so many power hierarchies. As Alice asked him the question one more time, he paused and became much quieter, "I want at least a few people to care for me." Both sensed that he had arrived at the heart of the matter.

> When we risk exposing what we really long for deep down, we become more vulnerable, more open to God and to each other.

Such insight and candor cannot be produced on demand. Various spiritual traditions have discovered ways to prepare the soil in which individual awareness and vulnerability might grow[1]—over a period of months, and years, and generations. In the history of Western spirituality, we can see examples of such wisdom in Ignatian practices of spiritual direction and in Quaker clearness committees. Both of these traditions of discernment are still alive today. A contemporary program called *Listening Hearts* (described later in this chapter, under the heading, "Formal Methods for Communal Discernment") distills a variety of classic understandings and practices into materials suitable for use across many denominational groups.

Planning can seem superficial, dull, or exhausting if we give too little attention to the yearnings of the individual heart. Here's a common scenario. A planning committee undertakes a written survey to find out what programs the members want. Many respondents say: "More Bible study!" At the request of the planning committee, the pastor spends a great deal of time designing and promoting new study programs—only to find that the sessions draw the same five people who've been attending his Bible study group all along. In this example, the committee has asked people in writing for a general opinion, but has not invited them to notice what they—personally—are hungering for. While this congregation's questionnaire could have been improved, real soul-searching is most likely to occur in settings where people can explore together a sacred story or text; engage in quiet reflection and journaling about a few soul questions; then share (only what they wish to, of course) with a few other people. Planning processes go deepest in congregations that gather people frequently for this kind of faith sharing, in congregations that focus—year in and year out—on building an atmosphere of prayer and trust and attentiveness to soul matters in all of church life. Even if your church has no experience in this area and little apparent inclination, a very simple framework like "Story Circles for the Soul"[2] might provide a nonthreatening place to begin.

A parable from the business world, called the Abilene Paradox,[3] could help a planning team to understand conceptually how planning discussions go awry without due attention to the desires of the individual heart. Jerry B. Harvey, a professor of management science, first identified the paradox on a sweltering summer afternoon in West Texas, when his father-in-law suggested that the family eat supper at a cafeteria in Abilene, 50 miles away. Though they'd be taking the trip in a 1958 Buick without air conditioning, each person in the group agreed it was a great idea. At the end of a miserable trip for an equally miserable dinner, the recriminations began. Each person blamed the others for promoting such a foolish venture. The originator of the idea finally admitted: "I never wanted to go to Abilene; I just thought you might be bored."

In congregational life, the Abilene Paradox (group adoption of an initiative that no one really wants) might cause a congregation to build a new sanctuary or employ an associate minister—and then experience disastrous conflict because the result is contrary to the real desires of the people involved. Writing about this dynamic, Pastor Jerry Kirkpatrick imagines what a courageous planning-committee member might have to say at the eleventh hour in order to prevent such an unhappy outcome:

> I know I may have said things before that made you think I was
> supportive of what we are about to do, but I have had other
> thoughts. I don't think we will succeed in doing this. In fact, I be-
> lieve we will be acting against the church's interest if we do. I won-
> der if anyone else thinks as I do. . . . I need to know where you
> stand.[4]

Kirkpatrick's article is included in full as Resource V (page 279) for use
in the orientation of your planning committee members.

Our Desire

Congregational planning is most often seen as an exploration of
our desires. Ultimately, members expect a planning committee to
name a destination that we, together, want to reach; and they frequently expect the committee to lay out a route that we, together,
might travel in order to get there. Most of the first half of this book
focuses on the "our desires" corner of the triangle—on steps for
creating a shared picture of the world, eliciting shared aspirations,
and developing shared intentions. Each recommended activity is a
kind of discernment. Each task has spiritual implications, whether
or not we take time to consider those implications. For example,
when we make a pin-map and puzzle over the boundaries of our
ministry area, we are asking a question posed to Jesus long ago:
"And who is my neighbor" (Luke 10:29)?

The very act of conversation has spiritual significance. To bring
my personal desires to the table is a form of communion with others.
Just like the bread of the Lord's Supper in Christian ritual, the longings
of a sincere heart are *offered* and *blessed* (by being lifted into the context of God's purposes); *broken open* through conversation; then *given
back* to us (and to the world) transformed. *Broken* is an especially
important word in this four-fold spiritual process, which was described
so well by liturgical scholars in the middle of the 20th century. To enter
into honest conversation is to fall into the hands of the living God. We
risk the death of old assumptions, old ways of seeing the world, old
certainties about the life of faith. We risk an adventure as rich and
hazardous as any story we might find in scripture, in Midrash, or in the
lives of the saints.

God's Desire

We have said that God is at work, somewhere deep down, in all our individual longings. We have said that conversation with another person in the faith community can be holy and transforming ground where we are set off balance and opened up to divine interference. Still, we need to set aside special times and places to turn our full attention toward God's desire for us. I mean desire for us in both senses of the term—the desire of the Lover for the beloved, and the desire God has for our lives to unfold in particular ways (resembling the hopes a parent might harbor for a child who is getting old enough to leave home).

> Conversation with another person in the faith community can be holy and transforming ground where we are set off balance and opened up to divine interference.

In order to attend to God's desire more directly in our individual lives, we pray sincerely for illumination and guidance. We withdraw to a quiet place and listen for the still, small voice whispering within us. We talk with a spiritual companion about the ways God may be nudging us. We peer through the scriptures as if through a window—squinting to see the outlines of God's life and God's work in the world.

How, then, does a congregation attend to God's desire in the midst of a planning process? This depends a great deal on the congregation's culture. Practices should be selected that are congruent with the congregation's faith tradition at its very best. At the same time, the practices chosen should stretch the congregation a bit—especially where the planning process is intended to do some frame bending. (See "Types of Planning" in chapter 1.) If we are going to ask members to consider tough realities and to think new thoughts about the congregation's future, then we also need to help members tap into some fresh sources of spiritual energy.

> If we are going to ask members to consider tough realities and to think new thoughts about the congregation's future, then we also need to help members tap into some fresh sources of spiritual energy.

Fresh sources might be ancient—so old that they are new to this group of people (just as the album called *Chant* made medieval religious music the latest rage a few years ago). Here are updated examples of two ancient practices a congregation might weave into its planning format, and perhaps into the whole life of the congregation.

Lectio Divina (Pondering a Sacred Text)

For about 1,500 years, Christians have practiced this holistic method of biblical reflection, in which we connect ourselves deeply to a particular passage in a sequence of different ways. First, we imagine the concrete details of the story and identify the sense impressions the passage elicits. Next, we consider the passage as a whole, looking for its themes and for the particular spiritual message it brings to us at this moment. Third, we pray from the heart—bringing before God the actual condition of our life at this moment (sorrow or joy, fear or hope, shame or thanksgiving) and offering to God our deepest needs and yearnings. Finally, we offer ourselves for quiet communion with God, letting go of sensation, of thought, and even of conscious praise or petition: "Be still, and know that I am God" (Isaiah 46:10).

In preparation for a planning process, leaders could reintroduce this ancient practice in various groups across the congregation (adult classes, men's or women's groups, committees, youth retreats). An excellent introduction is found in chapter 2 of *Soul Feast* by Presbyterian minister and professor Marjorie Thompson.[5] A "Short Guide to *Lectio Divina*," created by psychotherapist, spiritual director, and author Corinne Ware is found in Resource W on page 285. You may teach both the more traditional form of *lectio divina* (individual, silent meditation), and a more contemporary, interactive form. We suggest "An Oral Tradition Approach," often called "African Bible Study," that is very easy to use in all sorts of group settings (see Resource X on page 286). Some congregations select one book of the Bible to study throughout a year of planning. As we pointed out in part 2 of this book, biblical reflection gains particular power once members have begun to identify the particular stories that belong to them—biblical narratives that mirror the story the congregation is living now or the congregation's deep longings for a different future. (See Resource D on page 211 for details.)

Centering Prayer

Spiritual writer Basil Pennington (a Cistercian monk) popularized the term *centering prayer* about 25 years ago. These words were meant to describe an attitude and an approach that would make contemplation—a heartfelt sense of returning home to the presence of God—available to the ordinary person living an active life in the modern world. Pennington sought to re-balance the kind of prayer familiar to most people in Christian congregations (speaking composed sentences of prayer to express praise, confession, petition, thanksgiving) with a mystical tradition that goes back to the early centuries of Christian practice. In his book, *Centering Prayer*, Pennington sketched a bold vision for the way contemplative prayer—if widely practiced by people of faith—could change everyday life:

> Each one of us Christians [who is now practicing contemplative prayer] does indeed know, by personal experience, that he or she is a much-loved child of God. Our lives are filled with love and security, joy and peace. Each one is in touch with his or her own contemplative dimension. Busy days flow out of a deep center. Space is found, time set apart, to enjoy a Father's intimate loving presence and to let him enjoy us.[6]

Pennington's workshops on contemplative prayer helped people learn to use the following four rules[7] to shape a brief time of quiet:

- First, the time of meditation begins by taking "a minute or two to quiet down and then move in faith to God dwelling in our depths"; as we move inward, we discover and rest in a "center of faith-full love."
- Second, once we have allowed our hearts to experience (at least a little) the security of being held in the hands of a loving God, we allow a simple prayer word to bubble up from within, in response to God's presence.
- Next, that prayer word helps us to stay in the divine presence for a time; "whenever in the course of Prayer we become *aware* of anything else, we simply gently return to the Presence by use of the prayer word."
- Finally, at the end of the time we have set aside for prayer, we take a few minutes to return to awareness of our surroundings, concluding with the Lord's Prayer or some other familiar words.

Marjorie Thompson[8] describes this kind of prayer as an "inner sabbath" or "resting in God."

As we suggested with the form of biblical reflection (*lectio divina*) described above, a congregation might use the planning year as a time to help members learn how to rest in God through centering prayer. This resting positions us to listen for the still, small voice. Such a practice would have a profound effect on members' awareness of their own yearnings, and on their ability to hear what lies behind the words of others. Learning centering prayer would also reduce leaders' anxiety about getting the right answer or meeting everybody's needs, and prepare people to notice the lives of neighbors around the church with new openness.

Just as *lectio divina* has a form for group reflection, centering prayer can also be undertaken as a group spiritual practice. In Resource Y on page 287, you will find a simple format for a pastor or other leader to guide a time of centering at the beginning of a meeting. Alban consultant Roy Oswald has led this centering exercise for many years with congregations of vastly different religious traditions. It could be used to open every meeting of the planning team, and also for times of larger group reflection or deliberation. To establish this practice as an element of your planning conversations, you might ask the pastor—or a lay member comfortable with leading times of silent devotion—to serve as chaplain to the group and preside over the opening time of centering at every meeting.

If you are serving in this chaplain role, you should create your own centering script based on Roy's framework. We suggest that you write it out, including notations of when to pause and approximately how long. At first you may have to count out the pauses mentally ("a thousand and one . . .") to prevent yourself from rushing ahead with more words too soon. Don't be embarrassed to rehearse before you lead the first centering exercise; although this degree of preparation may seem a little stilted, a firm script and advance practice will help you (and the group) to relax into a centering ritual that will soon become familiar and reliable. Repetition over time helps people sink more quickly and more deeply into that place of inner sabbath—just as the predictable sequence of organ prelude and opening hymn helps many congregations cross the threshold into a time of corporate worship.

Formal Communal Discernment Methods

Consistent use of one fresh spiritual practice throughout a year of planning can make an enormous difference, fostering first-hand awareness of God's still, small voice within the conversation. In some religious traditions, however, more formal systems have arisen for making important choices in the light of faith. Each system is made up of a whole pattern of different practices meant to reinforce personal awareness, excellent listening within the group, and an explicit search for divine guidance within the group deliberations. In a Quaker meeting, for example, distinctive practices have been employed for centuries to facilitate individual or group discernment.[9] When a particular member has an important life decision to make—whether to change jobs, for example—he or she chooses a Committee of Clearness, and undertakes with them a disciplined consideration of the matter. Members of the committee do not give advice—rather, they are completely dedicated to helping the person sort out their own inner voices and leadings. Group decision making in the Society of Friends (Quakers) is similarly respectful of each person's inner light. The Quakers' careful rules for developing group consensus have greatly influenced secular decision-making practices (though some processes called *consensus* today reflect little of the Quakers' discipline or spiritual depth.)

The Roman Catholic religious order known as the Jesuits has carried forward a dynamic tradition of individual and group discernment based on the work of its founder, Ignatius of Loyola. In his work *Spiritual Exercises*, Ignatius offered an innovative set of "Rules for Discernment of Spirits."

Though many of the rules were drawn from time-honored traditions of discernment, others were new. The rules included the importance of imagination, reason, biblical connections, experience, testing the spirits, and feelings. The affective influences were central. People involved in Ignatian spiritual discernment put matters to the test—resting them in the heart, looking for consolation, which leads toward God in peace, or desolation, which leads away from God in distress.[10] At Jesuit Spiritual Centers around the country, you can find spiritual guides who are trained in Ignatian practices of discernment, both for individuals and for groups.

Today, two important cross-denominational movements are developing and teaching contemporary patterns for spiritual discernment that draw together the best practices from the whole sweep of Christian tradition. One movement is called Listening Hearts Ministries.[11] They describe themselves as offering "uncomplicated and practical" help for any prayerful community that wants to distinguish God's voice from the cacophony of voices calling for attention:

> The practice of discernment has been embedded in the contemplative tradition of every major spiritual tradition for centuries, yet has been inaccessible to the majority of people. . . . Drawing on

Quaker, Benedictine, Carmelite, Ignatian, Anglican, Protestant, Orthodox, and Jungian insights, Listening Hearts Ministries has taken the practice of spiritual discernment and presented it in a way that almost any adult who wants to cultivate the practice of spiritual discernment can do so.[12]

Facilitators trained in the Listening Hearts methods can teach a church board or planning team how to incorporate into their work suitable practices for spiritual discernment. For groups that have already received this training, these facilitators can also guide a discernment process in relation to a specific issue.

> Today, two important cross-denominational movements are developing and teaching contemporary patterns for spiritual discernment that draw together the best practices from the whole sweep of Christian tradition.

The second cross-denominational movement fostering practices of spiritual discernment is called Worshipful-Work.[13] Located in Kansas City, this organization grew out of research on the revitalization of church boards conducted by Dr. Charles Olsen. Individual leaders or working groups are invited to the Kansas City location for training, for a time of reflection, or for facilitation as they seek God's guidance in a particular decision. In many parts of the country, Consultant Mentors trained by Worshipful-Work are available to help clergy, boards, and congregations as they incorporate discernment practices into their ministry and as they seek God's leading around specific parish decisions.

Almost any congregation undertaking a planning process could benefit from a fresh look at their own understanding of spiritual discernment. If you suspect that an upcoming strategic-planning process will lead to watershed decisions—about changing location, adopting a dramatically different ministry focus, or handling culture clash within the body—you may want to seek training in spiritual discernment a year or more before any decision is to be made. Take time to consider how a climate of discernment might be fostered and how formal discernment dimensions could be built into the whole process, not just the final decision. Plan significant orientation in the theology and practice of discernment for the planning committee, board, staff, committee leaders, and congregation.

Finding Powerful Images

Use of specific spiritual discernment methods in the course of a planning process helps members and leaders to tap into deeper levels of meaning—to perceive with greater insight the soul of the congregation and the soul of the surrounding community. In his work on perceiving and naming the invisible powers that shape our lives, biblical scholar Walter Wink[14] points out that the Revelation to John is not addressed to the seven churches of Asia, but rather, as we noted in Chapter 4, to the *angel* of each of those churches. He encourages contemporary congregations to discern their angel:

> It is not easy for those of us who have been schooled in the Western outlook to discern the angel of a church. We are faced with two hurdles. First, our worldview is individualistic to an extreme; consequently, most of us regard a group of people as a mere aggregate of individuals, with no organic properties of its own. We do not perceive it as a Gestalt or whole, with its own history, character and calling. Second, our way of seeing the world is materialistic, and denies that a group could have a spirit. Consequently we do not perceive the angel [the intangible spirit of the church] because we have been trained not to live as seeing the invisible. . . . If we wish to discern the angel of a church, then, we first need to *see what is there*. Once we have become acquainted with its personality, we can ask about its vocation.

In order for our spiritual perceptions to generate sustained energy and action, they need to be expressed in some evocative symbolic form. This is a little like packing a suitcase. When we travel, a careful selection of items from home gets condensed into about a cubic foot of space, inside a portable shell. From the moment we zip it up, we no longer have to hold in memory all the details of what's inside; instead, we keep mental track of just one object, the bag, until we are ready to use the contents.

Images are like suitcases. Because the human brain is so adept at making associations at lightning speed, images can become packed with information and meaning. We can carry them around easily in our minds and hearts; we can exchange them with other people; we can combine them with other people's images in novel ways—creating new meanings together.

In the work of planning and discernment, many feelings and ideas are shared, many concepts are discussed, and many pages of material are produced. What will people remember?

> Images are like suitcases. Because the human brain is so adept at making associations at lightning speed, images can become packed with information and meaning.

What will they carry around in their minds and hearts? What will influence their daily thought and action? The answer to all those questions is—images: imaginative visual cues that give us easy access to larger experiences, conversations, and intentions. I've used an image in this section already—the suitcase.

One cliché of planning processes in the second half of the 20th century was the mission statement—as a memorable slogan that would fit on a bumper sticker. It is certainly not a bad idea. Occasionally, we run across such a statement that actually does powerful symbolic work. "Like a rock," the slogan for Chevrolet trucks, spoke not just to the customer but also to the workers, engendering commitment to build a solid vehicle. More often, we get the feeling that an image has been slapped on like a label—a thin veneer of color added at the very end of the manufacturing process.

In the work of congregational planning, a different attitude toward imagery is needed. Our job is to listen closely to the deep symbolic language of our people and our tradition. Memorable images arise from spiritual receptivity and attentiveness, expressed in contemplation, listening and play. In "Finding Our Biblical Story" (Resource D on page 211), Gil describes the congregation referenced earlier that found its aspirations reflected in the psalm text about being lifted up on eagle's wings, but also noticed its own tendency to chicken out when confronted with an important choice. They were playful enough to combine the two images into a new church logo—a flying chicken—that would help them both to laugh and to act when they were confronted with a difficult choice.

> Memorable images arise from spiritual receptivity and attentiveness, expressed in contemplation, listening and play.

Powerful images are not always visual. One tiny congregation near the Canadian border discovered an important image that was primarily auditory. This was a lively little church with intense bonds among the members. They loved and fought with each other. They loved and fought with their denominational officials. They loved and fought with the consultant who came to work with them. During a planning retreat, a half-dozen leaders were asked to write down their favorite hymn, and a few sentences about why this particular selection was powerful for them. Then each person was given a few minutes to share what he or she had written. People often share remarkably touching stories when they do this exercise together. Sometimes a powerful faith-image bubbles up. One man in the group said this. "My favorite hymn is 'Be Thou My Vision'—but not just the regular version we sing on Sunday. My favorite is the Van Morrison version. Morrison has that gritty voice, and he is such a gritty character.

His version of that hymn is like us in this church. We're cranky and cantankerous, but still, there's this longing for God." The auditory imprint of Morrison's song, combined with those few sentences of interpretation of the congregation's truest character, is probably the only thing anyone really remembers about that planning retreat. (See Resource L on page 260 for details of the "Favorite Hymn" exercise.)

If such moments cannot be manufactured, what can be said about them in a handbook about strategic planning? Several things. First, notice the natural poets, and artists, and shamans within the group. Some people (the natural poets and artists) have a real flair for verbal or visual imagery; others (the natural shamans) possess an unusual awareness of the spiritual forces at work in the congregation's life. We are not looking for the performer who can dazzle everybody with his or her brilliance; ego gets in the way of powerful communal images. We are looking for the person who can offer to the group an *evocative* statement—expressing clearly an experience or a longing that resonates with the whole group. As a planning leader, you can simply *notice* who seems to be able to do that. You can pay careful attention when they speak. You can occasionally invite them to make an observation.

Second, particular members of the planning team might take on the role of *collecting* images that emerge throughout the process. Write down the memorable statements. Save the cartoons people bring in. Snip out the rough diagram that someone jumped up to sketch on the chart-pad during a lively meeting. Collect the cards on which people wrote down their favorite hymns and their reasons for choosing them. Find tape or CD versions of songs that people have mentioned along the way. Look in a book of religious art to find images for biblical stories that have been especially meaningful to the group. All of these symbolic materials could go into a scrapbook, to be pulled out periodically for consideration by the group—but especially at the *mission and vision* stage of the planning process, when the team needs to synthesize what has been discerned into a form that can be communicated powerfully to others. (See chapter 6.)

Third, the most evocative images and symbols can be *amplified* within the planning team. In the church that lifted up the Van Morrison song, the planning consultant was recording on a chart-pad the exact phrases that people were offering during the exercise. During the wrap-up of the retreat, the consultant went back to the chart and read out some of the key phrases and images that had been offered. By returning to this symbolic material, by reciting some of the phrases once again, the meaning-making work of the group was amplified and fed back to them. A facilitator might ask: "Do any of the statements or images we generated resonate strongly for you now?" This question allows the group to select from the whole body of conversation certain symbolic elements that they can claim and validate together.

Notes

1. See Danny Morris and Charles M. Olsen, *Discerning God's Will Together: A Spiritual Practice for the Church* (Bethesda, Md.: Alban Institute, 1997).
2. Story Circles International. See www.StoryCirclesInternational.com.
3. Jerry B. Harvey, *The Abilene Paradox and Other Meditations on Management* (San Francisco: Jossey-Bass, 1996), chapter 2.
4. Jerald L. Kirkpatrick, "The Abilene Paradox Goes to Church," *Congregations* (May-June 2002): 28–30.
5. Marjorie J. Thompson, *Soul Feast: An Invitation to the Christian Spiritual Life* (Louisville: Westminster John Knox, 1995), 44.
6. M. Basil Pennington, *Centering Prayer: Renewing an Ancient Christian Prayer Form* (New York: Image Books, 1980), 247.
7. Ibid., 657.
8. Marjorie J. Thompson, *Soul Feast*.
9. This discussion comes from Morris and Olsen, *Discerning God's Will Together*, 32–33.
10. Ibid., 29–30.
11. Listening Hearts Ministries, 2015 St. Paul Street, Baltimore, MD 21218. Web site: www.listeninghearts.ang-md.org
12. This quotation comes from the Web site in note 11.
13. Worshipful-Work, 17000 NW 45 Highway, Kansas City, MO 64152. Web site: www.worshipful-work.org
14. Walter Wink, *Unmasking the Powers: The Invisible Forces That Determine Human Existence* (Philadelphia: Fortress Press, 1989), 73.

CHAPTER TWELVE

Key Roles in the Planning Process

Let's rehearse some key concepts. Planning is a structured conversation—which may last just one evening or continue intermittently for as long as 18 months. In the course of this conversation, people make meaning together: they discern and interpret what already is, and they listen together for a call that will draw them into the future in a faithful direction. Such listening must take account of the yearnings of individual hearts, the shared desires of the congregation, and God's yearnings for us who live as God's people in God's world. A key challenge in the process is to read with sensitivity the culture of the congregation, the culture of the communities the congregation is called to serve, and wider cultural trends that affect our lives as individuals and congregations.

As we structure the conversation, several important roles need to be considered and clarified: the planning team and its chairperson, the board, the pastor and other staff, and possibly a planning consultant.

The Planning Committee

Since the nature and role of the planning team is discussed at length in part 2 of this book, we will only highlight some key points here. In this handbook we have been using the terms *planning committee* and *planning team* interchangeably—not because the distinctions are insignificant, but because each congregation will shape the planning unit's structure and title according to its own organizational culture. However it is labeled, the group to whom the planning work is delegated has a crucial task—to create (and to become) a holding environment[1] where a set of questions, tensions, and learnings can bubble creatively for a certain period of time, until the congregation is ready to make decisions about them. A holding environment consists of times, places, processes, and people that are set aside to give special attention to complex or controversial matters. The steps you select from the hypothetical, full-blown process outlined in part 2 become elements of this holding environment. They provide a skeleton to support the flesh-and-blood conversations the congregation needs to have at this time in its history.

All of the roles outlined in this section are also part of the holding environment. By honoring the proper role of pastor and board, you create safety and structure for potentially stressful conversations to occur. By engaging other leaders and groups in the conversation, you invite the wider congregation to get their arms around these questions with you. By informing the congregation frequently and in a variety of media, you reassure the system that the deliberations are orderly, responsible, and open.

> A holding environment consists of times, places, processes, and people that are set aside to give special attention to complex or controversial matters.

The Planning Chair

This individual should be a trusted figure in the life of the congregation, known for open-mindedness, ability to work with other leaders, and concern for the good of the whole congregation. One essential gift is the capacity to serve as the key spokesperson for the committee's work. We recommend that someone other than the pastor chair the committee. This ensures that there is a lay leader authorized to represent the planning process and the committee's findings. When the time comes to make announcements about the progress of the planning work, it is common for the pastor to introduce the planning chair, who then delivers most of the remarks. The congregation gains confidence from the image of planning chair and pastor—side by side—interpreting the planning work.

> The congregation gains confidence from the image of planning chair and pastor—side by side—interpreting the planning work.

The Pastor

We encourage the pastor (the senior pastor in a multistaff congregation) to participate fully in the work of the planning committee. While the role of the pastor will vary according church size and according to other features of the congregation's (and denomination's) culture, here are some possible aspects of the pastor's role:

- *Chaplain:* The pastor helps the committee to set its whole work into a spiritual context by suggesting appropriate forms of prayer and scriptural reflection to use at each committee gathering; coaching committee members who agree to lead particular spiritual practices; and engaging the rest of the congregation in times of prayer about the planning work. *Chaplain* does not mean "the only person who can pray or comment on a Bible passage." If committee members share responsibility for prayer and theological reflection, the committee will be better equipped to articulate the spiritual mission and values of the congregation as they present the plan.
- *Professional:* As a person whose primary vocational energies are immersed in the life of the congregation, the pastor has a philosophy of ministry and a significant stake in the outcome of the work. The pastor should offer his or her own perspective on the matters being deliberated—then listen carefully to the responses of committee members. Where there is genuine dialogue, both the pastor and the committee will be stretched in their perspectives.
- *Information source:* Clergy have access to many kinds of information about the congregation's life, running the gamut from attendance statistics, to church politics, to the condition of the boiler. One danger, of course, is that the committee will rely too heavily on the pastor, and not develop its own independent assessment. Picking the pastor's brain should never be the sole method of gathering data about an important subject. Multiple sources of information provide both a reality check (valuable to the pastor) and the basis of a more credible presentation to the congregation.
- *Staff link:* In most congregations, the (senior) pastor is usually the only staff member who serves on the committee. This boundary is maintained so that the committee develops its own voice as a group of lay leaders. In the largest congregations (churches with average attendance over 1,000), a parish administrator may work closely with the planning chair in the week-to-week management of a

complex planning process; however, the senior minister will be deeply involved in the substantive discussions about the congregation's life and direction.

- *Denominational link:* In some traditions, the pastor is expected to bring the goals and values of the wider faith community to bear upon the work of the congregation. The pastor might bring in information about denominational goals, programs, and best practices. Better still, the pastor might urge the committee to invite a denominational representative (like an area minister or a member of the bishop's staff) to talk with the committee. Such a person may also be able to provide an outside perspective on the congregation's history and dynamics, on the church's community context, and on best practices of peer congregations.

- *Communicator:* In the course of preaching, worship leadership, pastoral visitation, and committee work, the pastor has an opportunity to make the rest of the congregation aware of the planning committee's efforts. While the pastor should not take primary responsibility for such communication, he or she will want to encourage various groups and individuals to stay in touch with the planning committee by mentioning specific topics or events that might spark interest. And the pastor can encourage planning committee members to build on relationships they already have with various people and ministries. (If John taught a Sunday school class recently, he might be the natural person to explore with this year's teachers the impact of a change in the Sunday morning schedule.)

In congregations with an average attendance between 50 and 150 (pastoral size), the pastor must usually initiate, or at least champion, the planning effort. Otherwise, lay leaders will probably hesitate to undertake the process.

The Governing Board

The church board[2] (which may be called the council, session, vestry, or administrative board) needs to stay connected to the substance of the planning work throughout the process. Otherwise, the recommendations have little chance of being adopted and implemented. The planning committee should report to the board on much more than the mechanics of the committee process; they should bring some meat for the board to chew on. Here are some ideas:

- In the needs assessment stage (see chapter 4), the planning team identifies which holy conversation is most crucial for the congregation to have at this time. The team also sketches out the simplest possible methods to get the right people talking about the right questions in the right settings. By making these decisions, the planning team is shaping the lens (the planning process) through which the congregation will look at its own life. As the team gains focus on the main holy conversation the church needs to have at this time, it is crucial to share the focus and the rationale for it with the board. By doing so, the team is taking an active role in shaping the expectations of other leaders about the planning process. If the board is surprised or disconcerted by the team's definition of its own work, the team will need to assess the meaning of this response and continue to negotiate its contract with the board.

- To keep the board engaged with substantive questions throughout the process, the team could approach them as a focus group and put them to work. Show them, for example, a graph of data you've recently collected, and ask them what they make of it. Ask the board to do the favorite hymn exercise (discussed in chapter 11 and included as Resource L on page 260); then help them to identify how the exercise connects to parish culture, to spiritual discernment, and to the need for powerful images. If you do some form of survey, or a cottage-meeting process (see chapter 13), try it out on the board first. Later, bring back one or two preliminary findings for board conversation—letting them know when full analysis of the data will be ready.

- Near the end of the process, as a report is taking shape, bring to the board a draft version of findings and recommendations. Don't get involved in any motions or amendments. Simply gather response—both on an individual reaction sheet (that people fill in before the discussion starts) and from the group conversation. Such a trial run gives the committee a very good chance of producing a report that will make sense to the board when it comes back to them later for formal approval.

The Consultant or Facilitator

Since strategic planning is a structured conversation, the question immediately arises: "Who provides the structure?" This question has two aspects. Someone (or some group of people) must *devise* the basic shape of the conversation, work out the connections between the separate steps, and make needed adjustments as the process unfolds. And someone must *facilitate* the conversation—clarifying the overarching process, encouraging people's participation, and ensuring a safe enough environment for honest and vulnerable sharing. Continuity in the facilitator role helps people develop trust; they have a sense of what to expect from session to session.

Smaller congregations (those with an attendance under 150) often use internal resources (pastor and lay leaders) and denominational resource persons to accomplish the design and facilitation of a planning process. Transitional and midsize congregations (those with an average attendance between 150 and 400) frequently seek guidance from a professional consultant within their own region, or ask their denominational office to recommend a consultant. Larger congregations tend to look across the national landscape for prominent agencies and individuals with a reputation for church planning expertise.

If you are going to choose a facilitator from inside the congregation, seek someone with the appropriate gifts. Here is a list prepared by consultants Roy M. Oswald and Robert E. Friedrich, Jr.:[3]

- Process skills
- The respect of the congregation
- The trust of the pastor
- A grasp of the theoretical material (in a book like this one, for example)
- Leadership skills
- A rich, consistent prayer life
- A deep sense of commitment to the long-term health of the congregation

- (*Optional*) Some experience in strategic planning in the corporate [or nonprofit] world, yet an appreciation of the difference between a spiritual discernment process and corporate planning.

If you can find the right kind of person and the funding, however, there are some distinct advantages to engaging an outside planning consultant who is experienced with the dynamics of religious systems:

- *Stewardship of the congregation's energy and attention span.* You want to get the greatest learning from the time people will put in, with a minimum of wheel spinning.
- *Reduction of unnecessary conflict within the committee.* Everybody seems to have a favorite planning method, and you cannot use all of them. A consultant provides common language and frameworks around which the group can unify.
- *The authority of the outside expert.* You may have within your congregation talented individuals who can (and sometimes do) lead excellent planning work with congregations. Like the "prophet without honor in his own country," this person will not be given the same authority as an outsider to whom you pay a fee. While this authority can be misused, the respect accorded to the outsider is an important resource when there is demanding emotional, intellectual and spiritual work to be accomplished.
- *Independent perspective.* As a person who is not immersed from week to week with the culture of your congregation, a consultant can raise questions and make observations from a different point of view.
- *Benefiting from the experience of other congregations.* A practitioner experienced in the dynamics of congregational planning will know the possibilities and pitfalls.
- *Leadership development.* Those who serve on the planning team will have a positive, enriching experience. This will affect their willingness to accept other challenging church assignments in the future.

Routine problem-solving work may not require external facilitation. But in congregations where the anxiety level is moderate to high, where sharp cultural differences are present within the congregation, or where real frame bending is needed (see the discussion of different forms of planning in chapter 1 and the summary in Resource C on page 209), a carefully chosen consultant is a good investment.

Possible Places in the Process to Use a Consultant

If you are going to work with a third-party consultant (whether from your denomination or from another source), involve them as early as possible in your thinking about a planning process. Later consultation doesn't compensate very well for a committee with a poorly framed assignment from the board or with the wrong people already recruited. Here are some possible times you will want to consider involving your consultant:

> If you are going to work with a third-party consultant, involve them as early as possible in your thinking about a planning process.

- Before you form a planning committee or shape its assignment, to help the pastor and board to clarify the congregation's planning needs and lead some balcony work. (See chapter 4 for discussion of balcony work.)
- When you are ready to form a committee, to help you develop criteria for committee membership and a process of selection. (See "Committee Selection and Training," chapter 4, for discussion of the issues.)
- When the committee has been recruited, to conduct an initial retreat for team building, orientation, and sketching of committee tasks. (See step 4 of "The Four-Step Process for Committee Selection and Training," in chapter 4.)
- During the gathering of data about the congregation's life, to facilitate a Time Line exercise. (See "Collecting Data," chapter 5, for general considerations; and the Time Line section at the beginning of chapter 10 for specific approaches.)
- After the committee has gathered some data about the congregation's life, to help the committee reflect more deeply on the congregation's culture. (See chapter 9.)
- When interpreting community demographics and psychographics, to help the committee sort through complex information and glean key learnings. (See chapter 3 on the seductive quality of statistical data and chapter 10 on reading the community context.)

- When drawing together overall learnings near the end of the process, to help the committee see the forest and sketch out statements of mission and vision. (See chapter 11 on discernment dimensions of planning.)
- When preparing major presentations for the board or congregation, to help the committee consider possible response and prepare for hard questions.
- After adoption of the plan, to help the board consider its crucial role in guiding implementation.
- Six to twelve months after adoption, to reflect with board, staff, and key leaders on implementation progress, unexpected difficulties, and new learnings.

Choosing a Consultant

The selection of a consultant is an important decision in the life of your congregation. Solicit as many referrals as possible from other congregations (especially those of a similar size), from your denomination, and from parachurch agencies like the Alban Institute. Ask specific questions about the nature of the work the person has done; the approaches they have used; the results the congregation has achieved with their guidance; and any concerns they might have about the work. It is wise to interview more than one consultant as you make your choice— you need to get a first-hand sense of this person's style and presence. When you narrow your list to a top choice, ask this person for the names of several previous clients you might contact. Make the calls, ask questions, and listen to the tone of the answers. When congregational leaders have undertaken a thoughtful selection process, the consulting relationship is likely to be more fruitful and collegial.

> When congregational leaders have undertaken a thoughtful selection process, the consulting relationship is likely to be more fruitful and collegial.

Notes
1. This psychological term is applied by Ronald Heifetz to the work of leaders in his book, *Leadership Without Easy Answers* (Cambridge, Mass.: Belknap Press, 1994).
2. Some congregations have multiple boards and councils. In that case, you may either select the one that has the most general oversight role or invite several different oversight bodies to join

together for key conversations with the planning committee. If, for example, financial and spiritual oversight are divided between trustees and deacons, see if you could involve them both.

3. From Roy M. Oswald and Robert E. Friedrich, Jr., *Discerning Your Congregation's Future: A Strategic and Statistical Approach* (Bethesda, Md.: Alban Institute, 1996), 20.

CHAPTER THIRTEEN

Involving the Congregation

Strategic planning is a structured conversation that helps a congregation make important choices. Those choices won't stick if they take members by surprise, or if they are finalized prematurely—before the necessary holy conversation has been fully engaged. Using the formal and informal communication networks of the congregation in a persistent way over many months, the planning team must somehow convey

- a clear picture of the current situation;
- compelling reasons to leave the comfort zone and try something different;
- a fresh articulation of the congregation's call in response to a changing context; and
- some well-imagined stories that help members see themselves engaged in new patterns of ministry.

Since planning is a conversation—not a monologue or an edict—the flow of information goes both ways. Members react and question. They affirm and resist. They offer their own language and their own images. Ideally, there is a constant circulation of facts, assessments, hopes, ideas, and proposals throughout the entire period of planning, so that no key findings or recommendations come as a surprise to the active members.

This desired flow of information happens in its own organic (and apparently chaotic!) way. Except in the tiniest congregations, the whole congregation is never in one room—or even in a whole collection of rooms, such as a series of home meetings. As we have seen in chapter 4, a smaller group of members (whom we have called the *productive 24 percent*, though the number may vary a bit) actually does the work on behalf of the whole faith community. If they are called to the holy conversation in thoughtful ways, this group will do important spiritual work and give other members confidence that the right matters are being considered in the right way. As we have noted before, there is a large group of people—between two-thirds and three-quarters of the congregation—who have neither a fixed opinion on the issues nor a strong wish to invest energy in extensive planning conversations. They are waiting for others to work it out and tell them what's going to happen. These people do not promise to like the results; if you change the worship schedule, for example, some of these good folk may find the new pattern so uncomfortable that they stop attending or join another church. Even so, they have little energy for the demanding process of learning and deciding what the congregation needs at this particular moment.

Most church leaders lament this reality, but this pattern may simply be the God-given shape of human community. In spiritual terms, we might say that some people are called by God to be among the *productive 24 percent*—to serve the whole congregation through a more intensive level of involvement. This service frees other members to respond to the call *they* hear from God to pay attention to family, friendship, work, school, civic involvement, individual prayer, recreation, personal growth, health concerns, bereavement, or even lying fallow for a time. Rather than fight this natural distribution of involvement, parish leaders may choose instead to navigate within it creatively by focusing most of their attention on the people who are ready to get engaged.

> In spiritual terms, we might say that some people are called by God to be among the *productive 24 percent*—to serve the whole congregation through a more intensive level of involvement.

In addition to asking, "Who feels called to engage in the congregation's holy conversation at this particular moment?" it is also helpful to ask, "Who exercises the gift of influence?" Words like influence and power sometimes cause discomfort to people in faith communities. Certainly, we can think of many cases in which power has been misused, just as money is often misused. But if we take the stigma away from the word, if we lift up influence as a gift to be used for the good of all, we can approach the subject with greater transparency and bring to it an attitude of stewardship and accountability. How do we acknowledge the gift of influence in a healthy way?

Identifying De Facto Leaders

Beyond the planning committee and the board, one circle of people to involve deeply in the work might be called your de facto congregational leaders, people from among the productive 24 percent who exercise gifts of influence. The people in this circle talk to, and are respected by, others in the congregation. If you reach this circle effectively, you will go a long way toward building a critical mass of support for the planning process itself and for any recommendations you may eventually bring forward.

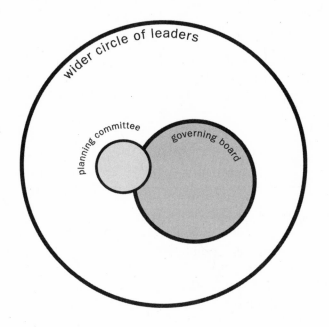

Almost every congregation has this wider circle of de facto leaders. These are people to whom the rest of the members look when they are wondering whether to support or resist a project. Some are in visible, official leadership roles on boards, committees, and ministry teams (like choir or Sunday school). Others are informal leaders—people whose opinions others take seriously when they are deciding about an important issue.

Most congregations—the 80 percent of faith communities with 200 or fewer attending—will typically have 25 to 50 people within the wider circle of leaders. (As you can see from the diagram, the wider circle includes as subsets the board and the planning committee.) One of your most crucial tasks is to become clear about who these people are and where their influence comes from. An exercise devised by Alban senior consultant Roy Oswald (summarized on the next two pages) is designed to do just that.

Power Analysis of a Congregation
Roy M. Oswald[1]

To complete this exercise, you will need a sheet of paper divided into four columns, like the chart below.

REPUTATION POWER	COALITION POWER	COMMUNICATION POWER	OFFICIAL POWER

Under Official Power, list all those persons who hold elected offices in the parish. For a large parish, limit this list to those in official decision-making positions.

Under Reputation Power, list that handful of people who have the respect of most persons in the community (that is, the congregation). These people have a certain charisma about them. When tough decisions get made in the parish, people usually look sideways to see where these people stand on the issues.

Under Coalition Power, first list all the formal and informal subgroups that exist in the parish. This should include every group from the choir to the church bowling league. Include also the informal groups that cluster together on Sunday mornings. Also list the key individuals within each of these subgroups—those one or two individuals who are ring-leaders. Depending on how the ringleaders feel about you or an issue, these subgroups can be mobilized either for or against you.

Under Communication Power, list the informal communication networks within the parish. Try to answer the question, "Who has whose ear?" Who calls whom when there is some news to share? Include here people who spend a lot of time around the church building (e.g., church secretary, janitors, retired workers, and so forth). These people usually have a lot of information about the activities of the parish. Those people who know "what's going on" are far more powerful than those who are in the dark. In this column, list those people who always seem to be in the know.

You now have people listed under four categories who represent power currencies within a parish. Go over all four lists and note names that appear on more than one list. Those names that appear on two or more lists are the most powerful people in the parish.

Write these power people's names on a special list. Spend a few minutes with each name and rate your credibility with each person:

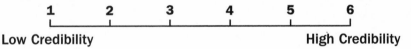

Low Credibility   **High Credibility**

This rating may give you some idea where you need to do some work if certain issues are to be resolved. You may decide you need to spend some time with certain folks in order to build a power base for yourself within the parish.

You may also want to rate each of these people with regard to their positions on specific issues. For example, if you are up against a key vote at a congregational meeting, rate each person's views on that issue:

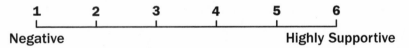

Negative   **Highly Supportive**

If the majority of these key persons are for the proposal, you can be fairly sure it will pass. To make sure, you may decide to visit a few key leaders who seem to be sitting on the fence. We do not recommend taking an issue to the parish as a whole unless you are fairly certain it will pass. When key issues fail to pass, your credibility and reputation may be diminished. This makes you less powerful when other issues arise.

Power dynamics affect each local parish. Most congregational members have their own assessment of power and control issues within their parishes. This is a given. So deciding whether or not you will undertake a power analysis of the parish is not the issue. At issue is whether you will be good at the process and disciplined in your approach or ignore the issues and handle power poorly. You may have to confront your personal feelings of comfort or discomfort with the use of power and clarify your theology of power.

When you have finished with the power analysis exercise, you will have a better idea whom you will want to recruit with special care for certain broader planning events, such as a time-line exercise or a goal-setting event. Remember that a personal conversation is always the best way to make an invitation. Least effective is a general announcement in the newsletter or in church, though you will certainly use announcements to reinforce individual invitations, to expand the group, and to let everyone in the congregation know what's going on. Never use your power analysis to limit the conversation to an influential elite; use it to *make sure that the people with the gift of influence in this congregation are in the room for the crucial conversations.* If these people are on board, any resulting project will have legs.

> **Never use your power analysis to limit the conversation to an influential elite.**

In a strategic-planning process, there are particular moments when it is especially beneficial for a planning committee to convene the wider circle of leaders (and anyone else who's interested) for conversation. Here are some suggestions:

- *Early in the process—even before the committee is formed.* You may wish to bring the wider circle of leaders together for an experience that broadens their horizons (balcony work). (See "Congregational Training for Planning," in chapter 4.)
- *Exploration of the congregation's history and culture.* (See chapter 9 for suggestions about exploring the congregation's culture and chapter 10 for information about time-line exercises.)
- *Exploration of the community context, including demographics.* (See chapter 10 on reading the community context.)
- *Testing the committee's synthesis of key learnings, mission, and vision.*
- *After adoption of recommendations, assigning implementation projects to existing groups and newly created action teams.*

Staying Visible on the Congregation's Radar Screen

If you are doing a good job of involving the wider circle of leaders, many others beyond that circle will already be aware of the planning conversations. People in that circle talk to others—to spouses, friends, fellow committee members, and those they run into at coffee hour or in the supermarket. It is still important, however, to bring aspects of the planning work into public view as frequently as possible, for several reasons. First, such communications will reinforce awareness on the part of those who have already become involved; busy people are paying attention to dozens of other important matters in the course of a given week and will quickly forget much of what you have told them. Second, public communication provides a link to people who are not connected to the planning conversation in any other way. For some of them, this information may open a door to deeper participation in the life of the congregation; for others, it will simply prevent them from feeling out of the loop. Finally, public communication venues provide the committee with an opportunity to crystallize key questions, facts,

> **Busy people are paying attention to dozens of other important matters in the course of a given week and will quickly forget much of what you have told them.**

ideas, learnings, and options. As they fashion this stream of communication, they are creating potential elements for a final report, month by month, as their conversations go forward. A committee that waits until the end to articulate findings will lose a great deal of valuable learning.

Let's move from the *why* to the *how* of public communications. Here are some guidelines:

- Apply St. Benedict's dictum about times of prayer to all your communications: "Better that they be frequent than long."
- Don't rely on just one medium; use all the channels simultaneously to reach more people and to reinforce awareness in the more active folks.
- Include a well-designed "Did you know...?" box on the front page of every issue of the newsletter.
- Offer a polished, one-minute presentation of a provocative question every couple of weeks at announcement time.
- Send members an e-mail message every month with a link to new information that has gone up on the strategic planning section of the Web page; provide an interesting caption in the e-mail to pique curiosity.
- Feature a *single* question, fact, idea, or opportunity in each communication.
- Don't just file your idea by title. Tell a story, show a diagram, give people a half-page handout with a few key points on it.

People remember stories, pictures, and objects much better than they remember oral communications.

- Tell the story in different voices. While it helps to have the planning chair visible all the time to symbolize lay leadership in the process, the chair can introduce someone else to speak or write a particular part of the message.

- Speak to people where they are—literally. If church-school teachers and parents seldom make it into worship for the announcements, have a committee member hang around downstairs and hand a half-page update to each person with a word of greeting. If some of your retirees gather for breakfast after an early worship service, ask if a committee member might join them occasionally to share findings. If a few of your more influential people never turn out for meetings, request a time for two members of the committee to meet with them at home to fill them in on what's happening. (After you visit them, it will be much easier to say: "Harry and Janet, your perspectives on this question are so valuable; we really need you to attend the goal-setting meeting next month so that others can benefit from your views as we make decisions.")

Use of Surveys

Many congregations assume that a planning process always includes a lengthy survey. We would like to challenge this preconception. Among the possible forms of information gathering in a planning process, surveys frequently create the most trouble for the least payoff.

A survey is an intervention—that is to say, asking a question changes the system. Take the area of worship, for example. It may seem logical to ask people what time they would prefer the worship service to begin. Putting that question on a survey immediately raises some members' expectation that they are going to see a desired change; for others, it raises uncertainty and anxiety about their ability to participate. The resulting scatter of responses may give no useful guidance for a decision. Imagine the conversation in the planning committee: "Let's see.

> Among the possible forms of information gathering in a planning process, surveys frequently create the most trouble for the least payoff.

We received the survey back from one quarter of our active members, mostly people over 50. A slight majority of them would like the main service to be earlier. Gosh, that would completely unsettle the church-school schedule. We don't really know how the younger members feel about this change, and we don't know how intense anybody's preference is. But now that we've asked, people are pressing us about our conclusions!"

Congregations rarely anticipate the consequences a questionnaire may set in motion. The committee may spend an exorbitant amount of time creating, administering, tallying, and interpreting the survey—then handling the anxieties it raises. A few well-framed conversations within the wider circle of leaders will usually produce more valuable information at far less cost in time and stress. In such a meeting, the committee might elicit viewpoints on a key issue by posting several statements on a chart pad, then asking people to rate their level of agreement with each statement using a scale from one to six. (Such rating can be done on an index card to keep things informal.) Responses can be tallied during a break and presented back to the group for immediate discussion. Or, you could ask those present to line up across an open space in the room to create an opinion spectrum right on the spot; such physical movement generates a great deal of energy and discussion. Real-time conversations have the enormous advantage of building relationship and allowing the group to interpret its own response through discussion. Committee members can probe any puzzling responses, or ask for opinion on a new question that emerges in the conversation.

> Real-time conversations have the enormous advantage of building relationship and allowing the group to interpret its own response through discussion.

Here are some guidelines about written surveys:

- Use other methods of information gathering, if possible.
- Late in the planning process, when key issues have been researched in other ways, a narrowly focused survey with a few questions on a single issue may be helpful. Take time to construct questions carefully, and pre-test the questions on a small sample group, so that you can find and fix the bugs.
- Some professionally prepared surveys can be helpful, if the planning committee has identified a clear need and has verified that a particular instrument will address that need, in a style the congregation will accept. Hartford Seminary Center offers congregations

a well-respected and comprehensive Parish Profile Inventory,[2] often used as preparation for calling a new pastor. While the entire survey might overwhelm the average planning process, a committee could select one of the eight sections that relates to a specific planning need. The U.S. Congregational Life Survey[3] offers a similarly comprehensive inventory which they describe in their promotional material as a "tool for discovering your congregation's strengths," designed to be administered at all worship services on a selected weekend; this survey was originally developed for a study of congregational life in four English-speaking countries. Both the Parish Profile Inventory (Hartford) and the U.S. Congregational Life Survey are designed to be useful across a broad theological spectrum. Natural Church Development[4] is an instrument that has been used in many parts of the world, operating from a moderate evangelical perspective. Eight "quality factors" are measured, and congregations are encouraged to focus efforts on their limiting factor (that is, their weakest area) in order to increase vitality and allow numerical growth to occur naturally.

- If you work with any ready-made survey, be sure you know why you are using it. Find out how other churches applied the results. Make sure it fits the culture of your congregation. Consider using a coach from the selected organization. Be prepared to work with the findings over several years and to make action on the findings a top priority—otherwise, don't do it.

Use of Home Meetings

Within the culture of some churches and synagogues—especially those with a congregational form of governance—there is a strong expectation that small home meetings (sometimes called cottage meetings) will be used to reach out to the membership and gather grassroots aspirations. While organizing and conducting these meetings requires a huge amount of work, they are often well received. People usually value the opportunity for face-to-face connection. In order to use this method most effectively:

- Consider recruiting a separate team to organize the home meetings. You probably have people in the congregation who love to organize gatherings and do it very well. Identify people with a good-sized living room and the gift of hospitality to serve as hosts. The hosts should *not* be asked to lead the meetings—that's the job of a team of two people from the planning committee.

- The questions asked need to be few and simple. For example: "What brought you to this congregation? What keeps you here? Where is God calling us next as a congregation?" (An alternative set of home meeting questions is found in chapter 5.) To make the information easier to collate, you might give people three index cards of different colors to write on.

- Here is a sample process: On a flip chart, reveal the first question and say, "Please write a brief response on the blue card." Allow a couple of minutes for writing, and remind people that there will be time for discussion after all have written answers to the three questions. When most people seem finished, reveal the second question (to be answered on a card of a second color); then continue with the third question in the same way. This process ensures that you get individual response from each person, and it helps the quieter people get prepared to participate. Divide the discussion time into three roughly equal periods. Encourage each person to respond to the first question before moving on to the second. We recommend that one member of the committee facilitate the conversation, while another member takes notes; even though you will collect the cards at the end, material pops up in the discussion that isn't recorded anywhere else.

- Leaders of the cottage meetings should expect to spend a considerable amount of time collating the information and organizing it into meaningful categories. You may find that there is not a lot of fresh thinking in the ideas proposed—this process is not particularly well suited to generating innovation, but it's great for building trust, affirming strengths, and getting a rough sense of people's priorities.

- Some congregations use home meetings toward the end of the process, to test a list of key learnings and possible goals. In that case, we suggest that you give each person a worksheet with the key learnings and possible goals listed out. You might use the following sample format for each key learning, and each possible goal:

Key Learning #1

The older and younger members of our church tend to have different worship needs, but they want to stay in contact with each other on Sunday morning. God calls us to work with this tension over the next few years, and to find worship patterns that respect the needs and gifts of both groups.

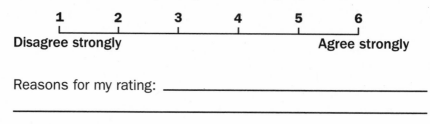

```
   1        2        3        4        5        6
   |--------|--------|--------|--------|--------|
Disagree strongly                        Agree strongly
```

Reasons for my rating: _____

_____

In this process, you might break for dessert after people have filled in the feedback sheets. During the break, do a quick compilation on one page of a chart pad showing the range of numerical responses for each item.

Learning # 1: Different worship needs.

1	2	3	4	5	6
	✓✓	✓	✓✓	✓✓✓✓	✓✓

When people return from the break, take a brief look at each item and note the distribution of responses. The goal is *not* to come up with a consensus, but rather to explore why people rated the item the way they did. Again, have one of the planning committee members facilitate while the other takes notes. At the end of the meeting, let people know when and how the committee will report back findings from the whole process.

Use of Large-Group Exercises

When done well, one of the most fruitful forms of data gathering is the large-group meeting, involving the wider circle of leaders (discussed earlier in this chapter) and anyone else who wishes to attend. The "History Grid" exercise (Resource N on page 263) is one example of a design for gathering information from a group of 25 to 50 people. If you have a facilitator available to you who has real expertise with open-space design, you may find other energizing ways to engage a large group in exploration of key questions. (Harrison Owen's book *Open Space Technology: A User's Guide* is a resource you may wish to consult.[5]) In order for large-group data gathering to succeed, the committee must

- Clarify one or two key questions to explore, so as to create helpful boundaries around the conversation
- Suggest ground rules for the conversation, and solicit group commitment to the ground rules
- Make it clear that the purpose of the event is learning, not decision making
- Provide clear steps in the conversation, and stick to them
- Engage an able and unbiased facilitator, familiar with the dynamics of larger groups, to lead the process

Toward the end of such a meeting, one or two committee members might summarize what they have heard on newsprint, and ask the group to verify whether these statements fairly represent the drift of the conversation. Checking out what you have heard right on the spot will make it easier to report the findings in other settings, and to integrate the findings into your overall plan. Allow some time for this checking process —new issues, concerns, or disagreements may surface at this point. If these second thoughts are acknowledged clearly by the committee, people can usually relax and allow the meeting to come to closure.

> Checking out what you have heard right on the spot will make it easier to report the findings in other settings, and to integrate the findings into your overall plan.

Retreats

A parish-wide planning retreat is an extended version of a large-group meeting. Though it is billed as congregation-wide, you will still need to do careful recruitment to make sure that your wider circle of leaders is in the room.

The extended time period (often Friday evening through Saturday afternoon) can allow greater continuity in the conversation, more informal time to build relationships and consider questions, and more opportunity to integrate personal sharing, Bible study, and prayer into the process. The drawback has to do with participation. Whole segments of your congregation (those who work weekends, those with younger children, those who cannot afford the suggested cost) may be missing from pivotal conversations. When you plan such an event, take a realistic look at who is actually going to come and make sure the agenda is appropriate for that group to undertake together.

> Take a realistic look at who is actually going to come and make sure the agenda is appropriate for that group to undertake together.

Retreat weekends can of course be extremely helpful for the planning committee. At the beginning of the process, when the committee is getting oriented to its task, a weekend away with the planning consultant can get the work off to a positive start. Toward the end of the planning process, when the committee is drawing together learnings into a sense of mission and vision, a weekend apart with your consultant may be the best vantage point from which to survey the whole forest of data you have collected, listen attentively (to self, other, and God), play with images, and test perceptions about the direction of God's call at this time.

A Final Note

We would offer one final reminder before leaving part 3. No congregation should use all of the recommended steps or resources. Ask yourself the diagnostic questions lifted up in part 2 of this book:

- What is the holy conversation your congregation most needs to have at this particular time?
- What kinds of resources are most appropriate to your congregation's culture and situation?
- How much energy and time is available for planning conversations?
- What can you do well, given the talents and resources at hand?
- What is God nudging you to pay attention to?

Notes

1. Excerpted from Roy M. Oswald's *New Beginnings: The Pastor-ate Start-Up Workbook* (Bethesda, Md.: Alban Institute, 1989). Used by permission. For a full exploration of power issues, see Roy M. Oswald's *Power Analysis of a Congregation: Revised and Updated Edition*, available for download from the Alban website, www.alban.org.

2. See Nancy T. Ammerman et al., eds., *Studying Congregations: A New Handbook* (Nashville: Abingdon Press, 1998), Appendix A. For information about the full Parish Profile Inventory, visit www.hirr.hartsem.edu/cong/cong_church_inventory.html

3. For information, contact U.S. Congregations, 100 Witherspoon St., Louisville, KY 40202. Phone: 1-888-728-7228, ext. 2040. Web site: www.USCongregations.org.

4. Christian Schwarz's *Natural Church Development* (Carol Stream, Ill.: ChurchSmart Resources, 1996) describes the assumptions and methods of the Natural Church Development approach. Both the book and the inventory are available from ChurchSmart Resources. Find them online at www.churchsmart.com.

5. Harrison Owens, *Open Space Technology: A User's Guide* (San Francisco: Berrett-Koehler, 1998).

PART FOUR

What Planning Looks Like in Practice

We have presented a conceptual basis for planning (Introduction and part 1). We have laid out the possible phases and elements of a hypothetical, full-blown planning process (part 2). We have addressed a variety of planning issues and pointed to a variety of methods and resources (part 3).

So what does it look like in practice? This section of the book is meant to help planning leaders move from possibilities to practice, by identifying some of the concrete circumstances in which planning commonly takes place. We will look at:

- Planning in congregations of different sizes (chapter 14).
- Planning when there are clear focal issues (such as adding staff, expanding space, clergy retirement, growth pressures, or persistent decline) or none at all (chapter 15).
- Planning in the context of an annual retreat for church leaders (chapter 16).

Once you have identified the concrete circumstances that apply to your own congregation, you will be in a better position to select appropriate concepts and methods from the wide range of material provided in the rest of this book.

CHAPTER 14

Planning in Congregations of Different Sizes

Over the past two decades, the Alban Institute has based a good deal of its work with congregations on several observations about size:[1]

- Congregations fall into distinctive size categories, and congregations of different sizes organize in different ways. Each has its own recognizable way of being church.
- Average Sabbath attendance—all ages, all Saturday evening or Sunday worship services combined, over the whole year—is the best single indicator of size for Christian congregations. Synagogues consider a wider range of factors in judging size.[2]
- Congregations do not grow or decline smoothly, but tend to plateau at certain predictable levels of attendance.
- In order to break through an attendance plateau, a congregation must deliberately relinquish familiar patterns of behavior and begin to act as larger congregations act.

These descriptions of congregational dynamics relate to a growing body of theory about the way human beings organize themselves.[3] Humans tend to form primary groups of 12 or so, and clans of about 50. At about 150, a qualitative shift (the *tipping point*) occurs and a true organization comes into being, with official roles and structures, formal communication, and explicit procedures. Larger organizations seem to work best when built of combinations of these natural-sized groups.

How Size Affects Planning

The numerical thresholds of 50 and 150 underlie the particular size theory most often used by Alban in its work with churches—a framework originally developed by church sociologist Arlin Rothauge. Using Rothauge's names for four church sizes, we would describe the categories in this way:

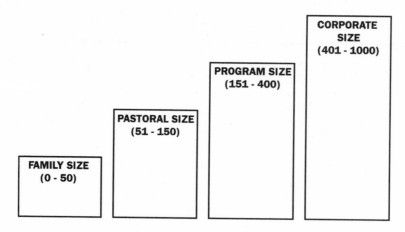

Rothauge's Church Sizes

Family-Size Church (Up to 50 Adults and Children at Worship)

This is a small congregation that operates like an extended family (and may in fact *be* a biological family network). Just as in the famous tavern from the television series *Cheers*, "everybody knows your name." This church is organized around one or two anchoring figures, called matriarchs and patriarchs by Rothauge to indicate their tacit authority in the system. Such congregations often have part-time pastors, and their clergy tend to adopt a chaplain role—leading worship and giving pastoral care. A pastor who challenges the authority of a patriarch or matriarch, or who presumes to be the primary leader of the congregation, generally will not stay long.

Planning in the family-size congregation often has the character of a kitchen-table conversation: casual, personal, and low tech. The work may, in fact, happen in the home of a key family; the get-togethers often have no official mandate from the board and no formalized roster of participants—just the tacit endorsement of a matriarch or patriarch and the participation of unofficial delegates from all the key families. There are real assets to this style: at their best, planning conversations in the small church are brief, direct, and practical. Problem planning is the long suit of these congregations, who often take pride in having survived against all odds. Development does not usually happen through planning, but rather through the passing of the mantle to a younger member of a key family or to newer person who has been fully adopted as a member of the tribe.

Because they are built on intense, family-type loyalty, congregations of this size may find it nearly impossible to engage in frame-bending conversations—even when faced with the threat of extinction—without considerable external support. Denominational offices can help by offering regional gatherings, in which teams from small churches can temporarily step outside the family circle, develop new skills, and learn about innovative patterns that other small congregations have found successful. One caveat about denominational resourcing: small congregations sometimes have a bit of a Napoleon complex. If they feel they are being bullied by the system, they may resist fiercely.

Pastoral-Size Church (50–150)

This congregation is a coalition of two or three family and friendship networks, unified around the person and role of the pastor. Clergy time is largely taken up maintaining a direct pastoral relationship with each member, coordinating the work of a small leadership circle, personally conducting worship, and leading small-group programs such as Bible study. The governing board usually operates like a committee, arranging much of the day-to-day life of the congregation. Members recognize each other's faces, know most people's names, and will notice if someone new is present at worship.

Planning usually won't happen in pastoral-size churches unless their clergy communicate a strong desire for it. It would be wise for the minister to identify several issues he or she would like a planning process to address; with these statements in hand, the minister will need to make the case for a special committee to develop some recommendations for the board. Since the governing board in a pastoral-size church does not usually delegate very comfortably, board leaders will need lots of informal conversation with committee members in the course of the planning work—but will also need to be reminded that the committee must have freedom to explore the options before bringing back recommendations.

Congregations of this size have traded a bit of their rugged self-reliance for the reassurance of a longer-term pastoral presence. As a result, problems that are ignored by the minister may also be ignored by the congregation until there is a crisis. On the other hand, these systems are more likely than the family-size church to do a bit of developmental thinking—provided, of course, that the pastor leads the way. Such planning usually begins with the minister taking a few people off to a workshop to hear about new models for church school or stewardship or new-member ministry.

Pastoral-size churches often make excellent use of local denominational consultants and staff. Because these resource people are part of the wider circle of relationships within which the congregation lives, churches of this size tend to feel comfortable inviting them in. Such denominational resource people are appropriately asked to help a church clarify its planning issues through active listening; to suggest appropriate planning methods or books; and perhaps to facilitate a retreat day as part of the process.

Program-Size Church (150–400)

This congregation is known for the quality and variety of its programs. Separate programs for children, youth, couples, seniors, and other age and interest groups provide entry points for a wide range of people. The pastor's crucial role is to recruit, equip, and inspire a small circle of key program leaders—lay and ordained, paid and unpaid. This ring of leadership might include, for example, the choir director, the church-school superintendent, the youth-group leader, the coordinator of lay visitors, and the head of a committee that tracks new-member incorporation. Working as a team with the pastor, they reach out to involve others as program participants and as leaders. Decision making is broadly distributed within the wider leadership circle (25 to 50 people) and pastoral care is shared by laity. While Rothauge originally identified the maximum attendance for program size as 350, we suggest an upper figure of 400.[4]

Congregations of this size begin to feel the need for a more extended and comprehensive planning process—to help leaders get their arms around a more complex organizational life, and to help them articulate an overarching purpose that can hold together diverse constituencies and needs. Such churches often contain a significant number of leaders who are involved with organizational planning and change management in their day-to-day lives (in business, school systems, scouting programs, human services, and so forth). These members are familiar with the use of consultants and facilitators—and may play this role themselves in other settings.

As we work with planning committees in program-size churches, Alban consultants meet many energetic members of Generation X. The oldest members of this cohort—now in their 30s and early 40s—have been dubbed *nomads*.[5] Accustomed to coping with organizational change and uncertainty, they are often willing to jump in and help with a planning process that asks big questions and uses the latest techniques for group involvement. Expect laptops on the table for taking real-time minutes, PDAs beaming calendars around, e-mail meetings, Web updates to the congregation, priority-setting exercises using sticky dots, and PowerPoint presentations of the committee's findings. This is a breathless generation that seems to thrive on having too much to do; they will cooperate with well-structured times of prayer or scriptural reflection, but often need the pastor or a seasoned lay leader to bring these elements firmly into the process.

Program-size churches are especially likely to include cottage meetings in a planning process. At the smaller end of program size, congregations are usually experiencing considerable tension between relational and programmatic ways of being church. In this environment of ambivalence, cottage meetings reaffirm a value on relationships while demonstrating the benefits of a multi-cell program. ("We don't all have to be in the same place at the same time in order to feel connected as a faith community!") Program-size congregations often say that these gatherings were, in themselves, one of the most significant products of the whole planning process.

Mission and vision statements developed by churches of this size are rarely bold or memorable. Nevertheless, they are crucial to the extent that they are born of deep conversation about the glue (shared identity and purpose) that holds the church together. As congregations move through program size, they experience increasing pressure for quality in their key programs. Debates intensify about the allocation of staff positions and program funding. Unless a shared sense of mission begins to develop, the various program units are likely to become alienated and to compete with each other in destructive ways.

The small circle of key program leaders (described in the first paragraph of this section) must be kept abreast of planning conversations about overarching mission and vision, perhaps through a separate staff retreat. The pastor and the planning chair keep good communication flowing with the staff at every step of the planning process, but prevent staff members from dominating important discussions about identity, mission, and vision. Member ownership is vital.

Corporate-Size Church (400–1,000)

This congregation is known for excellence in worship and music, and for the range and diversity of its programs. Specialized ministries are provided for narrowly identified groups of people; several of these programs may be known beyond the congregation for their excellence. Often, distinct subcongregations form around multiple worship services. The senior pastor spends more time preparing to preach and lead worship than most clergy, and must be skilled at working with a diverse staff of full-time professional leaders. Decision making is carried out by a multilayered structure of staff, boards, and committees. While clergy continue to provide pastoral care, especially in crisis moments, most members find their spiritual support in small groups or from lay visitors.

Strategic planning in the corporate-size church is a formal and elaborate process that may take up to two years from first mention to final, glossy report. Formal initiation of the process typically comes from the board. A consultant search may include nationally known individuals and agencies, as well as respected planning facilitators from the corporate and nonprofit worlds. At the request of the planning chair, members of the staff will likely be expected to undertake statistical research tasks, handle logistics of retreats, produce communications materials, or create time and task logs for their own positions. The parish administrator may be assigned to provide staff support to the committee itself.

In congregations of this size, the senior minister is expected to be a high-profile leader. As a result, the planning process must include frequent formal dialogue between the senior pastor and the planning chair, and also between the senior pastor and the planning committee. While the senior pastor will not usually attend every planning committee meeting, the committee will consciously seek the perspective of the senior pastor on such matters as:

- Key issues to be addressed in a planning process
- Strategic choices the congregation faces in today's environment
- Primary conclusions to be drawn from the data gathering
- Mission and vision formulations to energize the next era of ministry
- Major goals and initiatives to be advanced and funded

Beyond these interactions with the senior minister, the planning committee will also establish a dialogue with

- The second tier of parish leadership (major boards and programs)
- The congregation at large (often through professional-quality surveys and carefully constructed focus groups)
- The wider community, where this congregation tends to be an important player

The planning committee chair, consultant, and assigned staff person will constantly monitor the plan for the whole planning process to make sure that each activity is competently implemented and that all the pieces are coming together to create a coherent picture of what is and what might be.

A Final Note on Size

Differences based on size are not, of course, as cut-and-dried as these descriptions. Many congregations live in the plateau zone between two sizes—and so may hold conflicting expectations about planning (as they do about many other things). If this describes your situation, you may wish to refer to chapter 9, where we discuss the impact of size on a congregation's culture.

Notes
1. This chapter draws together descriptions from several sources: Alice Mann's book, *The In-Between Church: Navigating Size Transitions in Congregations* (Bethesda, Md.: Alban Institute, 1998); contributions by Dan Hotchkiss to an article written with

Alice Mann and David Trietsch, "Searching for the Key: Developing a Theory of Synagogue Size," *Congregations* (January-February 2001); and the recent work by Gary McIntosh, *One Size Doesn't Fit All: Bringing Out the Best in Any Size Church* (Grand Rapids, Mich.: Fleming H. Revell, 1999). "The tipping point" has become a household term because of Malcolm Gladwell's book *The Tipping Point: How Little Things Can Make a Big Difference* (New York: Little, Brown, 2000). Elements of this section are also found in Alice Mann's *Raising the Roof: The Pastoral to Program Size Transition* (Bethesda, Md.: Alban Institute, 2002), chapter 1.

2. Mann, Trietsch, and Hotchkiss, "Searching for the Key: Developing a Theory of Synagogue Size," 24.

3. British anthropologist Robin Dunbar, for example, has demonstrated a biological basis for the way primates organize themselves into groups. See R. I. M. Dunbar, "Neocortex Size as a Constraint On Group Size in Primates," *Journal of Human Evolution* 20 (1992): 469-93. Cited from *The Tipping Point*, chapter 5.

4. This change is partly based on my observation that congregations rarely accomplish the full shift to a program identity and structure until attendance hits a critical mass of about 250. Gary McIntosh, author of *One Size Doesn't Fit All*, offers the number 400 as the upper limit of medium size.

5. The term comes from William Strauss and Neil Howe. An excellent application of their theory to congregations can be found in Carl Eeman's *Generations of Faith: A Congregational Atlas* (Bethesda, Md.: Alban Institute, 2003).

CHAPTER FIFTEEN

Common Driving Issues

In the needs-assessment phase (see chapter 4), one key task is to specify any particular impending decisions that may be driving the planning process. In this chapter, we will discuss some of the driving issues we run into frequently in our work as planning consultants, and also consider the implications of planning when there is no urgent question identified in advance.

We Are About to Expand the Staff

Congregations often step back to plan when they are feeling the need to add staff. This is a healthy impulse. It is wise to clarify the assumptions leaders are bringing to the table before you write a job description and start a search. Staffing questions may seem pretty simple on the surface:

- Shall we employ a children's church-school coordinator, instead of expecting a volunteer to do it?
- Should we add a youth minister?
- Do we need an associate pastor?

But under the surface, a bundle of assumptions probably lie waiting to be clarified and tested.

Planning around any of the three questions just identified might reveal a more complicated picture:

- *Church-School Coordinator:* We assume that our children's program will continue to grow quickly, but we have not looked at any child population projections from our local school system. We have an obvious inside candidate for a coordinator position, but we have not considered the impact that employing a member[1] may have on staff dynamics or on the motivation of other volunteers. Furthermore, we have not looked at our overall staffing pattern to assess how *all* the staff positions now function—and interrelate—to support our agreed mission. (We are not referring here to a performance review of the *person* holding each office; rather, we are talking about an analysis of the way each staff *position* is defined, and the way the staffing pattern as a whole advances the congregation's work.)

- *Youth Minister:* We assume that employing a youth minister will cause the youth program to grow, but we have no agreed parish strategy for reaching more young people and no shared picture of the difference we want to make in a teenager's life. Many people seem to want a pied piper—a twenty-something layperson with a charismatic personality—with whom high school students will easily relate. But wouldn't a solo performer job description undercut our emerging team of volunteer leaders? Wouldn't a ministry based solely on charisma leave the program vulnerable—to burnout of the youth minister, to potential abuses of emotional power, and to complete collapse at the moment when the current piper moves on?

- *Associate Pastor:* With an average weekend attendance nearing 200, we think our current minister needs help. She's doing a lot of administration. Many of our leaders think that's terrible because she is losing her direct pastoral link with every household. Should we employ an administrator and then ask the pastor to make more visits? Should we fund a second clergy position with a generalist job description? Should we hire a retired pastor part-time to be a minister of visitation? Should we look for an associate who is a specialist in building lay pastoral care teams—and if we did, could our current minister successfully renegotiate her pastoral role with the parish?

Congregations are wise to pause—at least for a few months—to examine strategic questions related to staffing before they authorize a position and launch a search. An outstanding guide to planning for staff expansion is *Staff Your Church for Growth*, by Gary McIntosh.[2]

We Are Overcrowded

Space is another question that drives congregations to plan. For lack of an adequate facility, many congregations have failed to reach new waves of population growth in their communities—especially congregations that reach the plateau between pastoral size and program size. On the other hand, we all know disaster stories of churches that adopted the philosophy, "Build it and they will come," only to find that a baby boom had already gone bust, or that the arriving populations had quite different religious preferences. Further, even in congregations with demonstrable potential for numerical growth, there are more questions to address than square footage and style:

- Does the congregation have a strong sense of vocation to make room for the new people God is sending? (See the section below on growth pressures.)
- Is expanding the building the best option, or should the parish focus on reusing the facility at several different times each weekend? (This second alternative will generate issues of staffing, worship styles, and a possible shift from relational to programmatic orientation in the church's culture.)
- Should a change in location be considered? Moving to a well-chosen new site can often boost a congregation's potential to incorporate new people. As in a new congregational start, people may be attracted by the chance to get in on the ground floor of an exciting new venture.
- Is the congregation able and willing to expand *all* the elements of its facility that are necessary to allow natural growth to occur? More worship seating won't help if parking is a major problem, or if a deteriorating education wing turns off parents with high standards of quality for children's programming. Parking and classrooms probably won't help if worship capacity has been ignored because the historic building is a sacred cow.
- How much money are we actually capable of raising for a building project? Building programs generate plenty of inherent conflict on their own. Once a congregation arrives at agreement to support

a particular proposal, it is very demoralizing to face a whole new battle over which elements to cut for lack of funding.

Congregations frequently skip over these fundamental planning questions and proceed too quickly to retain an architect.

As we noted in the case of staffing questions, it is usually wise to engage in a cycle of broader strategic conversation (using, for example, selected activities from part 2 and part 3 of this book) before developing a specific plan to expand facilities. If you are certain that *something* must be done about the building, you may want to review *A Congregational Planning Process* from Episcopal Church Building Fund.[3] This guide incorporates a good deal of practical wisdom into a suggested structure and process for tackling a potential building project.

We Are Anticipating a Capital Campaign

Some congregations undertake strategic planning a year or more in advance of any anticipated capital campaign—regardless of the purpose for which the funds are likely to be raised. Such a move might be wise in situations like these:

- The church has a dynamic music program with its own base of loyalty. The music committee is beginning to imagine a massive restoration of the church's historic organ.
- The congregation has just moved from one major service to two (alleviating immediate pressure), but recognizes that facilities are still an issue to be addressed.
- Major bequests are anticipated in the next five years. While this is not a capital campaign, it is another kind capital infusion that merits careful thought before the fact.

The advantage of beginning with a wide-angle strategic-planning process is obvious—leaders develop a broader sense of vision before they zero-in on costly initiatives. The problem with strategic planning at such moments is that some people may become suspicious that the whole process is organized to produce a preconceived answer. ("We know we're only doing this plan because the pastor is against the organ project." "The powers-that-be have decided to build that new wing—

a campaign will be recommended no matter what the congregation says!") Sometimes, these suspicions are well founded.

Strategic conversations could happen in two ways at this moment. If a capital campaign, or its primary purposes, are *not* already a done deal, then an honest exploration of mission, vision, and goals could help the congregation determine whether a campaign would be appropriate at all, and if so, what its focus might be. If a capital campaign *is* presumed, then say so. Use the strategic conversations to: (1) place that effort in the perspective of the congregation's mission, and (2) test assumptions about the importance and viability of a capital project. If you go forward and engage a campaign consultant, ask this person to build the feasibility study and case statement on what you have already learned. Otherwise, the consultant may inadvertently duplicate the work. This will confuse and annoy the congregation, and will waste an opportunity to sharpen and deepen the conversation through the fundraiser's involvement.

Our Long-Tenured Pastor Is Nearing Retirement Age

Clergy sometimes encourage the board to undertake strategic planning a few years ahead of their likely retirement date. Especially when the minister has served the church for a long time, he or she may be concerned that the system will simply coast through the last few years, then find itself unprepared to grapple with questions about its next era of ministry.

Here's the dilemma. Even if no one is talking about the impending retirement, the congregation is subliminally aware that these are the closing years of a long ministry. If things have gone relatively well in this pastorate, leaders are loath to do anything that might be interpreted as hurrying the minister out the door. Clergy are often hesitant to speak the "R" word (retirement) for fear of becoming a lame duck. Further, clergy usually want to keep their options open about their exact ending date. Denominational officials often discourage any conversation that might cause the congregation to short-circuit the necessary work of closure and grief—or that might tempt current clergy to try to call the shots about who will succeed them.

We indicated before that frame-bending conversation arises from the combination of pain and possibility. The congregation may not experience a great deal of either until the current pastor announces a departure date. In the meantime, however, developmental planning may help keep the congregation's ministries vital, and may help leaders gain planning experience with each other that will stand them in good stead at the time of clergy transition. Congregations anticipating a clergy retirement would benefit from Alban consultant Roy Oswald's recent work on transition committees, *Beginning Ministry Together*.[4]

We Are Experiencing Tensions over Growth

We have already identified two driving issues that may be related to overall numerical growth—adding staff and expanding space. Beyond these specifics, some congregations undertake strategic planning in order to engage the growth question head-on: "Is this congregation called to reconfigure its life to allow further numerical growth? If so, are we prepared to make the necessary changes?"

Especially in the transition zone between pastoral and program size, these questions can be daunting and divisive. Congregations with an average attendance between 150 and 250 are likely to experience profound ambivalence. They sense that the relational orientation is no longer working well—newcomers are slipping through the cracks; old-timers are uncomfortable with the pace and complexity of the congregation's life; the pastor is expected to maintain personal contact with every household, but can barely keep up with hospitalized members. While there is a growing demand for excellent programs, the congregation has not yet attained critical mass (of attendees, pledging households, leaders) to function well in the programmatic orientation. Alice's recent research suggests that churches do not reach that critical mass until average attendance is sustained at 250 or more. Congregations in the in-between zone (150 to 250) may want to draw on her book, *Raising the Roof: The Pastoral-to-Program Size Transition*[5] as a resource during strategic planning. Chapter 4 of that book describes learning and planning steps that may help shape the strategic conversation.

We Are in Persistent Decline and Need to Redevelop

On the other end of the spectrum, we find congregations whose driving issue is long-term decline, not growth pressure. Depending on how far they have proceeded down the decline curve, these congregations may be experiencing big doses of pain, and little sense of realistic possibility.

Congregations in decline often imagine that the solution is simply to find the right pastor. However, the profile of the right pastor depends upon the congregation's strategy. Most congregations in decline *do not have a clear strategy* for relating their ministry to the surrounding community in a new and more viable way.

All the questions involved in strategic planning are relevant to a congregation in decline. What is usually missing is the energy to engage in frame-bending conversations persistently enough to break through to a new sense of mission and vision. Often, it takes wise coaching from outside (a denominational resource person or external consultant) to help the congregation face up to reality and to consider hard choices.

For a broad discussion of the dynamics and steps of redevelopment ministry, see *Redeveloping the Congregation: A How-To for Lasting Change* by Mary K. Sellon, Daniel F. Smith, and Gail F. Grossman,[6] or *Can Our Church Live? Redeveloping Congregations in Decline* by Alice Mann.[7] An outstanding guide to redevelopment is available on Alban's Web-based Congregational Resource Guide (www.congregationalresources.org). To find the tutorial on redevelopment, search for "Spiritual Strategic Pathways," by George Bullard. Using Bullard's material, you can explore up to 13 strategic options for redeveloping churches. In a congregation whose planning questions revolve around the reality of decline, this online resource could energize the learning and planning process, provide helpful structure to the conversation, and sharpen the choices.

We Do Strategic Planning as an Organizational Discipline

Some congregations begin to plan just because planning is a good thing to do. For example, in congregations with a relational orientation (typically those with an average attendance under 200), a new pastor may spend the first year getting to know the church and addressing one goal identified as a high priority during the search. In the second year, this minister may ask for a new round of goal setting—based in the reality of this particular pastoral relationship. If the church created a useful profile of parish and community during the search period, don't start over from scratch. Rather, revisit that work. Ask which statements are still valid, and which need revision now—because the situation has changed, because we now perceive it differently, or because the pastor brings particular gifts. Leaders may be amazed at the amount of useful information lying dormant in the search profile. By the time that document was completed, people were probably so fixated on meeting candidates that the findings got little study. Descriptions that still seem accurate can jump-start the planning conversations; material that seems off base may hold up a mirror—this is how we perceived ourselves (or our neighborhood) back then.

Churches with a programmatic or organizational orientation will benefit from a regular cycle of strategic planning; the size and complexity of the parish system demand the discipline of longer-term thinking and goal setting. What do we mean by longer term? Most congregations today cannot cope with a planning horizon longer than about five years. Leaders should not wait five years, however, to start the cycle over again. For these midsize and large congregations, we suggest that the five-year plan should be revisited, revised, and extended after three years.

Notes

1. For a discussion of issues related to hiring members, see the article "Becoming Staff" by Dan Hotchkiss at www.danhotchkiss.com. To access the article, click on articles and then click on the title "Becoming Staff."
2. Gary McIntosh, *Staff Your Church for Growth: Building Team Ministry in the 21st Century* (Grand Rapids, Mich.: Baker Books, 2000).
3. Episcopal Church Building Fund is located at 815 Second Avenue, New York, NY, 10017 and online at www.ecbf.org.
4. Roy M. Oswald and James M. Heath and Ann W. Heath, *Beginning Ministry Together: The Alban Handbook for Clergy Transitions* (Bethesda, Md.: Alban Institute, 2003).
5. Alice Mann, *Raising the Roof: The Pastoral to Program Size Transition* (Bethesda, Md.: Alban Institute, 2001).
6. Mary K. Sellon, Daniel F. Smith, and Gail F. Grossman, *Redeveloping the Congregation: A How-To for Lasting Change* (Bethesda, Md.: Alban Institute, 2002).
7. Alice Mann, *Can Our Church Live? Redeveloping Congregations in Decline* (Bethesda, Md.: Alban Institute, 1999).

CHAPTER SIXTEEN

Annual Planning Retreats

Many congregations hold an annual planning retreat, either for the pastor and board, or for a wider circle of leaders. This is an extremely helpful discipline in the life of the congregation. Such an annual gathering—running, perhaps, from Friday at supper through Saturday afternoon—can serve either a developmental or a frame-bending (as described in the Introduction) purpose.

Developmental Planning at an Annual Retreat

The most common type of planning retreat serves several functions. It helps recently elected leaders to get a big picture of the congregation's work. It provides an accountability loop—an opportunity to review progress on last year's goals. It allows an opportunity for times of team building, prayer, and discernment that are harder to incorporate into an evening meeting.

We indicated earlier that about 80 percent of congregations see an average attendance of 200 or fewer. These churches—with their relational orientation—may use the annual retreat as their primary venue for developmental planning. Congregations with a programmatic or organizational orientation may use it to supplement and reinforce a three-year cycle of longer-range planning. In either case, here are some possible elements of an annual planning retreat for developmental planning:

1. Identify the scope of the event (topic). Will we look broadly at the whole life of the congregation? Will we focus on a few key program areas or a particularly pressing issue? Will we look at the development of the board as a leadership body, and on the teamwork between board and pastor?
2. Identify the scope of the event (participants). Once you know what the topic will be, you can consider whom to involve—

board only, board and committee chairs, board and wider circle of leaders (see chapter 13 for ways to identify this wider circle). Congregations with a relational orientation often invite everybody through the newsletter and chancel announcements; if this is a cultural expectation in your church, we recommend that you also make specific, personal invitations to your wider circle of leaders, emphasizing that the event will not be effective without their input. Also remember that you probably will not get wide participation for more than a few hours. You could do an all-parish supper and quick assessment on Friday evening, and then continue the conversation with a well-defined circle of leaders on Saturday.

3. Celebrate accomplishments—planned and unplanned. One energizing way to begin is with a catalogue of accomplishments for the year. This serves two functions: it starts people off with a focus on the positive, and it often surfaces fruitful work that would have gone unnoticed if we started out with fixed categories.

4. Discern—"How have we experienced the presence and leading of God in our life together this year?" Take people into the church or chapel for a time of silence. Begin with a prayer for God's guidance. Give each person a pencil and piece of paper with just this one question on it; ask them to make a few notes for themselves. After five to ten minutes, ask them to pair up quietly with someone else and share their responses. Return to the meeting room and collect responses on newsprint.

5. Revisit last year's goal statements. The idea of bringing back these statements may make some leaders nervous, but this is an important step. Often, there has been more progress than people realized. Goals not accomplished provide an opportunity for learning:

   • Did the goal articulate a deep aspiration of our faith community?
   • Did we pursue the goal using appropriate methods?
   • Did we identify who would take responsibility for this goal?
   • Did we provide leaders with the necessary training and resources?
   • Did we expect too much progress (or not enough) in one year?

6. Identify potential goal areas for the coming year. These may be steps to follow up on the previous year's work, or new areas to address. You will probably end up with a long list of possibilities; avoid editing the list or critiquing the ideas until you have everybody's items on your list.

7. Prioritize. You might give each person some one-inch sticky dots to apply to their preferred items on the list. (If you have 15 possible choices, give each person five dots, to be distributed among the five items they see as most important to work on in the coming year.)

8. Create a rough action plan for each of the top-rated goals. It helps to get some more specifics on paper before people leave the event. One way to do this is to form self-selected subgroups to flesh out the three highest priority goals (one goal per subgroup).

9. Bring the action plans back for discussion and endorsement by the whole group. If possible, have someone transcribe the endorsed action plans right on the spot. A laptop is one good way to do it—but a handwritten version on loose-leaf paper is okay, too! Make sure that everyone present gets a copy of the notes within a few days.

10. Bring the action plans back to board meetings for regular follow-up. Turn the notes on the top goals from the retreat into an integrated one-page plan—distributed to each board member, staff members, and committee chair. Discuss the integrated action plans at the beginning of the very next board meeting. Then, at least quarterly, begin the board meeting with a check on progress on those same goals.

This is a very humble process. It's not sexy, not high tech, not all encompassing. You won't bend a lot of frames with this one. But this work builds trust in the ability of leaders to think, pray, decide, act, and reflect together. Nothing could be more important.

Frame Bending at an Annual Retreat

Remember the premise we have been offering throughout this book. Congregations are generally unwilling to bend the frame unless there is a significant amount of pain plus some glimmers of new possibility. When the pain is intense enough and persistent enough, an annual retreat might be devoted to strategic—rather than developmental—work. In this case, you will have to shelve the annual review of goals. (You might do such review at a board meeting instead.) Instead, create an environment that says: "We are now doing a different kind of thinking about our life together." Everyone needs to know that the weekend is for exploring questions, not generating answers. If all goes well, these will be good, big, energizing questions—but they will also be unsettling.

For this retreat, you will need an outside facilitator who doesn't mind making people uncomfortable, and some stimulating experiences for the group to undertake together. Here are some options to consider when frame bending is the purpose of the retreat.

- Suspend decision making for the time of the retreat. Tell everyone at the beginning that making decisions is not the purpose. Rather, critical thinking and prayerful discernment are the focus of the day. Some will be relieved that they will not be pushed into solving problems they do not understand, while others will be given a signal that they should not evaluate the retreat as a bad meeting because nothing (decisions or actions) happened.
- Get people moving out onto the balcony in advance by circulating some new and different ideas. Is there a book that everyone should read prior to the retreat so that participants consider a larger context when talking about their congregation? How about a video? Ask yourself what helped you to see things in a new way, and consider sharing that resource or experience with retreat participants.
- In a sense, the purpose of the retreat is to unsettle your leaders—to shake loose some old certainties. Uncertainty elicits anxiety; when anxiety goes up, people often behave badly (or at least with less civility than usual). This is normal, natural—even healthy. But you may want to set some norms about how the group will work. The question is not whether everyone will agree but rather how people will treat each other when they disagree. For a helpful resource on setting safe and healthy boundaries see Gil's book on behavioral covenants in the congregation.[1]

- Use the "History Grid" (Resource N on page 263) to help people talk about what has been changing, in both the community and the congregation. As trends are uncovered, don't forget to identify which factors church leaders can actually influence (such as the time and style of worship) and which lie outside their influence (the number of choices members have about ways to spend Sunday morning other than church). When leaders assume they should be able to fix everything, they become demoralized. On the other hand, when leaders realize there is a great deal that they cannot control, they are freed to find those arenas where they do have influence and to work with new energy.

- When talking about the cultural and community changes that influence the congregation, people may find it threatening to identify what's wrong with the congregation (that is, how the congregation may be failing to adapt to its environment). Invite people to talk about the impact of a particular trend on their own lives (for example, "How does marketing and consumerism affect you?"). Then ask about their larger experience ("Where else at work and in the community do you see some impact of marketing and consumerism?"). When that groundwork has been laid, it is usually much safer to discuss the life and ministry of the congregation ("How does this impact our work and our faith as a congregation?"). This crucial sequence—self, larger context, congregation—prepares people to see larger dynamics at work in the life of the congregation without assigning blame.

- Invite participants to work in small groups to find the biblical story that the congregation is currently living out (or wishes it were living out). Invite full group sharing and collect the stories with the greatest energy for later study. (Resource D on page 211, "Finding Our Biblical Story," provides background for this task.)

- Invite people to move into small groups to share *stories* that illustrate "My greatest fears and disappointments about my congregation" and "My greatest (realizable) hopes and dreams about my congregation." Call the people back to the full group; ask, "How did it feel to engage in these conversations?" The person leading this conversation should ask the group to leave aside the specific ideas and complaints they discussed in the small group; this reflection focuses on the holy work of conversation *in itself*.

As a way of summarizing the work of the retreat, brainstorm two lists: (1) things we can actually do something about; and (2) things we need to learn more about. Make some quick agreements about how both lists will be taken back to the board, planning team, and staff for further work.

A frame-bending retreat might be used in the *congregational training for planning* stage to lay the groundwork for a longer exploration of strategic issues. If a fuller strategic-planning process is not intended at this time, you will need to identify, at minimum, some group or setting where these provocative and unsettling questions will live within the system. Otherwise, everyone will probably return to business as usual—with increased anxiety but no way to keep the learning process in motion.

Note

1. Gil Rendle, *Behavioral Covenants in Congregations: A Handbook for Honoring Differences* (Bethesda, Md.: Alban Institute, 1999).

A Final Reflection

This is the end of one stage in a spiritual journey. For Gil and Alice, the trip has included new appreciation for each other's thought and practice and new challenges to clarify, extend, or reconceive our own material. Just like strategic planning, this venture has been exciting, unsettling, challenging, frustrating, and energy producing.

How has the journey been for you? Do any of the same descriptors apply? By reading this book, you have allowed two authors to make an intervention in your life and leadership. You have allowed us to start up a holy conversation with you. Now the conversation continues—inside your own mind and heart and inside the systems you will engage using these perspectives. This holy conversation is the real action, the critical outcome of our work. We trust the Spirit to keep that conversation going, and (behold!) to make all things new.

Resources

Copyright and Reproduction Notice

The resources in this section are intended for use in the congregation in a variety of settings. Some are appropriate for a smaller group, such as a planning committee; others will find broad usefulness within larger groups in the congregation. Because many of these resources are used most effectively within the context in which they are presented in *Holy Conversations*, we recommend that congregations purchase copies of the book for each individual in those small-group contexts. Due to copyright protection issues, the materials printed in this resource section may not be reproduced in any form without written permission from the Alban Institute.

Recognizing that many congregations will want to reproduce some of these materials for use in larger-group settings, the Alban Institute has made many of these resources available for free download from the Alban Web site. These resources have been formatted for easy and clear printing on 8-1/2" x 11" paper and may be printed and reproduced in limited quantities for private use in the congregation without obtaining written permission. For more information, go to www.Alban.org/BookDetails.asp?ID=1803 .

For more information on reproducing resources that do not appear on the Web site, or other materials in *Holy Conversations*, go to www.alban.org/permissions.asp

Questions for Leaders to Ask Continually throughout the Planning Process

There are some basic planning questions that can continually help leaders diagnose their situation and be appropriate in their leadership. There are no right answers to these questions. However, a willingness to ask the questions is an important way a leader prepares to engage others:

1. What holy conversation about the congregation's future do I believe we need to have at this moment in history?
2. When I consider the full planning process, what part is most important and appropriate for us to work on at this moment?
3. What strategies can I develop and use to invite people into this conversation in a structured, open, and positive way?
4. What tools or information will we need in order to have this healthy, holy conversation?

Questions for Leaders to Keep in Mind When Planning to Plan

A part of the task of the leader is to reflect continually on the progress of the planning team in order to identify the most helpful next steps. Below are a number of general questions to be used by the leader following each planning meeting:

1. What just happened in the last meeting?
2. With whom do I need to test my perceptions about what happened?
3. Where are we in the planning conversation?
4. How do I need to suggest that we adjust our conversation path or time line because of where we are at this moment?
5. What resources will we need to take the next step?
6. Who should we be telling about what we are learning and how will we tell them?

Types of Planning

What are your congregation's planning goals?

Type 1: Problem Planning

- Short-term planning
- Problem-solving methodology designed to fix things
- Goal: to return things to the way they were before the problem.
- Timetable: immediate and short-term

Type 2: Developmental Planning

- Long-range planning
- Asks the questions: "What's next?" and "What do we do now?"
- The assumption is that things are good. What we are currently doing in ministry is faithful and appropriate.
- Goal: to determine the next steps, building on what is presently being done
- Timetable: takes 3 to 6 months to complete; commonly revisited or revised every 1 to 2 years

Note: Type 1 and Type 2 planning are continuous. They are examples of gap planning, which proceeds according to the following steps:

- Here's where we are in the present.
- Here's where we want to be in the future.
- Here's the gap between the two.
- Here's what we have to learn or do in order to get there.
- Here's our action plan: *Who* will do *what* by *when* at *what* cost?

Type 3: Frame-Bending Planning

- Strategic planning
- Asks essential formation questions: "Who are we?" "What are we called to do?" "Who is our neighbor?"
- The assumption is that things are not working. What we are currently doing in ministry is not faithful and effective.
- Goal: to go back to the beginning and examine our purpose and call from God
- Timetable: takes 12 to 18 months to complete, commonly revisited or revised every 3 to 5 years

Finding Our Biblical Story

Adapted from chapter 3 of *The Multigenerational Congregation: Meeting the Leadership Challenge* by Gil Rendle (Bethesda, Md.: Alban Institute, 2002). Used by permission.

What can be said about the spiritual life of congregations? Many times the description and interpretation brought to congregations come from the social sciences, systems theory, and the experience of working with leaders in real-life decision-making situations. Daily life in a congregation has a sense of immediacy that seems best explained by the tools of our sciences and an analytic mode. The sights, sounds, and smells of close human encounter will often suggest a distance from the biblical and spiritual truths that are meant to be conveyed by life in these congregational communities.

In his memoir of his first pastoral call in southern Illinois, *Open Secrets,* Richard Lischer of Duke Divinity School recalls the impromptu weddings, the counseling sessions that led to reconciliation, the hateful accusations spoken by a member in anger, the prayers and confessions—all of which took place in his study while he was pastor of a small rural congregation. Connecting that daily stuff of real-life encounters with the faith that it represents, he writes: "That room contained our community's version of faith, conflict, and love."[1] It takes the continual work of leaders to connect the daily moments of congregational life to the large landscape of the biblical record. Each congregation has its own version of that connection.

The congregation is a spiritual community in temporal space. Called together through shared faith, members need help in daily living to stay connected to the congregation's biblical purpose as part of a larger tradition, and they need help to stay connected to the vision or mission that called the congregation into being. Regular monthly board meetings seldom reflect this connection well. Yet negotiating the differences in a congregation and finding a future are deeply spiritual functions that keep both faith and community alive.

I have been convinced of the spiritual nature of this negotiation as I work as a consultant to congregations deeply enmeshed in their differences. One of my favorite and most productive exercises with leaders is to invite them to find the biblical story that their congregation is living at that moment. I invite them to find their spiritual space by locating the biblical story in which they see themselves—the story or idea in the text that they would intuitively say describes them.

This is neither a literal nor a historically critical way of approaching scripture. The exercise is metaphorical play—but deeply spiritual play that can instruct us in new ways. Old Testament theologian Walter Brueggemann has offered the exile experience of the Israelites as one of the most productive metaphors for the current state of faith in the United States. His reflection on the metaphorical power of scripture inspires leaders to connect the mundane and often frustrating experience of daily life in community with the biblical promise that makes it purposeful.

The usefulness of a metaphor for rereading our own context is that it is not claimed as a one-on-one match to reality, as though the metaphor of exile actually described our situation. Rather, a metaphor proceeds by having only an odd, playful, and ill-fitting match to its reality, the purpose of which is to illuminate and evoke dimensions of reality that will otherwise go unnoticed and therefore unexperienced.[2]

The exercise I use is simple and straightforward. I invite a small group of leaders to find the story they are now living and, when they return to the larger group, to explain why they believe they are living that story. I will often expand the possibilities, allowing the group to use a denominational hymnal if they prefer to find the hymn they are living. Some congregations and individuals are more sensitive to sound and music than to words or word pictures. I usually give the group an hour for its work. Many groups need more time.

The conversations of these groups are rich and instructive (I listen in when I have the opportunity). People go through their own personal repertoire of Bible stories looking for a connection. Fragments of stories are recalled, and people begin flipping through the pages in search of the full story. When the proposed stories are found in the text, they are read aloud. Details long forgotten or never known are discovered. As the stories are read, it is the details that convince. Listening to the reading, the group will often conclude that something about the story fits, but it isn't really us. And then, one or more times, the details will connect and the moment of insight will hit the group. I once worked with a group of leaders in a troubled church who returned from their assignment with the announcement that they had found five stories that belonged to them—two that they wished they were living and three that they wished they were not living. I would argue that their hour or so of spiritual leadership in discerning their biblical place was more centering and helpful than the many hours of organizational leadership they had committed to solving people's problems. Without the biblical connection, they had been working hard to become good leaders in a difficult situation. With the biblical connection, they shifted to the behavior of spiritual leaders and found their responsibility to be much more purposeful.

I am often surprised at how accurately the story chosen by a small group lays open the motif that rests at the heart of their differences. When the larger leadership team claims the story, it becomes the focus of Bible study for the full group. The Bible study may include textual criticism, or it may more appropriately be playful or introspective. Once the story is found, I encourage the leaders not to leave it until it is fully digested.

The biblical stories are told in congregations to keep focus on the spiritual life being negotiated in these congregations. As Brueggemann suggests, the stories are metaphors to be played with. Ill-fitting but accurate, they are told in the congregation not with the aim that people learn more about the Bible but so that through the biblical story the people may know more about themselves and their purpose.

The following story was claimed by a Protestant congregation amid planning by the governing board. I was invited to work with the board over two weekends several months apart, and we agreed that a self-study of congregational data and introduction to big-picture cultural dynamics would fill a part of our time together. As a part of the self-study, the leaders were asked to prepare a tenure study graph of their members and other participants. As we explored their graph, I asked the leaders to place themselves on the graph by their own length of membership or participation. We discovered that fully 85 percent of the leaders at the center of this congregation were long-tenured members of 20 years or more. Only 12 percent had been members between 10 and 19 years and fit into the smaller middle segment. Only one person within the core leadership had been active in the congregation for less than 10 years, though a substantial portion of active members and other constituents of the congregation were short tenured. Clearly the leadership group did not reflect the makeup of the membership. Much of our planning was focused on the leaders' concern over the apathetic response they had received over the past few years to the congregation's traditional programs and projects.

Asked to find their biblical story, a small group of leaders set off somewhat reluctantly but came back with high enthusiasm. They had found the post-resurrection story of the appearance of Jesus in John 21:1-12 and claimed it as their own. This account of the disciples after the crucifixion shows them standing at a lakeside not quite knowing what to do or expect. Impetuous Peter announced that he was going fishing. The other disciples joined Peter in an all-night fishing expedition. Having caught nothing all night, the disciples were hailed by a stranger from the shore—later revealed to be Jesus. The stranger instructed them to cast their nets on the other side of the boat. Doing so, they hauled in a catch of 153 fish (which, I later learned, represented one of every type of fish known at that time). In encountering Jesus and in shifting their nets from one side of the boat to the other, they went from catching nothing to catching one of every kind of fish.

When I asked these leaders why this story struck them as theirs, they pointed to our planning work and to the fact that 85 percent of the leaders at this church were long tenured, coming from only one side of their boat. It had become clear to them that they knew how to fish only out of one side of the boat, following the preferences of the established leaders. This insight helped them see why they had been getting an increasingly smaller response to their traditional programming. "If we hope to catch anything in the future," one said, "we are going to need to learn how to fish out of the other side of the boat."[3]

The leaders still faced a significant challenge of changing well-established behavior and expectations. But where their work might have bogged down in organizational diagnosis, this group exercised spiritual leadership and discovered a much clearer reason to redesign their leadership-development process to meet their new bimodal needs.

Finding Your Biblical Story

The following exercise is designed to help a congregation search for its own biblical story in the midst of a strategic-planning process.

After the planning committee has gathered information about the congregation, the surrounding community, and wider trends, the following spiritual reflection can help the committee crystallize its learnings and discover powerful images for the church's life today:

1. **Time.** Allow at least one hour for this exercise. A two-hour time frame would permit more relaxed exploration of the material.

2. **Use with a planning committee.** An ideal setting might be a committee retreat for drawing learnings. In a space and time set apart, people can more easily shift into the mode of play, imagination, and symbol. During a retreat day or weekend, time frames can be adjusted more flexibly than in a single meeting. The next best option would be to devote one full meeting to this exercise, with prayer or other centering activities to prepare people's minds and hearts for a different kind of conversation than committees usually allow themselves to have.

3. **Use with a larger group.** Another setting would be the wider circle of leaders (including members of the board and planning team, along with other key leaders—see chapter 13 on "Involving the Congregation"). The exercise would work best if those attending had already digested (in a previous meeting) some of the key data collected by the planning team. As far as possible, set this session for finding our story apart from other kinds of work. For example, schedule this activity as the primary focus of one whole session; use a special space or at least get away from the work table; open the time with quiet music, prayer for discernment, or the lighting of a candle to symbolize God's presence.

4. **Steps.**
   a. Provide Bibles (perhaps in a variety of translations) for the groups to use as they wish.
   b. Divide the planning team or wider circle of leaders into subgroups. Three to five people per group would be a good size.
   c. Describe the task: "Find the story our congregation is now living. Identify why that story belongs to us in a special way." (People sometimes panic a bit if they don't feel they know the Bible well. Assure them that they have all the knowledge they need, and encourage them to give it a try.) Allow up to half an hour for this exploration.

d. When people return, ask each group to propose its story or stories and to say why the story seemed to fit. You may wish to appoint one or two scribes to take notes during the presentations, assigning them to capture the key phrases that were used. As the preceding step indicates, what people say *about* the story is crucial.

e. Listen for signs of recognition in the total group of a story that really belongs to them—laughter, silence, tears, a group "Yes!"

f. Don't force a conclusion. If the group is struggling, help them talk about the struggle. That may result in the suggestion of another story, or the struggle itself (to know who we are and where we are in spiritual terms) may in fact *be* the story.

g. When a story does surface that has resonance for the total group, allow it to become a focus of study and discussion over time (later in the retreat, at subsequent meetings, perhaps in a sermon or in a parish Bible study group) until it has been fully digested. The imagery or language of this story often finds its way into statements of mission or vision or into the introduction of a planning team's report. Remember that those less involved in the process will probably need help seeing why and how this story applies. Take time to help them connect to the biblical reflection—a powerful story, well told, might be the only thing the average person will remember about the plan.

Notes

1. Richard Lischer, *Open Secrets: A Memoir of Faith and Discovery* (New York: Doubleday, 2001), 237–238.

2. Walter Brueggeman, "Preaching among Exiles," *Circuit Rider* 22, no. 4 (July-August 1999): 22.

3. Additional examples of congregations and their biblical stories can be found in Gil Rendle's *The Multigenerational Congregation: Meeting the Leadership Challenge* (Bethesda, Md.: Alban Institute, 2002), chapters 5 and 7.

Understanding Your Congregation's Life Cycle

An adapted excerpt from chapter 1 of *Can Our Church Live?: Redeveloping Congregations in Decline*, by Alice Mann (Bethesda, Md.: Alban Institute, 1999). Used by permission.

Social organisms—including faith communities—differ from biological ones in that they may outlive their individual members; nevertheless, they manifest similar patterns of emergence and decline. Key stages in the life cycle of a congregation can be described initially as a developmental arc[1] as illustrated below.

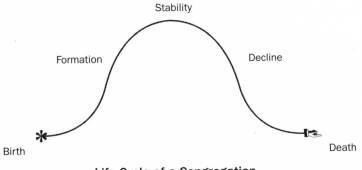

Life Cycle of a Congregation

Congregational Life Cycle Stages

Birth

Congregations identify their birth moments in a variety of ways: for example, the evening a group of people decided to start a church, the first worship service, or the occasion of official recognition by their denominational body. These earliest moments in the congregation's story contain powerful bits of genetic information that will express themselves in the rest of the life cycle. I recall the rather dramatic story of a suburban church founded by members of a downtown congregation during a period of "white flight" from urban areas. Decades later, members of my own nearby congregation would comment to me that they had—on their first or second visit there—been told how awful the city was and why the church had moved to the suburbs. The fearfulness and alienation present at its moment of birth expressed itself in many other ways far into that church's life cycle. Though a new suburban ministry might have been needed to reach shifting populations at that moment, the negative tone of this congregation's founding impulse still resounded in the ears of every newcomer decades later, beyond the life span of most of the original members.

One vital piece of genetic coding has to do with size.[2] Those who study the planting of new churches have noticed how the number attending the first worship service "imprints" the congregation with a certain potential for natural growth. New churches tend to reach an attendance peak at five to ten times the number present at the first service, regardless of the population or receptivity of the surrounding community. Forty years ago, mainline congregations often started out with a dozen enthusiastic souls, only to level off with too few members for vital and sustainable ministry in their particular settings. Today's "church planters" are trained to spend a year or so organizing small home groups that never come together for public worship until critical mass can be reasonably assured.

Formation

The moment of birth gives way immediately to a period of formation, when the congregation's basic identity is established. During this time, the congregation develops its own tacit answers to three powerful questions:

1. Who are we (especially at a faith level)?
2. What are we here for?
3. Who is our neighbor?

In a "nation of immigrants," the religious identity of American congregations has often been shaped by cultural difference. Immigrant churches easily define "who we are," because "we" are noticeably different; our language, ethnicity, race, customs (or all of these) differ from the norm of the communities in which we have settled. "What we are here for" is also clear—to assure a transplanted people that our God is with us in this new (and perhaps inhospitable) place. Many Lutheran congregations, for example, were founded in the middle of the 19th century by German and Scandinavian populations arriving in America. Both their language and their sense of theological distinctiveness (forged in the crucible of European religious controversy) gave them a sharply defined identity within the American landscape.

Many congregations formed by past generations of immigrants can readily tell you when they stopped offering at least one service in the language and style of the "old country." Often this is a moment of identity crisis for the faith community, revolving around a painful question: "If we speak and dress and eat just like our neighbors, if our children have succeeded educationally and moved into the economic mainstream, why do we need our own congregation?" Lutheran churches founded in the colonial era were already losing their ethnic and confessional identity by the time those new waves of immigrants arrived in the 19th century. The ensuing conflict between proponents of Americanization and defenders of European-Lutheran particularity persisted for decades and shaped the character of Lutheranism in America.[3]

Even without a language difference, such an identity crisis can occur. In the late 1980s, I served a Trenton congregation that had been founded at the turn of the 19th century by pottery workers from Stoke-upon-Trent, England. These immigrants, who had come to work in New Jersey's booming ceramic industry, built a small, neat church building a few blocks from one of the largest potteries. Nicknamed "cheeseheads" because of the cylindrical firing containers they carried on their heads—yellowish ceramic boxes resembling wheels of aged cheese—these workers merged successfully into the city's population and provided an education for their children. Their children's children came of age in the 1950s and 1960s, and moved out into the emerging suburban communities—a process accelerated by an outbreak of urban violence. The potteries eventually closed, along with much of the industrial base of the city; the church's neighborhood along a main route was transformed into a backwater by a highway bypass; and the remaining congregation dwindled, aged, and began to feel embattled. Their self-definition as an immigrant community at prayer had clearly run out of steam.

As congregations are born and develop, their answer to the third formative question—"Who is our neighbor?"—flows from the other two. If we understood ourselves at the beginning as an immigrant community at prayer, if our purpose was to "sing the Lord's song on foreign soil" in our own cultural idiom, then the neighbor on whom we focused our attention would be the household from our own cultural group. If, on the other hand, we started out as the "church around which the town was built" (a statement of historical identity by a Congregational church in a centuries-old community outside Boston), we would probably be accustomed to thinking of our neighbors as the whole town.

Both types of congregation may be facing a crisis today in the definition of "neighbor." The Trenton congregation, now surrounded by an extremely diverse mix of peoples, has been grappling with ways to relate itself to its fragmented environment. Could it minister to a newer immigrant group and function once again as an ethnic church? Could it develop a multicultural identity and attempt the hard work of building a place where cultures meet? Could it move five miles outside the city limits, where some of its old constituency still lives? Could it forge a clear identity around a distinctive style of worship and faith community that might draw people from a 10-mile radius? This church has chosen the last of these paths I have described, but it may have waited so long to make the transition that its resources will run out before the new reality can take root.

The congregation that helped to establish its historic Massachusetts town is also facing a crisis in its way of defining "neighbor." In the circle of communities just inside the Interstate 495 beltway, the strong identity of individual towns is giving way to a more regional reality. This church now draws members from the new housing developments constantly emerging in surrounding communities, a population more likely to be concerned about program quality and adequate parking than about the nuances of the town's history and politics. Many members have come and stayed because this congregation occupies a specific niche on the theological and political spectrum (they call themselves "open-minded") that may distinguish them from several surrounding churches of a similar tradition. The result of these internal and external forces is a crisis in defining self and other. Are we still the one, comprehensive Congregational church for neighbors in this one town? Or are we now a regional church, drawing people from a 10- to 15-mile suburban radius with our fine programs and our relatively liberal faith stance? What will our choice imply about the civic role of the congregation—our responsibility toward neighbors who are not members of this church? Are we still, in any sense, a cornerstone institution in public life?

Stability

Ideally, the formative period in a congregation's life paves the way for a period of fruitful and sustainable ministry. Such stability has both institutional and spiritual dimensions that will, in the healthiest congregations, nourish and inform each other. When a congregation has forged a clear faith identity, and has organized its life to express that faith effectively and persistently within its community context, we might call that state "stability."

Sometimes only part of that equation is present. Many churches skip over the issues of spiritual formation early in their lives, devoting all their creative energy to the work of selecting a site, constructing buildings, paying off a mortgage, calling their clergy, and gaining ecclesiastical status as a "real" church. If the demographics are favorable and leaders make some unusually good judgments early on, this church might build a coherent spiritual identity around an effective long-term pastorate early in its life.

More often, the lack of priority given to faith development in the church's first years will leave an indelible imprint on its personality. Even the most able pastors may find themselves frustrated that money, buildings, and the togetherness of the founding group always seem to take priority over matters of ministry and spiritual formation. Perhaps the men who manage the investments rarely come to church. The women who painted the hall and sewed the curtains may not want smoky AA groups spoiling the interior.

None of these devoted leaders can understand why the pastor doesn't care more about them and give them more credit for their hard-won accomplishments. Nor can they understand why clergy are turning over so frequently or getting into so many fights with a group of friendly people. A church like this may begin to grapple seriously with spiritual questions only after a major crisis provokes a soul-searching look at its own history and values.

Congregations may also come out of the formation phase with a clear faith identity but inadequate organization to live that faith effectively over time. For example, one of those churches that began with a dozen people at its first worship service may have become a spiritually vital congregation with aspirations of drawing many people from its community, but still find itself unequipped to navigate its first predictable size plateau. (Two-thirds of the American Baptist congregations planted in the 1950s, for example, hadn't broken through the 150-member mark by the 1960 denominational census.[4]) At first, the "glass ceiling" of a size plateau may provoke frustration and disappoint the outgoing spirit of the church. But if leaders can't diagnose the trouble as a common developmental crisis, the congregation will usually begin to rationalize its small size and denigrate ministries of invitation as "growth for growth's sake." At that point, an institutional crisis has damaged the congregation's soul.

If a congregation does attain both spiritual and institutional stability, it will always arrive at a moment when it is tempted to rest on its laurels, feeling that it has nothing more to learn except techniques for fine-tuning what already exists. As stagnation sets in, attendance and participation typically fall off, while membership and total giving continue to rise. Leaders commonly ignore or bury the earliest indications of decline and continue (with some strain) to focus on the positive. At this point in the life-cycle curve, congregations resemble the cartoon coyote who speeds off the edge of a cliff and keeps going straight ahead from sheer momentum—until he looks down and discovers there is nothing under his feet! Stagnation could be defined as the beginning of a decline we are not yet willing to acknowledge.

Decline

At some point, even the coyote realizes that he is falling. The congregation finds it can no longer dismiss as temporary or random the noticeable falloff in worship attendance, church-school registration, volunteer energy, pledging households, first-time visitors, new-member retention, and so on. After refusing for months, years, or even decades to "look down" at its situation, the congregation arrives at a moment of painful recognition.

Unfortunately, the most common reaction is blame. The board blames the pastor for letting fine old members drift or stomp away.

The pastor blames the board for not leading the congregation in evangelism or tithing. Members blame their leaders, or the denomination, or the visitors who didn't return. Everyone blames the surrounding community and the wider culture for changing in ways that have threatened the congregation's survival. While there may be at least a kernel of truth in all these accusations, a blaming response is likely to accelerate the decline. Few people wish to join, attend, or lead an angry, depressed congregation.

Because congregations often feel helpless about changes in the external context, they are likely to focus their attention on matters they feel they can control: selling more clothing in their thrift shop, pressing the pastor for monthly reports on the number of visits made, resisting changes in worship that might upset well-established members. Little energy is devoted to fresh learning about the surrounding community, where fewer and fewer members may actually live as time goes by. Decisions are made by a shrinking core group of long-tenured members.

Death

If a congregation never replaces the blame response with a learning stance or waits too long to try something new, death is the likely result. But death does not come easily. Denial and blame, the same responses that allowed the decline to continue unabated for decades, become the enemies of a holy death. Just as physicians and families once avoided the word "cancer" at all costs, many severely diminished congregations do not speak openly about the prospect that they may soon have to close. If a visiting denominational official raises this possibility, the church may have a sudden surge of energy to fight the outside threat, but that kind of activity rarely makes a difference to the church's basic viability.

This stage in the life cycle can drag on for a long time. I recently listened to the story of a 30-year-old congregation that had been founded and supported financially from the national level as part of a denominational church-planting program. After 10 years, the denomination's mission department realized that early demographic projections had overestimated the opportunity in this location; the agency terminated the subsidy with the intention that the congregation would close. How did the church react? "They can't close us!" The congregation vowed to use its own modest resources to keep up the mortgage payments and to employ a pastor, creating a budget that was the institutional equivalent of a starvation diet. One leader spent her time collecting drippings from the altar candles and forming the wax around new strings so that the purchase of candles could be avoided. Until they had paid off the mortgage and proved they could survive, members would not consider the possibility of closing or merging.

Sometimes a congregation dies because it has completed its task or because a changed environment is now calling forth an entirely different kind of ministry. What would constitute a holy death in such a situation? The hospice movement has helped many individuals to make their last months both dignified and emotionally rich, but this cannot happen if the person keeps waiting for a cure. When a congregation faces its impending death sooner, while there are still enough members around for a wonderful "funeral" event, the concluding days of that faith community can be spiritually powerful. Bestowing a financial legacy on some other ministry that carries forward the congregation's values can provide an additional sense of self-esteem and continuity.

The Redevelopment Loop

Sometimes a terminally ill person will risk trying an experimental treatment—a radical and somewhat unpredictable intervention that could conceivably offer a new lease on life. Similarly, some courageous congregations facing serious decline attempt the difficult path of redevelopment, which involves:

- Recognizing the death of the congregation's previous identity and purpose
- Reallocating the bulk of the congregation's resources to discovering and living out a new identity and purpose
- Finding and empowering leaders who can, in effect, start a new congregation on an existing site
- Caring for the remaining members of the previous congregation—sometimes by providing a separate chaplaincy ministry as long as it may be needed

The redevelopment congregation finds substantially new answers to the three formation questions: Who are we? What are we here for? Who is our neighbor? Let's return to the life-cycle chart, to see where the redevelopment loop fits in (figure 2).

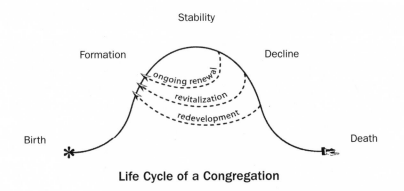

Life Cycle of a Congregation

Ongoing Renewal

In a time when stability is drifting toward stagnation, a congregation might find a way to take a fresh look at the three formation questions. In the evangelical tradition, periodic revivals may have served this purpose to some extent, long before anyone started to study congregational development; in more catholic traditions, teams from religious orders would come to a church and conduct a preaching mission. These periods of intense proclamation, prayer, song, and study would interrupt "business as usual" and press the church back to fundamental questions of faith. Because they were systemwide interventions, they introduced common language and frameworks to which leaders could later refer as church decisions were made. Today it is common for churches to engage in strategic planning—even in times of relative stability—to refocus the congregation on fundamentals and to ask challenging questions about identity, purpose, and context. Other congregations rely on the self-study process that accompanies the selection of a new pastor to help them take stock.

Two tendencies prevent churches from revisiting the formation questions when everything seems to be working. First, the renewal event, self-study, or planning process may be rejected outright under the banner,

"If it ain't broke, don't fix it." The new perspective provided by a revival leader, consultant, or self-study process may seem quite unnecessary, since the congregation's key programs are humming along successfully. Second, the congregation may undertake the process but discount any disturbing trends or hard questions that come to the surface. Some theorists argue that a system will never question its fundamental assumptions until the pain induced by present practices becomes intolerable.

Revitalization

In the early stages of decline, a congregation might gain some motivation to revisit the formation issues. If some way is found to look hard at the facts, avoid blame, and engage in new learning, we might call this process revitalization—a term implying that there is still substantial vitality present that can be refreshed and refocused. Though congregations usually expect that the call (or appointment) of a new pastor will accomplish this work automatically, a change in leadership will not, by itself, alter the curve. If the new pastor has the skills, information, and political support to raise the formation questions again effectively, a new era of vitality might ensue. More typically, the forces driving the decline—internal dysfunction, external change, or both—will be ignored until things get worse. In that case, the new pastor will experience (and often collude with) the congregation's two most destructive illusions: the fantasy that growth can occur without change and the fantasy that change can occur without conflict.

Redevelopment

When a congregation has been declining steadily for years and even decades, when it has sustained significant losses in people, energy, flexibility, and funds, then the path back to the formation questions is far more costly. The farther you slip down the decline side of the curve, the more capital it takes—spiritually, financially, and politically—to create the possibility of a turnaround. Yet there may still be tremendous potential for spiritual growth, invitational outreach, and community ministry.

In my experience, redevelopment efforts are often "undercapitalized" in all three ways. Many are set up for:

- *Spiritual failure:* The congregation has not really faced the fact that it is dying—that most elements of an old identity and purpose must be relinquished if anything new is to occur.
- *Financial failure:* Leaders are working with an inadequate budget or overly optimistic revenue projections.
- *Political stalemate:* Leaders—at both the congregational and denominational levels—severely underestimate the amount of political resistance that redevelopment efforts can provoke.

Those are stark assertions. I have presented them not to discourage the work of redevelopment—which has occupied a great deal of my ministry—but to increase the chances that specific redevelopment efforts will succeed. Redeveloping congregations are important to the whole church for several reasons:

- Often they are located in communities where the needs for ministry are enormous.
- Since all congregations will eventually face similar issues, these churches are engaged in important learning.
- Whether or not they succeed in establishing a new era of stability, redeveloping congregations live out the mystery of death and resurrection by "losing their life to find it."

Notes

1. Various writers have described the life cycle, including sociologists Martin Saarinen and Arlin Rothauge and consultant Robert Gallagher. While the discussion in this section draws to some extent on each of these, the diagram comes from Gallagher.
2. For an extensive discussion of size transition, see my book *The In-Between Church: Navigating Size Transitions in Congregations* (Bethesda, Md.: Alban Institute, 1998).
3. Robert T. Handy, *A History of the Churches in the United States and Canada* (Oxford, England: Clarendon Press, 1976), 210–212.
4. George D. Younger, "Not by Might Nor by Power," in Clifford J. Green, ed., *Churches, Cities, and Human Community: Urban Ministry in the United States 1945–1985* (Grand Rapids, Mich.: Eerdmans, 1996), 28.
5. Mike Regele (with Mark Shulz), *Death of the Church* (Costa Mesa, Calif.: Percept Group, Inc., and Grand Rapids, Mich.: Zondervan, 1995). This quotation is the subtitle of the book.

Healthy vs. Unhealthy Conflict Index

HEALTHY	UNHEALTHY
ATTITUDE: Conflict is inevitable; it is a chance to grow.	**ATTITUDE:** Conflict is wrong or sinful.
IMPERSONAL: Disputants are clearly able to see the difference between the people and the problems—and do not mix the two.	**PERSONAL:** Disputants quickly mix people and problems together and assume that by changing or eliminating the people, the problem will be solved.
COMMUNICATION is open. People speak directly to one another and everyone has the same information.	**COMMUNICATION** is diminished, with people speaking only to those with whom they already agree. Third parties or letters are used to carry messages.
THE BALANCE SHEET is short. The principals address the issue at hand, not what happened months or years ago.	**THE BALANCE SHEET** is long. The list of grievances grows and examples are collected. People recall not only what they think was done to them but what was said or done to their friends.
INTERACTIVE: There is give and take, an exchange of ideas, and a spirit of cooperation and openness. There is careful listening and thought-out statements.	**REACTIVE:** Problems cannot be "touched" without exploding. I write a memo to you and you immediately fire back a nasty letter to me.
ACCEPTANCE: Disputants acknowledge the existence of a problem and the need to solve it.	**DENIAL:** Disputants tend to ignore the real problem and deny what is going on.
TIMELINESS: Resolution takes as much time as needed. The parties take the time to go through the journey together, to experience the pain, and to come out together on the other side.	**LACK OF TIME:** There is a strong need to solve the problem too quickly. People are very solution oriented and seek to avoid the pain of conflict by saying, "Let's get it over with."

Adapted from *Mediation: The Book: A Step-by-Step Guide for Dispute Resolvers* by Sam Leonard (Evanston, Ill.: Evanston Publishing, 1994). Used by permission.

A Road Map to the Full Planning Process

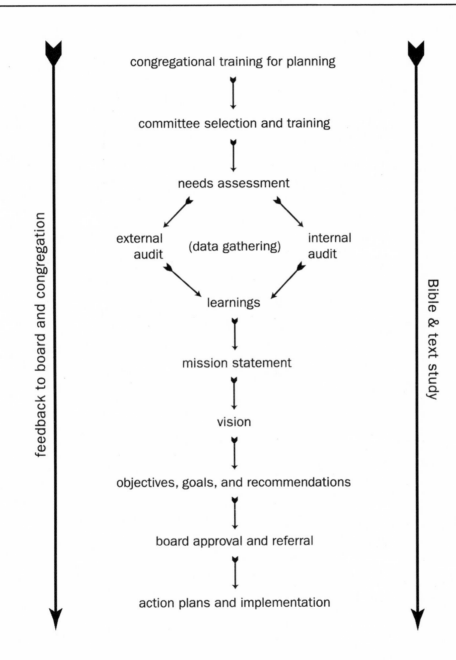

Building a Planning Committee

SIZE
- ideal size is 5 to 7 persons, including the pastor
- maximum size is 9 persons, including the pastor

PEOPLE NOT TO INVITE
- people not good at decision making or unable to consider potential consequences
- people who are unwilling to change themselves or their church to accomodate the needs of other people
- people with "axes to grind" about the church
- the pastor's #1 opponent
- people who want to go back to 1947, or whatever year is remembered as the favorite time in your church
- people too busy to be effective
- people who focus on managing the details instead of looking at the big picture

PEOPLE TO INVITE
- people who would be open to what God is calling your church to be and to be about in the future
- people who understand your church's strengths and weaknesses
- people who understand the "political realities" of your church
- people who can understand the value of open deliberations and the need for a redundant system for keeping membership informed
- people actively supportive of the current pastor
- people willing to learn new things and think new thoughts
- people who have a "voice" back in the congregation and are listened to when they speak
- people who are willing to put time, energy, work, and prayer into the effort of the committee
- people comfortable discussing ideas ("purpose," "role," "mission")
- people active as volunteers in the life and ministry of the church

WHO SHOULD BE THE CHAIRPERSON?
- not the pastor
- a person with a strong voice and credibility in the congregation and who will be listened to when reports are offered

How Many Triangles?

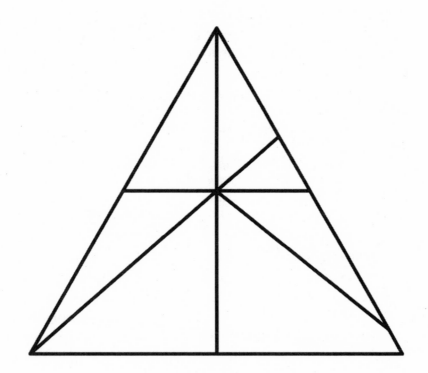

Excavating the Religious Cultures of the Congregation

Adapted from chapter 3 of *Raising the Roof: The Pastoral to Program Size Transition* by Alice Mann (Bethesda, Md.: Alban Institute, 2001). Used by permission.

In June and July of 2000, Alice Mann studied the experience of seven congregations—all UCC churches in southeastern Massachusetts—moving through the transition zone between pastoral and program size. While their stories are complex and contain much that is particular to their specific situations, these congregations have helped her to understand what it might mean to "lay the foundation" for a difficult size transition. In this excerpt, Alice encourages congregations to excavate their religious cultures.

"Excavating the religious culture" sounds a bit like archaeology, doesn't it? A fine new resource called *How We Seek God Together: Exploring Worship Style*[1] makes the case for viewing congregations as distinctive cultures. The authors define congregational cultures as "tool kits" made up of "stories, symbols, rituals, patterns of thought, world views with which people build a way of life." A congregation's culture (or cultures, since more than one distinctive culture may be manifest within a single congregation) can be explored by studying various cultural products such as worship, buildings or other physical artifacts, and mission activity in the local context.

Congregations with different cultures will define a term like "mission to the surrounding community" in different ways and will assign different religious meanings to an apparent opportunity for numerical growth. Using categories developed by church sociologists David Roozen, William McKinney, and Jackson Carroll (*Varieties of Religious Presence*, 1984[2]) we might characterize these different stances toward growth in broad terms.

For congregations with an *activist* religious culture, "God calls the *congregation* to speak out on issues and engage in corporate action, working for social change. . . ." Some activist churches see no need to be more than small cadres, more concerned about commitment than numbers; others seek to "build their base" of ministry (and consequently their numbers) through community organizing techniques.

The congregation with a *civic* culture promotes the public good through involvement with existing social and economic institutions. Internally, it "provides a forum in which social issues can be discussed and debated in a way that enables *individual* members to act responsibly as Christians. . . ." Civic churches tend to see themselves as part of the community fabric. They may view sabbath attendance as a minor measure as compared to the total number of people whose lives are touched by the ministries of the congregation and by the leavening influence of members scattered throughout the community. On the other hand, they may see building membership as a way to foster strength, openness, and diversity in their "little public." (I will elaborate on this last point in the discussion of task 3.)

In a more *evangelistic* church culture, the "spirit of the Great Commission is at the center of congregational life"; congregants are "encouraged to witness to their faith, sharing the message of salvation with those outside the fellowship. . . ." Generally speaking, this religious tradition tends to value numerical growth as a sign that the Good News is being proclaimed effectively and that more people are being called into a life of discipleship. Numerical aspirations may be affected, however, by the degree of theological conformity required of new members.

Where the congregation sees itself primarily as *sanctuary,* members are called across the threshold into the congregation to experience divine transcendence over the trials of daily life. Christians are "expected to live in the world, accepting it as it is, and to uphold its laws; but they are to be 'not of this world' in their deepest loyalty which belongs only to God." Since weekly worship is a key spiritual discipline, growing attendance may be seen as an indicator that the congregation is engaged in effective spiritual formation of its members and inquirers. On the other hand, members may understand themselves as the "faithful remnant" and may expect few others to join them as they seek to enter through the narrow gate.

These four congregational cultures are "tool kits"' available to faith communities as they interpret shifts in their context and reimagine their own role in a changed environment. As you explore the culture of your faith community to lay the groundwork for a size transition, *How We Seek God Together* would be an excellent guide.

"Golden Rule" Christianity

No single set of categories can adequately describe all the nuances of congregational culture. Recent work by church sociologist Nancy Ammerman ("Spiritual Journeys in the American Mainstream," 1997[4]) offers another perspective on cultural differences that helped me understand the seven churches in the study—as well as other congregations I have worked with on issues of numerical growth. Her analysis of extensive data from 23 churches (ranging from fundamentalist to Unitarian) revealed that about half the members overall shared an approach to religious life which she termed "Golden Rule" Christianity. This group was at least a substantial minority in even the most conservative congregations. Her appreciative portrayal of this cultural subgroup found within a wide spectrum of congregations may help you interpret some of the growth-related conversations (and silences) in your own church.

Based on Ammerman's interviews, here are the kinds of phrases an imaginary group of Golden Rule Christians might use to describe their own spiritual path:

- The most important attributes of a Christian are caring for the needy and living one's Christian values every day.
- The most important task of the church is service to people in need.
- The Bible is important (even though few of us would call it the "inerrant" word of God).
- We are less concerned with answering life's great questions or developing a coherent theological system than with practices that cohere into something we can call a "good life."
- Our goal is neither to change another person's beliefs nor to change the whole political system. We would like the world to be a bit better for our having inhabited it.
- We have not given up on transcendence. The church's "sacred space" and the "sacred time" set aside for worship give many of us an

opportunity to set our priorities in order, "feed the soul," and know that we have been in a presence greater than ourselves.

Most of the leaders I met in the course of my study expressed their faith using a Golden Rule idiom.[5]

If Ammerman's findings were shown to be representative of the general population, Golden Rule Christians would constitute the largest subset of church members in the United States. This could help explain why so many congregations have difficulty with the topic of numerical growth. Since Golden Rule Christians place a very high value on diversity and tolerance, they are not eager to challenge other people's religious beliefs or even, in most situations, to verbalize their own. One woman wrote me a letter explaining her feelings.

> When I visited my grandparents in a small northern New York State town as a child of seven, I was reprimanded for going down by the railroad tracks with my friend to try to peek at those "strange people" who set up a tent to shout out the glory of God, sing boisterous hymns, and pray. . . . I don't think that was an unusual social stigma [i.e., any association with the religious culture of "holy rollers"]. Those of my age now . . . sometimes find it difficult to speak publicly about our faith and so we dedicate ourselves to the work of God and His Church. Doesn't the Church grow in spite of that type of faith?

Golden Rule Christians often exhibit an appealing modesty about their faith. Where this reticence is more intense, however, leaders may vehemently reject invitational outreach of any kind—even gentle communication with people who share (or who would readily appreciate) the congregation's approach to faith. This "allergic" reaction stands in tension with other core values of the Golden Rule path, such as offering a caring welcome for newcomers in the community. Though American culture in the 1950s operated like a dump truck, depositing people at the church's front door on Sunday morning so that mainline Protestant Christians could greet them, it now whisks prospective members off to the mall, the soccer field, the office, or the weekend getaway. Congregations that want to show "hospitality to the stranger" may need to build a more visible path (metaphorically and literally) to the doors of their spiritual home and provide more explanation about their faith tradition for those who do appear on the doorstep. But the "allergy" must be addressed in order for this kind of outreach to occur.

Across the sample of churches in the study, a number of specific issues emerged that related to the prominence of Golden Rule Christianity within each congregation's cultural makeup.

Intending growth. Congregations with a Golden Rule religious culture have an especially hard time forming, expressing, or endorsing an intention to grow numerically. Though all seven churches I studied were located in growing towns and were visited regularly by newcomers, many leaders disavowed any goal to increase church attendance. When my questions included the word *growth,* interviewees often prefaced their answers with a definition of the term that did not involve an increase in numbers. The subject seemed to provoke more than intellectual disagreement; in many conversations, the idea of *seeking growth explicitly* seemed to provoke slight twinges of discomfort, embarrassment, or distaste. Growth that "just happens" may be acceptable (and even a source of quiet satisfaction for some), but numerical growth intentionally sought seemed somehow to be regarded as an unworthy or shameful goal.

Only a few of the leaders I interviewed volunteered a clear moral or theological case for stepping up to the next size in order to make room for the people moving into their communities. In several of these congregations, leaders were surprised to see that their worship attendance had been stuck at a plateau for several years; tracking attendance trends was not part of their annual self-assessment.

Emphasis on children. With an apparent preponderance of Golden Rule Christians in the pews, what motivated the seven churches I studied to work at the tasks required for a size transition? By and large, concern for children and their parents was the biggest driving factor that pressed these congregations to expand their capacity even in the face of their reluctance to embrace numerical growth as an overall goal. "Religious and moral training for their children," says Ammerman, is "central in the circle of care" which defines a virtuous life for Golden Rule Christians. Within the seven churches in the "Raising the Roof" study, the

Christian Education Committee typically played a key role in advocating for growth plans. Dynamic younger women often led the charge, and a few of these gifted leaders were later selected to serve as paid Christian education staff. In one of the churches, the elder generation expressed a high value on reaching children even before younger families had arrived in any number. Their long-range plan called bluntly for a transition to a new generation.

Children in worship. In the churches I studied, parents tended to want their children with them in worship at least part of the time each week. Children were typically attending the first part of the service and participating in communion when it was offered; one church went further by creating a new "early service" that involves children throughout. For some of the empty-nest and elder adults in these churches, weekly connection with youngsters in worship is a joy. For others of them (and even, perhaps, for some younger parents), this practice seems to collide with a longing for transcendence that they may have a hard time articulating. Ammerman's work sheds light on these particular yearnings. When she asked Golden Rule Christians about their experience of God, they often paused to search for words; some then responded that they felt "close to God in Sunday worship, especially in the music and in the opportunity for quiet reflection." Since Golden Rule members are less likely than others to attend programs designed for adult spiritual formation, especially in small-group settings, many of these adults may cling to those familiar worship patterns as their one reliable touchstone with transcendence. This group may feel bereft of their particular experience of the holy when worship becomes more focused on children (one argument for multiple worship services).

Spiritual growth. By understanding and respecting the congregation's existing culture(s), leaders may develop the trust required to guide each cultural group—including the Golden Rule Christians—toward appropriate forms of spiritual growth. Religious cultures are dynamic; they evolve over time in response to external circumstances, internal needs, and the overtures of individual leaders. Ammerman challenges congregations to help Golden Rule adults and their children to develop a "sustained religious vocabulary" and to "[build] up the store of moral resources on which they can call for living the good and caring life to which they say they aspire." She concludes that the spiritual yearnings of the Golden Rule group are "as real as they are vague" and deserve respectful attention. The difficulty comes in persuading these members that they should actually show up for experiences that would deepen their spiritual life—especially small groups.

Among the seven churches I studied, one has a particularly effective strategy for adult education and spiritual development that seems to fulfill Ammerman's challenge with considerable success. Headed by a volunteer director (a retired private school dean), this program currently includes 20 different adult faith-development offerings in the course of the year. Some are clergy-led, but most are not. Some last three or four sessions, while others are long-term study groups. The overall menu of choices addresses different styles of spirituality and learning.

It is probably not a coincidence that this same congregation scored especially high on two measures used in the study. The first instrument, developed in the course of this research, was the "System Change Index," which locates a congregation on nine dimensions of organizational transition required for healthy functioning at program size. (Factors in the index include congregational self-definition, pastoral role, size of staff, physical capacity, multi-cell functioning, delegation of planning tasks, aspirations to quality, infrastructure for member care, and conflict management.) This particular church received the highest possible rating on almost every dimension. Its adult-education strategy is just one example of its consistently "program" way of doing things— a variety of choices, high quality, and the deployment of staff (in this case a talented volunteer) to organize and direct a program delivered by many different leaders.

The second instrument was the "Margin in Life" inventory developed by nursing researcher Joanne Stevenson.[6] This inventory measures the impact of various factors, including religious practice, on a person's available reserves of energy, vitality, and resilience—a surplus she calls "margin." Adults draw upon these reserves when they embrace an opportunity for personal growth and learning, or when they confront a challenge such as illness, grief, or unexpected change. I administered this inventory to about 30 people in each church. Members of the particular congregation I have been describing seemed to have more "margin" in their daily lives; on average, these congregants scored highest among the seven congregations. While this finding caught my attention, the variations in average "margin" scores might well have arisen from demographic differences among towns and congregations rather than from differences in church structure or programming. But the specific contribution of religion to a member's "margin in life" was also the highest in this particular church. It seems reasonable to speculate that differences in scores on the religion factor might indicate a real difference in the impact each congregation makes on its members. Since my study involved such a small sample of congregations, this finding is only suggestive, but it reinforces a strong hunch: Remaining stuck in the transition zone seems to drain the margin (personal reserves of energy, vitality, and resilience) out of the lives of leaders and active members. Full transition to a "program" way of operating—combined with explicit attention to the spiritual development of adults—seems to allow the congregation to enhance people's "margin in life" more effectively.

Notes

1. Linda J. Clark, Joanne Swenson, and Mark Stamm, chapter 2 in *How We Seek God Together: Exploring Worship Style* (Bethesda, Md.: Alban Institute, 2001). This book comes with a powerful video comparing the style (and therefore the culture) of three congregations.
2. David A. Roozen, William McKinney, and Jackson W. Carroll, *Varieties of Religious Presence: Mission in Public Life* (New York: Pilgrim Press, 1984), cited in *Handbook for Congregational Studies*, edited by Jackson W. Carroll, Carl S. Dudley, and William McKinney (Nashville: Abingdon Press, 1986), 29–30.
3. The "tool kit" metaphor comes from "Culture in Action: Symbols and Strategies," an article by sociologist Anne Swidler in *American Sociological Review* (April 1986). The article is cited in *How We Seek God Together* (see n. 1 above), chapter 2.
4. Nancy T. Ammerman, "Spiritual Journeys in the American Mainstream," *Congregations* 22, no. 1 (January-February 1997): 11–15.
5. The study included a group exploration of the congregation's history, plus individual interviews with the (full-time) pastors and two lay leaders in each church.
6. Joanne Sabol Stevenson, "Construction of a Scale to Measure Load, Power and Margin in Life," *Nursing Research* 31, no. 4 (July-August 1982).

Generational Watershed

Adapted from chapter 4 of *The Multigenerational Congregation: Meeting the Leadership Challenge,* by Gil Rendle (Bethesda, Md.: Alban Institute, 2002). Used by permission.

Congregations are doing ministry in the context of a "major generational watershed."[1] This major divide separates "preboomers"—that is, people born before 1946—from those who came after. "Watershed" is an appropriate and helpful image. The term denotes a ridge or high place dividing a large geographic area drained by different rivers or river system (for instance, the continental divide). I live near such a watershed in Pennsylvania. On one side the water drains west toward the Susquehanna River and into the Chesapeake Bay, on the other side the water flows east toward the Delaware River and into the Delaware Bay. Surely the rain that falls in a particular place flows in multiple directions depending on immediate elevations and ground slope. However, gravity ensures that the overall flow of water from the watershed divides, heading eventually toward one bay or the other.

The "watershed" within bimodal congregations has similar qualities. Preferences about any decision or practice in the congregation may flow in many directions at one time. As with local water, multiple variables will influence the immediate flow. However, dominant and more determinant flows or pulls will direct a large portion of the behaviors and attitudes within the congregation. The dividing lines for congregations tend to be generational value systems, which function much like the watersheds that determine the flow of water from the large masses of a geographical area.

It is possible, using a pure-market approach, to differentiate specifically the preferences of generational cohorts such as GIs, early boomers, late boomers, Xers, and millennials. However, congregations more often find themselves negotiating the more basic differences between two primary cultural-value systems marked by the "watershed" of the birth year 1946.

This dominant value distinction to be negotiated is the difference between the *GI value system* and the *consumer value system*. Using that watershed distinction to identify differences, the bimodal congregation can be interpreted through three basic subgroups:

- The GI generation value cohort (pre-1946)
- The consumer generation value cohort (post-1946)
- The bridge people

Before we describe the bimodal congregation more closely, please recognize that this is an exercise in simplification. I acknowledge to the reader, as I do to congregational leaders with whom I work, that we are embarking on a conversation about people and groups in the congregation, described in a stereotypical manner. I further recognize that for almost any statement describing the values, behaviors, and preferences of subgroups within congregations, one can probably point to specific examples to the contrary. Nonetheless, leaders need to have a clear sense of the basic value differences that mark significant groups within congregations; through these the smaller and more confusing differences can be understood. The differences in the value structures of the GI and the consumer generational cohorts in congregations can be described using four "markers":

- Deferred pleasure vs. instant gratification
- Group vs. individual orientation
- Assumptions of sameness vs. assumptions of difference
- Spirituality of place vs. spirituality of pilgrimage

Exploring Generational Cohorts and Their Markers

In reading these descriptions, keep in mind that they point to life lessons that differ from one generational cohort to another. The question is not whether one set of values is better than another, but whether we can understand the values as life lessons appropriate to the people who went through critical developmental life stages when these value systems were dominant.

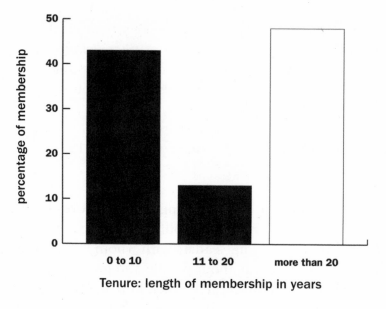

The GI Generation Value System

1. Deferred Pleasure

Let's begin this description of the GI generation value system with the marker of deferred pleasure, since it rests on a fundamental and broadly shared experience in the American setting. It can be understood through the American "giving/getting compact," described by noted market researcher Daniel Yankelovich as the "unwritten rules governing what we give in marriage, work, community and sacrifice for others, and what we expect in return."[2] The giving/getting compact that was central to the experience of people born before the 1946 divide was formed primarily by the Protestant work ethic: One did what was required in the current moment, and one delayed gratification for a future time when the reward would be appropriate.

Under this value system it was common practice for people to commit their labor to one company or industry for their full adult working lives. My grandfather, for example, began working for the Lehigh Valley Railroad at age 13. He remained with that railroad until he retired at age 65, when he reaped the promised rewards of a gold watch and a pension that would see him and my grandmother through the rest of their lives. That meant committing his working years to one company through good and bad, through agreement and disagreement, with a sense of responsibility and sacrifice. My grandfather could make that commitment with a belief that reciprocity or payoff would come in the rewards that would allow him to care for his family, buy and own a home, and live with a sense of control and security.

Such lifelong commitment is much like the "heroism of midlife" that *Boston Globe* columnist Ellen Goodman identified in a column about the popularity of the movie *Groundhog Day*. The film comedy centers on a TV weather forecaster sent to Punxsutawney, Pennsylvania, to report on the February 2 weather forecast, to be determined by whether the groundhog "Punxsutawney Phil" sees his shadow. The weather guy (Bill Murray) finds himself trapped in seemingly endless repetitions of February 2, each a virtually identical Groundhog Day. Morning after morning, he awakes to a clock radio playing Sonny and Cher's rendition of "I've Got You, Babe." The exasperating replays of February 2 end only when the Murray character learns to exchange his boorish, selfish behavior for more responsible and appropriate conduct befitting an adult—thus earning the love and respect of the woman he has fallen for (Andie McDowell). Only then can he move on to February 3. Goodman's description of the movie as a metaphor for the heroism needed to address the humdrum dailiness of life is a good example of the pre-1946 giving/getting compact. Whereas the years of youth and young adulthood are marked by choice—of mate, educational path, career, and location—Goodman notes that the heroism of midlife is remaining faithful to and responsible for the choices already made. Midlife is a time of commitment to the unvarying days that come as a consequence of choices made when one was younger, a daily commitment whose rewards will not be given right away but realized only over the long haul. The GI generation understood and accepted the concept of deferred pleasure, requiring daily responsibility and sacrifice whose full rewards would not be reaped until some later time.

This value system of deferred pleasure, known variously as the Protestant work ethic or the American way of life, spoke *the language of responsibility*. One's value and place in the community were measured by one's ability to be responsible and dependable toward commitments made and roles accepted. The valued husband or father was one who could "put a roof over his family's head." The valued church member was one who attended worship regularly, pledged regular financial support, and could be expected to show up for committee meetings. Immediate pleasure was not expected but rather deferred to a time when the present sacrifices and responsibilities would produce the intended results.

Because of this willingness to defer personal pleasure and gain and because of the sense of personal responsibility, it should not be a surprise that both the Social Gospel and the Great Society were religious and political expressions of this value system. In both cases, the underlying belief was that present sacrifices through the giving/getting compact would result in a better world or a closer approximation of the kingdom of God.

The GI generation's value system also brought a sense of responsibility to the congregation. To be a member of a congregation was also to be a good citizen to the larger community, a good spouse, and a good parent. Membership in this group is defined or measured by the amount of time, money, and attention sacrificed for the good of the whole. Not surprisingly, those who live closest to the cultural lessons of deferred pleasure point easily to responsibilities that are not equally perceived or accepted by newcomers to the congregation. It is common to hear this long-tenured group of members say that they have carried out their responsibilities long enough and "now it is time for others to step up and keep things going." Later, when we look at the value system of the consumer generation, it will be clearer why newer and younger members do not simply step into the roles, positions, and responsibilities of the group born before 1946. But it should not be missed that the assumption that newer people need to pick up the responsibilities of longer-tenured members is frequently based on an expectation that the newcomers should maintain the established patterns of the congregation rather than initiating changes. An attendant assumption within the GI generation value system specifies that once the path or pattern of how to do things has been determined, people should keep doing it the same way. That statement leads us to the second generational marker—a group identity.

2. The Group Identity of the GI Generation

The pre-1946 generational cohorts in our congregation tend to see themselves as a group. As cyclical historians William Strauss and Neil Howe note:

> The initials "G.I." can stand for two things—"general issue" and "government issue" —and this generation's lifecycle has stood squarely for both. All their lives, the G.I.s have placed a high priority on being "general" or "regular" (as in "he's a regular guy"),

since regularity is a prerequisite for being effective "team players."
They developed this instinct young, building in high school and
college what historian Paula Fass labels a "peer society"—a har-
monious community of group-enforced virtue.[3]

The life lesson that supported this group identity and cohesion—the
sense of team—came from the chaotic and threatening environment of
the Great Depression and World War II. The cultural lesson was to
band together and to take on these great threats as full communities or
as a nation, that is, as a group. It has been said that the learned response to problems for the GI generation was to identify the problem,
to find out who was on your team by looking for people like you who
agreed with you, to focus on the solution, and never to give up. The life
lesson was that if you followed this path, you could do anything, even
win a world war.

I have jokingly said to leaders that these are the people in your
congregation who show up without an appointment at the denominational executive's office in a rented bus with a petition stating that they
are displeased with what is going on in their congregation. In several
instances this example turned out not to be a joke, since it was a fairly
accurate description of what happened when a congregation was dealing with seemingly unresolvable differences.

I recall in particular working in several congregations where long-
tenured members held secret "by-invitation-only" meetings to organize their displeasure. In each case I identified these secret meetings
and described them publicly as unhelpful to the decision making and
community building that we were working on for the whole congregation. In each case, some long-tenured members expressed surprise that
I would object to what they were doing, since they assumed it was the
way people naturally handled such situations. Secret meetings among
people who already agree are, in fact, unhelpful since they break communication between the people who need to be talking—and listening—
to each other. However, leaders should recognize that GI-oriented folk
are not mean-spirited people trying to defeat the opposition unfairly.
Rather, these people are using their life lessons as a group-oriented
cohort that long ago learned the effectiveness of a coordinated team
with a strategy to accomplish what they believe to be "right."

Leaders should understand that those who hold the GI value system tend to have a clear idea of what is "right" and believe that "right"
is determined by the group. For these members, there is a right way and

a wrong way to do many things, and the "right" is determined by what is good for the group. The driving assumption is that if there is a right way to worship, then it is the right way for *everyone* to worship. Multiple worship services designed to speak to different groups or blended worship that brings together traditional liturgy with personal testimony or praise music are not natural starting places for this group when its members think about making their worship "better." Another driving assumption: There is a right way to build a budget and support it, and it is based on the principle that everyone pays a fair share toward an agreed-upon program agenda. The driving assumption of mission or outreach is that it is to be done with people who are "different" from "us" in ways that invite or enable those people to become more like us.

At the heart of this value, centered on group identity, is the conviction that the individual must change to accommodate and support the needs and preferences of the group. Since the group has priority over the individual, and since it is the individual who ought to change to accommodate the group, differences can easily and directly be dealt with by determining the will or the direction of the majority. For this part of our congregations, *Robert's Rules of Order* and majority votes make perfect sense, as they are decision-making methods that quickly capture a picture of the will of the majority and simultaneously identify the individuals who should conform to the greater will of what is "right."

3. Assumptions of Sameness

Highly correlated with the marker of group identity is the value of sameness—an assumption that one size fits all. This idea conforms well with the group identity of the GI, "general issue," part of the congregation that learned its cultural lessons in a time of uniformity. I often ask groups to think back to 1940 and ask, "If you wanted a telephone for your home back then, from how many models could you choose?" People laugh and describe the standard model, the only phone available—black, heavy, with a rotary dial, attached to the wall by a sturdy cable. To some extent, the selection of telephones was limited because the industry had not yet discovered computerization and digital and cellular technologies. Still, in the 1940s we did understand colors and shapes. Yet every phone was the same—black, boxy, and heavy.

This uniformity was acceptable because it fit the cultural assumption of sameness. If you needed a phone, you needed the same thing that everyone else needed in a phone. It was acceptable that they all be identical.

The same principle held true for congregations. It was assumed that if you needed a Lutheran or a Methodist congregation when you moved into a new community, you needed the same thing that other Lutherans or Methodists needed. Congregations were assumed, and expected, to come in "standard issue," so you usually went to the closest local congregation of your denominational or faith tradition. Congregations and their leaders were measured and evaluated not on the basis of their unique effectiveness for the location or their appropriateness for the specific people they felt called to serve, but for their ability to be like other clergy and congregations of their tradition.

Congregations and their leaders were measured by a general standard, and the standard was one that could be generalized across the board. It made sense, then, to print an order of worship in the front of a denominational hymnal to be followed by all congregations of that denominational family each week at the regular service of worship. Uniformity was a standard of effectiveness. It made sense, then, to report to a denominational middle judicatory or national office using standardized report forms or through formal reporting sessions with the denominational executive. A widely shared consensus prevailed as to what a congregation and its leaders should be doing. If all congregations were more or less the same, all reports on their practices could be filled out on identical forms. It was assumed that congregations were reporting on similar goals, using standard committee structures, and following standard financial practices.

In the language of management, the decisive question for congregations in the time of the GI culture was "Are we doing things right?" The measurement was then appropriately taken as leaders looked around them, across the landscape of neighboring congregations. Leaders could ask, "Does my congregation offer a Lenten Bible study series like other congregations of my denomination?" or "Do we participate in an Easter sunrise service like others?" or "Do we also have an annual women's bazaar to support foreign missions?"

The marker of conformity still holds great value for the GI-generation portion of our congregations. This committed portion of our leadership still asks the standard management question of whether we are doing things "right." Doing things right was once a measure taken by leaders looking horizontally across the congregational landscape at similar neighboring congregations. Was our congregation doing things the same way as everyone else? Today, however, the landscape is becoming more varied and confusing. It's harder to ask management questions about "doing things right." Today the measure is often taken by this long-tenured portion of the leadership and membership by looking not horizontally but historically to ask if what we are doing is being measured exactly as we did it in the past.

One challenge for current leaders in congregations is to help everyone see that the use of past practices as a point of evaluation is not simply a matter of older members who are stuck in the past and unwilling to change. Indeed, in many cases, older people in our culture and our congregations are leading change. A large number of people over 65 are active participants and shapers of the Internet—because they have the time and the interest. An increasing number of people use retirement and later life for spiritual experimentation and deepening. Many older people have found opportunities that allow them to explore in new ways. These members of our congregations are not by definition rigid and unyielding. They are, however, people schooled in life lessons and in a value system that underscores continuity and asks evaluative questions to determine whether we are doing things right— often meaning the way that has proved effective in the past.

4. Spirituality of Place

Robert Wuthnow, professor of sociology at Princeton University, distinguishes between the established spirituality of *dwelling* and the spirituality of *seeking*. One is located in a place, the other in the journey. He writes:

> In settled times, people have been able to create a sacred habitat and to practice habitual forms of spirituality; in unsettled times, they have been forced to negotiate with themselves and with each other to find the sacred. Settled times have been conducive to an imagery of dwellings; unsettled times to an imagery of journeys. In one, the sacred is fixed, and spirituality can be found within the gathered body of God's people; in the other, the sacred is fluid, portable.[4]

For the people of Israel the difference was between the settled time of the Temple and the wandering time of the tabernacle.

The generational cohorts of the GI value system are oriented to the settled time, to a spirituality of place. The sacred can be found in a place to which one can go. Wuthnow notes that a spirituality of place "requires sharp symbolic boundaries to protect sacred space from its surroundings."[5] The boundaries may be physical, behavioral, or relational. Clearly, physical boundary issues were a concern for the pastor who tried to negotiate a compromise to allow the drums to stay permanently in the chancel area for use in the contemporary worship service. But no compromise could be found to accommodate what GI value carriers regarded as secular drums in a sacred space. In the GI value system, locating the sacred in a place of spirituality reinforces the idea that the church or synagogue requires different norms or behaviors. People who hold this value system appreciate hushed voices in the sanctuary, more formal dress and behavior, and careful attention to physical order (with a place for everything and everything in its place).

I well remember and appreciate the man in his 80s who participated in a group interview that I conducted in a large Lutheran church in Minnesota. We were seated in a circle of chairs in a contemporary worship space—a marvelous auditorium designed specifically for contemporary worship. With deep concern for his congregation, this man began to catalog all that was wrong with the goings-on in this contemporary space. Because there were tables in the worship space, families could sit together around a table during worship. This arrangement led to inappropriate behavior, such as children coloring with crayons while the minister preached. Worse, some people's backs were turned to the altar when the communion elements were consecrated. The atmosphere also encouraged people to bring cups of coffee into the worship setting. And, the octogenarian concluded, obviously saving the most damning evidence for last, "they also bring those plastic water bottles that you can't get away from anywhere."

A spirituality of place has a settled nature that encourages tradition. Many homes, my own included, display the same holiday decorations in the same assigned place year after year. Once the Hanukkah candles or Christmas decorations are placed in an appropriate location, they reappear in that same place annually. As with seasonal decorations, so with seasonal practices. I grew up in a congregation that unfailingly sang Jean-Baptiste Fauré's "The Palms" every year on Palm Sunday. Today I still leave my current congregation feeling disappointed on a Palm Sunday when we haven't sung this "old chestnut."

A spirituality of place easily establishes traditions of dress and behavior as well. From the GI generation's perspective, the acolyte who allows her sneakers to peek out from beneath her robe has allowed secular clothing and behavior to cross inappropriately into sacred space. (It does not matter that her sneakers may be her "best" and most expensive shoes.)

For the GI generation, slightly bawdy jokes or occasionally spicy language allowed at the shopping mall or in the congregation's parking lot is disallowed once the threshold of sacred place has been crossed. To others who do not carry the GI value system, these distinctions may seem duplicitous or hypocritical. To those who live within this value system, they may simply seem faithful.

The Consumer Generation Value System

When we turn our attention to the short-tenured portion of the congregation, we may find a quite different, and often oppositional, value system undergirding people's assumptions, attitudes, and behaviors. Once again our description will be simplified and stereotypical. Once again, the goal is to describe cultural life lessons, not to establish or mark these values as right or wrong, better or worse than other values or value systems. Rather, these are the values learned and practiced because a group of people was born in a certain era and learned about life from the environment they encountered.

1. Instant Gratification

Where the GI value system honored and practiced deferred pleasure with its attendant disciplines and required patience, children of the

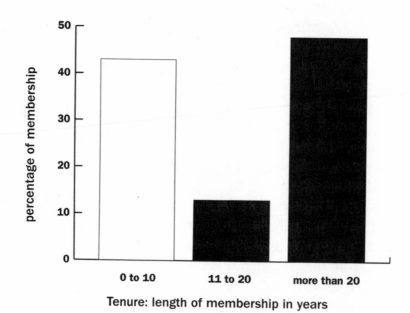

consumer value system learned the lessons of instant gratification. Yankelovich quotes sociologist Daniel Bell as saying:

> The Protestant ethic was undermined by capitalism itself. The single greatest engine in the destruction of the Protestant ethic was the invention of the installment plan, or instant credit. Previously one had to save in order to buy. But with credit cards one could indulge in instant gratification.[6]

Surely the advent of instant credit was part of a much larger and more complex matrix of changes that followed World War II. Nonetheless, the postwar economy emphasized production. Many people were weary of deferring pleasures through a depression and a major war and were now itching to "catch up." These factors account for the shift in life lessons absorbed by the younger generational cohorts. The lessons no longer centered on saving until one could afford to buy a car or a refrigerator. The new cultural penchant was reflected in advertising slogans that encouraged purchasers to "buy now and pay later."

This cultural value shift is discussed at some length in the Alban Institute video "Living into the New World."[7] In that video I point to the many examples of changes in assumptions and behaviors that shaped the "now" generation that came of age in the 1960s, the "me" generation of the 1970s and the "greed" generation of the 1980s. These changing values and their life lessons form a remarkable story when viewed as part of a big picture, and looking at them as a cultural pattern aids our understanding of our national and congregational experience over recent decades. These changing cultural values have a major impact on the ministry of congregations and faith communities that live in the "new world" of consumerism. But the overwhelming effect of the cultural value shift that came on the heels of World War II was to teach people to expect not to wait.

The rise of instant credit taught people that they could take their goods home immediately and pay for them later. McDonald's (and the fast-food industry spawned from its example) told people that they could get their food almost instantly—food that was cheap and good. A drug industry began to produce medications and supplements that could reduce or eliminate symptoms almost immediately, and even people with chronic illnesses went in search of doctors and medicines that could provide the "silver bullet" that would solve the problem simply and quickly. People earned money but spent it immediately. For the first time in modern economics, concern arose over the paucity of voluntary financial savings practiced by Americans in comparison to people in other countries. Out of concern for the long-term security of the American people, who seemed to pay little attention to the long view, the federal government began a retirement savings program in IRAs (individual retirement accounts), in which the money could not be used until retirement. But to appeal to the consumer mentality, immediate tax relief was offered to savers in the same year that they contributed to their account. Some wonder if the IRAs would have held any attraction at all for age cohorts that expected immediate gratification had an instant advantage not been attached to its use.

While the GI cultural value of deferred pleasure spoke *the language of responsibility,* the cultural values of the consumer generations spoke the *language of need.* One's value and one's place in the community were not measured so much by one's sense of responsibility and dependability as by one's sensitivity to self and one's ability to consume. To be a practiced consumer required a heightened sense of need—of knowing what one needed and wanted and how to get it from the marketplace.

Note the manner in which marketers have learned to observe and study each individual in our communities to give people access to whatever they think they need whenever they need it. In the process, the media and advertising industries have worked effectively together to help "teach people their needs" or to create a sense of need for specific products and services; Boomers and later generational cohorts have been thoroughly schooled in life lessons in consumption-lessons based on a language of need and a highly developed sense of uniqueness.

2. Individual Orientation

Whereas the GI value system found its identity in the group, the consumer value system focuses on the individual. Suddenly one is no longer expected to conform to group norms and practices; the individual is responsible for his or her own norms and practices based on a clear sense of one's own needs and "style." It is instructive to turn to the logos, mottoes, or sayings of the times that captured the moment. The GI value system emerged from generations that had been taught to "grin and bear it." The newer generations were taught quite different lessons. When it no longer sufficed for McDonald's to be fast, Burger King stepped in with its famous difference—"Have it your way"—and the importance of the individual was underscored. In the pivotal decade of the 1960s the youth movement reminded people, "Don't trust anyone over 30" (since people over 30 had the wrong value system for these young learners of new cultural lessons), and "If it feels right, do it," perhaps the ultimate slogan of individualism in which the final arbiter of right or wrong is the individual with his or her own feelings. Beer companies pointed out the sobering truth that "you only go around once" and advised beer drinkers to "grab all the gusto" while they could. Marketers of hair coloring conceded that their product was expensive, portraying young women with thick, shining tresses who concluded, "But I'm worth it."

Where once the culture was marked by deferred pleasure and assumptions of conformity, now immediacy and nonconformity held sway; and congregations, like schools, stores, banks, and an expanding array of service providers, were expected to identify and respond to individual needs. No longer did the individual conform to the group. Now the individual was to be elevated and served. Once it was sufficient to have a common, garden-variety credit card; now credit cards are individualized and customized with different interest rates, credit limits tailored to an individual's payment history, incentives that tie frequent-flyer miles to an airline of the user's choice, and even one's choice of art work on the laminated surface. Is it any wonder that congregations today find it necessary to clarify and claim a unique identity to fit a niche in communities and cultures finely tuned to the differences of individuals?

Once people assumed that a "right" way to worship should fit everyone in the group; now individuals go shopping for a worship style that best speaks to their preferences. Once consensus prevailed on the "right" way to build a budget and on the expectation that everyone would contribute a "fair share"; now finance committees look for ways to allow participants to designate their giving to a certain part of the budget, a particular program, or favored mission project. Once voting was the accepted way to measure the level of consensus and to decide the direction in which the majority would lead the congregation. Today voting and *Robert's Rules of Order* are tools that capture our differences and spark competition—often creating conflict rather than resolving differences. In the wake of these changes in cultural teachings, congregational life is simply not the same.

3. Assumptions of Difference

Where the focus of the GI value system was on sameness, the focus of the consumer value system is clearly on difference. I already noted the high correlation between a group identity and assumptions about uniformity. If the individual is assumed to conform to the group, it is relatively easy to behave as though one size fits all (or that one size *should* fit all). If only one type of telephone was available for those who wanted one in 1946, consider how many types of telephones consumers can choose from today—or how many telephone service providers are available, each of which is more than willing to talk with you by phone about their service during your evening meal.

In an earlier time, if you were a Lutheran or a Methodist just arriving in town, you went in search of the nearest Lutheran or Methodist church with some assurance that it would serve you well because it was like other Lutheran or Methodist churches. Today you shop for the church that best fits your own needs (individualism) for this stage of your life (instant gratification). And it is OK for you to try out different brands. If you were a Lutheran in your last community, it is acceptable to visit the Assembly of God, the Episcopal parish, and the Baptist church in your new town to see which has the schedule, the atmosphere, the music, the programs, and the friendly members that best match your needs or preferences. This approach may make you suspect that religion is being reduced to consumerism and marketing—and that risk is present. But such a search also grows out of people's sensitivity and ability to know what life questions and spiritual questions they want to ask and their willingness to go looking for a place where their questions can be addressed.

Congregational leaders can no longer assume that they are doing things right just by doing what they have always done or by doing what other congregations in their denominational family do. Now leaders have to practice discernment and ask the more difficult questions about what their own congregation is called to do, to practice, or to provide because of its distinctive setting in the community among its special constituency, using its particular gifts. Today two Lutheran churches located across the street from each other (a not uncommon occurrence because of historical events) can expect to be quite unlike one another because each has distinctive gifts and is doing ministry with different people in a time when differences count.

4. Spirituality of Journey

As noted earlier, sociologist Robert Wuthnow has observed that the two sides of the generational watershed hold different assumptions about spirituality. "In one (the spirituality of place) the sacred is fixed, and spirituality can be found within the gathered body of God's people; in the other (the spirituality of journey) the sacred is fluid, portable." Each value system looks to encounter the sacred in a different place.

A parallel difference: In the GI value system, if a person is displeased or dissatisfied, the learned response is to dig in deeper, organize, work tenaciously, and fix what's wrong. In the consumer value system individual differences are the measure of satisfaction. If something displeases or does not satisfy, one simply moves on. This lesson of choice and freedom to seek is a life lesson of the marketplace to address the diverse needs of its customers. When the consumer is roaming the shopping mall looking for black slacks and discovers that the store she's in has none that fit, she doesn't organize with others to make her displeasure known or to try to change the store. The shopper just moves on to the next clothing store to see if what she needs can be found there.

Similarly, the spiritual journey or quest simply continues. Those who pursue the spirituality of journey do not necessarily identify a special place as important in the encounter with God. People on a pilgrimage are willing to search and to encounter God in both likely and unlikely places; they are ready to move about to find God. This search can confuse the holders of GI values, who associate spirituality with place. The pursuit can lead to "multiple memberships" for those responding to consumer values. They may "belong" to one congregation because they prefer the style of worship there, but simultaneously "belong" to another congregation for the youth program, while also "belonging" to a third congregation because of a helpful support group or study course. In all of these "memberships," the carrier of consumer values may never take the formal step of officially joining the congregation but may be satisfied that participation is "belonging" enough. For an adherent of the GI value system, with its focus on the importance of the group and of belonging, the portable spirituality of the consumer group is confounding and displeasing. This intergenerational

discomfort is further exacerbated when encounters with the spiritual for
some in the consumer value group also include practices outside their own
tradition, such as yoga, Tai Chi, or 12-step programs.

The Bridge People

There is a third subgroup that has a separate character in the congregation. This usually smaller group of members resides in the middle between
the larger clusters of GI value carriers and consumer value carriers. These
really are people in the middle. As noted in the bimodal distribution model,
they have commonly been members of the congregation from 10 to 20
years. They come with their own life lessons from one side of the 1946
watershed or the other, with preferences for the GI or the consumer
value system. But functioning within the congregational system, they
tend to be sensitive to and understanding of both large clusters.

No matter how long-tenured the clergy and program staff of the
congregation may be (newly arrived or 20-year veterans), they nonetheless, as staff, live their lives in the congregation as part of this bridge
group, in the middle. They are expected to understand and to represent
both divergent value systems. They are expected to bridge the differences and make the sense of community "work" for everyone.

Bridge people are expected to be multilingual, able to speak the
languages and respond to the markers of both value systems that flank

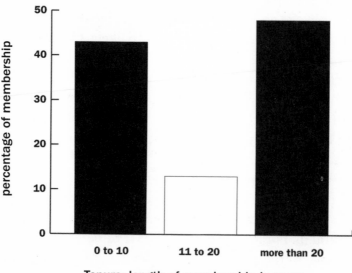

Tenure: length of membership in years

them. Because they stand in the middle and understand both languages, they are often looked upon as problem solvers, as people who are responsible to negotiate with the "other side" to make it work.

One difficulty often encountered by bridge people is the perception that they are "siding with" the newer members who represent consumer values. This reaction is a natural but difficult consequence of the misunderstandings of behavior dividing the congregation's two dominant value systems.

It is common in many established congregations for the GI value cohort to have a much more expressive voice in decision making. After all, these members have been around longer and know the norms better. But more than that, their life lessons encourage them to organize to make their preferences known. They willingly defer their needs and pleasures to devise strategies to get what they want. They're willing to work and wait for their views to prevail. Theirs is usually the voice most clearly heard at board meetings and congregational meetings. Theirs is the opinion most easily registered by surveys of the congregation, which often get the best responses from people who know how to register their opinion.

In contrast, many congregations find it difficult to hear and understand the voice of newer participants who carry the consumer values of immediacy, individuality, difference, and journey. These newer members do not necessarily see themselves as a group and don't organize to get their needs and preferences heard. They often don't assume that others need or want what they are looking for. The portability of their search means that if they don't find what they are looking for in one congregation, they can rather easily leave and move on to the next congregation to see if the fit is better. Often the first hint congregational leaders detect to indicate that members of this group are displeased or unsatisfied comes from noticing that they have been absent.

In such a situation, behaviors consistent with the values of the two groups give the longer-tenured members a more dominant voice. Realizing the importance of having the voices of short-tenured people heard, the bridge group quite naturally steps in to protect and to give a platform to the quieter and sometimes diffident voices of the short-tenured members who carry consumer values.

For the bridge people, representing the short-tenured members and attenders is often seen as a matter of fairness. For staff and key lay leaders, this act is often regarded as a critical issue of listening to the voice of the "future" that speaks too quietly and needs to be heard. But not surprisingly, for the long-tenured GI-value-centered members, this representation of the short-tenured people is often perceived as a betrayal. The bridge people suffer under this assumption made by GIs. The GI value holders are not mean spirited. Rather, they make different assumptions about their group identity, for they are people who value the group and their membership in the group. For them, if someone is not standing with them (in their group), that person must be standing against them (favoring some other group). When bridge people, especially clergy, program staff, and key laypeople, stand with the newer members to help their quieter voices be heard or interpreted, the long-tenured members (who still assume that, given enough time, even the new members will become more like them) can feel betrayed.

The experience of living and leading from the bridge position is draining and often uncomfortable. "Multilingual" people needing to speak both of the "languages" of the competing value systems find that they can tire quickly and become depleted from a lack of appreciation from either side. The difficulty of this bridge position and the personal toll that it can take was put into words by an active member of a congregation with which I was consulting. We had been working on differences in expectations between these two cultural value groups, and one point of discomfort had expressed itself in worship. Members were having a difficult debate about whether applause in worship was appropriate. The longer-tenured folk, with their value on the spirituality of place, were uncomfortable that community behavior, such as applause appropriate to a performance, was creeping over the boundary into their sacred space. The shorter-tenured people, with their value on immediacy and individuality, were eager to have a place where they could participate, and did not see worship as a performance but as a venue to express themselves in their own search. The lines were drawn and the conversation had been strained. The real burden on the bridge people was given voice by a man in his late 40s who had been an active member for about 12 years. He said that when the children's choir finished singing, he was one of those who applauded. He did so because he appreciated what the singers had put into their music; he wanted them to feel that they had a place in this congregation and that the members could accept them and meet their needs. But, the man continued, every time he clapped, he felt both sad and guilty because he knew that he was breaking the heart of his father, who was standing next to him.

Not for the Faint of Heart

Many established congregations have a daily life and rhythm determined by the cultural value differences held by their members. I have sat in competitive hymn sings in which long-tenured members called out the names of "old chestnut" hymns for the whole group to sing and short-tenured members responded with names of contemporary praise songs or the newest "global" hymns from the denominational hymnal. The energy of the group was high, but it was hard to tell whether the people really wanted to sing the hymns they named or whether they wanted to force others to sing the very songs those others would not have selected. In congregational listening groups I have heard long-tenured members complain that newer members would not join committees and serve on the board, while newer members complained that they were not permitted to participate in decision making—and both were right.

Leading and living in a multigenerational congregation is not for the faint of heart. But the experience can occasion rich and dynamic conversation about the presence of God in our lives, the fabric of faith, and negotiations for the values and truths that will be passed to the next generation. Often approached too seriously and in a win/lose spirit, this wonderful conversation needs to be held a bit more lightly and treated with more enjoyment and delight.

Notes

1. This image originated with church sociologist Jackson Carroll.
2. Daniel Yankelovich, *New Rules: Searching for Self-Fulfillment in a World Turned Upside Down* (New York: Bantam Books, 1982), 6.
3. William Strauss and Neil Howe, *Generations: The History of America's Future, 1584 to 2069* (New York: Quill–William Morrow, 1991), 264–265.
4. Robert Wuthnow, "Returning to Practice," *IONS Noetic Sciences Review* (August-November 1999), 34.
5. Ibid., 34.
6. Yankelovich, *New Rules,* 227.
7. Gil Rendle, *Living Into the New World* (Bethesda, Md.: Alban Institute, 2000, video).

Favorite Hymn Exercise

1. Gather in a place and time that allows for relaxed exploration. Stock the room with copies of any hymnals and songbooks that might be familiar to members of the congregation.
2. Give each person an index card and a pencil. Ask them to write down the name or first words of their favorite hymn. Say: "You may interpret the word *hymn* as broadly as you wish . . . anything from the Beatles to Bach." (Allow two or three minutes of quiet.)
3. Ask people to add to the card a sentence or two about why that hymn or song is powerful for them. Add: "Don't just write down "the words" or "the music." What about the text is meaningful to you? What about the tune do you find moving?"
4. If you are using this exercise in a smaller group like a planning team, each person in the group takes about one minute to share their response. Impromptu singing, humming, or playing of a verse is a completely appropriate group response to each person's sharing! (Allow about 20 minutes for a group of 10 to share and sing their way around the circle.)

   If you are using the exercise with a wider group of leaders or members, divide up into groups of five to seven people. Invite one minute for sharing of the material on the cards. Encourage the group to hum or sing a bit of each offering if they can. (Allow about 15 minutes.)
5. Ask the planning team (or the subgroups of a larger gathering) to reflect theologically using the following questions. Ask a group member to record responses on a chart pad. Allow 7 to 10 minutes for each question:
   - Based on the hymns we have shared, how do we see God?
   - How do we see human life?
   - What do we see as the purpose of a congregation?
6. If you have used subgroups: As the groups are finishing the above task, ask each group to select one of its hymns for the full group to sing (at least one verse).

7. Subgroups report back, identifying all the hymns chosen by the group, and the answers to the three questions. End each report with singing of the group's selection.

8. Reflect on similarities and differences among the responses. Is there a clear theological emphasis or theological division that comes to light? Does this emphasis or division sound like you?

9. As the planning committee goes to work on a mission or vision statement or on the introduction to a report, consider returning to hymns that seemed to resonate with the group to search for powerful imagery or language. A planning report might also comment on the theological emphases discovered in this process.

Wall of Wonder

WALL OF WONDER

—— EVENTS ————————————————— founding year ——————— current year ————————————————

—— PEOPLE ————————————————————— —— —— —— —— —— ——

—— OBSERVATIONS ——————————————— —— —— —— —— —— ——

History Grid

Adapted from chapter 4 of *Raising the Roof: The Pastoral to Program Size Transition* by Alice Mann (Bethesda, Md.: Alban Institute, 2001). Used by permission.

In this exercise, you will be asking leaders to reflect on the history of the congregation, using mainly the information they carry around in their minds and hearts. Instead of deferring to an "official" historian (if you have one) to provide all the information, you want participants in this session to become aware of their own impressions—no matter how incomplete or inaccurate these may be from a factual point of view.

To prepare for this session, you may want to interview your congregation's historian in advance to get some baseline information and his or her impressions of what this history might mean for the present. This would serve two purposes: to discover a basic time line of major events that could be helpful to the group, and to "release" the historian from needing to dominate the conversation. Ask your historian to allow members of the group to share their own impressions first, without "corrections." Toward the end of the event, you can invite him or her to comment briefly, offering some missing pieces or another interpretation of the story. Other occasions can always be planned to continue this conversation in more depth if there seems to be sufficient energy for it in the group.

Some congregations have an officially designated historian or archivist. In other churches, the historian or archivist is an informal role in the system, filled by the person who knows the most stories. This person may be a present member, a former member who now lives in a retirement facility, or a long-tenured member of the staff who has collected the lore. Occasionally, a congregation has no effective custodian of its history, perhaps because some traumatic event has demolished the cohort of long-term members. Through denominational archives, town historical societies, neighboring pastors, retired clergy, and elders in retirement facilities, a learning team could begin to reestablish that link. Of course, a careful search of the files, the closets, and the attic will often yield clues to past eras in the congregation's life.

The "History Analysis Chart" below provides the basic format for the history discussion. Some churches have more than one set of "glory days." It is essential to look at the most recent glory days (often, but not always, the 1950s). But you may decide in advance that there is another era you should look at as well. If that's the case, add another column to the chart, and work in four subgroups when you do the process outlined below. Make sure you have a copy of this chart for each person, and a very large version of it on the wall (perhaps the size of four pieces of chart paper in a square.) You will want to hold this session in a large room where there will be plenty of space for the group to spread out.

- Set the tone for the exercise: "We are going to be looking at the way this congregation has thought about itself over time. As we talk about the way the congregation defined itself in different historical eras, it's our impressions that matter, not what is written down in some book or document. So please share your impressions—no matter how new you may be to the church or how little you feel you know about its past."
- Hand out the blank grid to everyone and briefly explain each box on the left. (Some sample responses are offered on page

	FOUNDING ERA	GLORY DAYS	NOW
What was going on in our context? · local community · wider culture · wider church			
How did we understand our distinctive "calling" as a congregation? Clues: · name · location · building style and size · clergy strengths · primary programs			
What was our definition of the "right size"? How did that definition relate to: · our context · our distinctive calling			

History Analysis Chart

267 in the "Sample Grid from an Episcopal Church in a New England Town" to help you understand what fits in each box.)

- Define the eras you are going to look at. The person leading the meeting might say: "By 'founding era,' we mean the 1890s." I find that it works best if the learning team defines in advance when the most recent—other than now—"glory days" occurred (a decision you can check out with the larger group before you go into groups to work). Your 30-year attendance chart might provide a clue; so might the portrait of a beloved pastor on the wall. Basically, you are looking for the era that the largest proportion of the congregation might remember as the "good old days," about which there may still be some mourning or nostalgia.
- Identify the longest-attending person in the room. Then identify the newest church participant in the room. Ask them to stand on opposite sides of a large open area.
- Ask everyone else to line up in between these two people, based on when they started attending. (Chaos will ensue for a few minutes.)
- When people are more or less in a line, ask them to count off—1, 2, 3, 1, 2, 3. . . . (If you wish to reflect on two sets of "glory days," count to four.) Then ask people to move themselves into groups based on their numbers (still standing). This will result in three or four groupings with a wide mix of tenures in each.
- Assign each group one column on the grid (founding era, glory days, or now). Explain that they will spend the next 15 minutes filling in the three boxes in the column they have been assigned. Appoint one reporter for each group (a member of the learning team or someone else who will listen well and reflect the group conversation accurately).
- Send each group to a different part of the room to sit down and work.

Groups work (about 15 minutes, plus 5 minutes grace period to finish and return)

Reporters share findings of group (about 5 minutes each)

- Let people know there will be five minutes to hear the report of each group. Keep the reporting moving along.

- Record on a chart pad key words and phrases for each box. (Another member of the team may want to take notes on a pad, so that key phrases are captured for later even if they don't get onto the chart.)
- Thank each group for their great work.

Explore (about 15 minutes)

- Engage in dialogue with the group about the meaning of what they see on the chart. Often, the group working on the present has had a difficult time focusing a call; typically, they generate a long list of activities with no real focus. You may want to indicate that part of the purpose of this eight-month process is to discover what that focus might be.
- Invite your official historian to add other perspectives and information.

Closing comments (5 minutes)

- Review on a chart pad the next steps your planning team will be taking as the process continues. Let these leaders know how you will keep them informed as the work goes forward.

Follow-up after event

- Write up some of your findings and observations from this event, including a transcript of the grid responses.

Sample Grid from an Episcopal Church in a New England Town

	FOUNDING ERA (around 1900)	GLORY DAYS (early 1950s)	PRESENT
CONTEXT	• Small New England town (founded 1650) steeped in history • Close to a major city • Surrounded by farm country • Congregational and UU the main churches • Town attracted "Newfies" & "Novies" (Canadian immigrants) moving out from the city	• Great wave of post-war migration from cities turns town into an inner-ring suburb • Many new families with children • Challenge to town's sense of community was met by new alliances; e.g., Protestants and Catholics join to place a creche on the town green at Christmas	• New wave of growth: affluent, managerial folk drawn by schools, location, feeling of community • Ways the town used to build community don't work any more • Big fight over creche on town green reflects diversity in wider culture as well as in town
CONGREGATION	• Episcopal church a "newcomer" in old town • Located up a side street (not a dominant presence) • Naturally attracted the Canadians (Anglican) • Brought together farmers, blue-collar workers with other residents • Paternal, protecting style of clergy • Emphasis on community; everybody knew they belonged	• Rapid growth • Long-tenured pastor worked with developers (who were members) to build a bigger church across the street • New building more austere: "like a Yankee meetinghouse" • Newcomers and old-timers still found sense of belonging, but previous coherence was somewhat strained • Educating children a central concern; new education wing planned	• Wrestling for several years with diverse needs in worship • Recently established a second major Sunday service • Stressful; some older members feel intense grief or anger over changes • Our call today may still have to do with belonging, building community, but how do we do it in these new circumstances?

	FOUNDING ERA	GLORY DAYS	PRESENT
RIGHT SIZE	· Small, intimate building (wood, gothic); just right for 100 people · Pastoral-sized congregation · One pastor who knew everyone · Church seems to have provided a small "alternative space" (physical, religious, ethnic), protecting people who were different in some way from the norm	· Grew to program size with the baby boom, then dropped off from mid-1960s onward (trend similar to other mainline churches) · By the time new wing was finished, it was too much to support—was rented during week · Never really settled fully into program-size self-image and style	· We're unsettled about size · New worship service has grown, now exceeds the other · We worry that the new people will leave when they perceive the underlying stress · Our pastor wants us to grapple with these growth decisions together; some think he should be more directive

Membership Pin Maps

Location of Members

Using the "bull's-eye" map below, locate the households of active members of your congregation. Please place one mark for each family unit (or household) you identify.

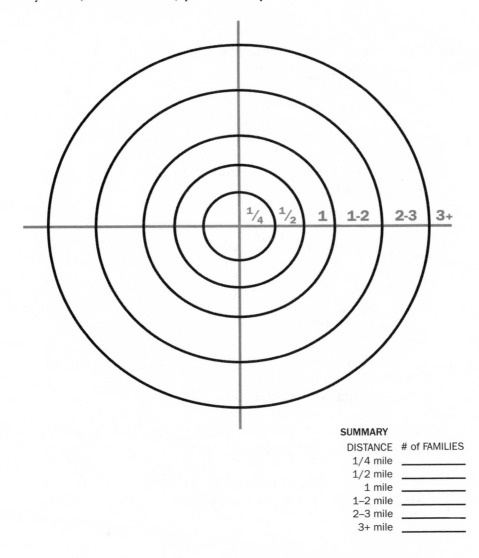

SUMMARY

DISTANCE	# of FAMILIES
1/4 mile	_____
1/2 mile	_____
1 mile	_____
1–2 mile	_____
2–3 mile	_____
3+ mile	_____

Whom Do We Draw?

What demographic groups or subcultures within your community does your congregation already have the greatest capacity to draw and incorporate?

Steps

1. Determine how many members you are going to study, based on your average Sunday attendance.

   over 151:   your last 100 members
   100–150:   your last 75 members
   under 100:   your last 50 members

2. Starting with your newest members, make an index card for each person, showing:

   name
   age
   education
   type of housing
   gender
   marital status
   employment
   type of vehicle
   income (high, middle, low)
   preferred entertainment
   length of tenure in the community

3. Play with the cards. While no one is exactly like anyone else, start arranging the cards based on similarities.

4. Try to describe the patterns that are emerging. What kinds of people does your congregation draw most naturally? Who is missing?

Neighborhood Walk

The purpose of this activity is to generate a fresh, first-hand impression of the neighborhood around the church. Have every member of the planning team spend an hour walking in the community.

Procedures

1. You should select a day when all members of your planning team will go out into the immediate neighborhood around the church.

2. Place yourselves in pairs and assign each pair a small section of the neighborhood that they will observe for one hour as they walk along.

3. Consider the following as you walk:
   a. People (what ages, sexes, races; in what activities at what times and places; languages and accents heard; etc.)
   b. Land-use patterns (single-unit residences, row houses, detached and semi-detached, multi-unit residences, stores, public services, educational, industrial, etc.)
   c. Condition of properties (signs of deteriorization, repair, decoration, etc.)
   d. Condition of streets (how wide, how heavily traveled, how clean, etc.)
   e. If you have lived in the area for a while or have attended the church for a while, ask yourself what has changed since you first started to visit the community.
   f. If you are new to the community, ask yourself what is surprising to you on your walk.
   g. What are you seeing on your walk that would not be noticeable or significant if you were traveling through this area by car?

4. Return to the church and write down as a group the learnings and observations from the walk.

5. Review the list of learnings and offer some guesses about the significance of your observations for the future ministry of your church.

Network Maps

From *Studying Congregations: A New Handbook,* edited by
Nancy T. Ammerman, Jackson Carroll, Carl S. Dudley, and
William McKinney (Nashville: Abingdon Press, 1998), pp. 51–52.
Used by permission.

For this exercise you will need several detailed maps of your city or
locale attached to corkboard, push-pins with colored ends, and yarn.
You will also need several large sheets of newsprint or butcher paper
and marker pens. Your work may be expedited if you have a copy of
your local telephone directory handy as well.

Members can have fun completing this exercise after a Wednesday-
night supper or as part of various classes or group meetings and then
sharing discoveries during an all-congregation gathering. The exercise
should take about 45 minutes to an hour to complete and discuss.

Begin by dividing participants into groups representing what
congregants feel are significant constituencies within the congregation.
Perhaps your congregation is composed of many long-time residents of
the community and numerous newcomers, or perhaps several ethnic
groups are prominent. In any case, you will want to ask representatives
of each constituency to sit together at a table. Identifying the various
constituencies in your congregation will likely be illuminating in itself.

Next you will want to ask for volunteers at each table who are
willing to speak about their activities and memberships in the community. You are not trying to find individuals who are strictly representative of everyone around the table. You will have opportunity to talk
about the differences later.

When the volunteers have been designated, ask each one to write
on the butcher paper answers to the following questions:

- Where do you live?
- Where do you work? Where do the other members of your household work? If you are not currently employed, where do you
  spend the most time during the day?

- If you have children, where do they attend school?
- If you have pets, where is your veterinarian?
- Where do your parents and siblings live? If your parents are deceased, where are they buried?
- Where do your two closest friends reside?
- Where do you do your grocery shopping?
- Where do you purchase your clothing?
- Where are the clubs or voluntary organizations you attend? If you participate in any other groups—for example, Bible studies, yoga groups, or support groups—where do they meet? If you play golf, tennis, or softball; work out at a gym; or attend football, basketball, or baseball games regularly, where do you do that?

When volunteers have written the answers to these questions, you will begin assembling the map for the volunteer at your table. Place a thumbtack on your map at the location of the volunteer's home. Then locate your congregation and place the first push-pin. After that, locate the places the volunteer identified in answer to each of the questions asked above. Insert a push-pin at each location. After each pin has been inserted, group members can cut the yarn to attach to each pin.

After the volunteer's map is finished, encourage those at each table to speak about the patterns revealed. Ask group members how they imagine that their own network maps might differ from or be similar to that of the volunteer. When you reconvene in the larger group, you will want to present each group's findings and discuss the similarities or differences among the maps. What causes these variations? How do these maps help you understand your congregation's context better?

Community Leader Interviews

Adapted from chapter 4 of *Raising the Roof: The Pastoral to Program Size Transition* by Alice Mann (Bethesda, Md.: Alban Institute, 2001). Used by permission.

This method produces more than information—it builds relationships.

- Make a list of four to seven community leaders from different sectors of life. Possible candidates might be: school superintendent, police chief, head of social services, town planner, a denominational official familiar with your area, and a few neighboring religious leaders.
- Assign one or two team members to handle each interview.
- Schedule a 30-minute appointment with each community leader.
- Tell the leader right at the beginning that you have three basic questions to cover during this short interview:

  1. What impressions, if any, do you have of our congregation?
  2. What trends and challenges are you seeing in our community today?
  3. What unmet needs do you see in our community?

- I strongly suggest that you do not ask, "What should our church be doing?" I have known many community leaders to balk at a request to tell the church what its business should be. That's your job. Ask them to talk about what they know best: the conditions and needs they confront every day in their own work.
- Be prepared for some awkward moments when you ask for impressions of your congregation. These leaders may not know who you are, where you are located, or what you have ever done as a church. Asking this question gives you a reality check on whether your congregation has much of a profile in the wider community—and whether the information others have about you is correct. Thank them for whatever they offer.
- From the notes you have taken during the interview, write up a brief summary of the responses you received to your three questions, using as many of the person's own words and phrases as you can.
- Bring these reports back to the planning team for discussion.

Snapshot Page, Ministry Area Profile

A "snapshot page" from a sample Percept Ministry Area Profile is reproduced on the following pages. Used by permission of Percept Group, Inc.

"Snapshot" Page from a Percept "Ministry Area Profile"

Snapshot

Coordinates: 42:23:02 71:11:79
Date: 6/11/99

Prepared For:
Massachusetts Conference UCC
ImagineArea #4
W. Cambridge, MA

Study Area Definition:
3.0 Mile Radius

Populations and Households

■ Population
■ Households

Primary U.S. Lifestyles Segments—1999

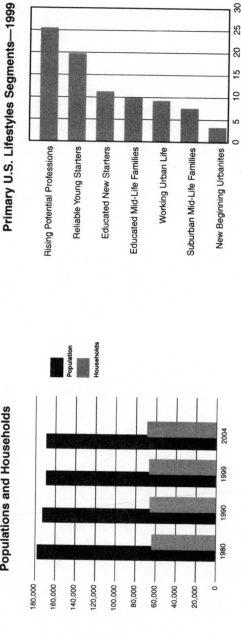

Rising Potential Professions

Reliable Young Starters

Educated New Starters

Educated Mid-Life Families

Working Urban Life

Suburban Mid-Life Families

New Beginning Urbanites

Percentage of Households

The population in the study area has decreased by 4142 persons or 2.4% since 1990 and is projected to increase by 41 persons, or 0.0% between 1999 and 2004. The number of households has increased by 1009, or 1.5% since 1990 and is projected to increase by 1662, or 2.4% between 1999 and 2004.

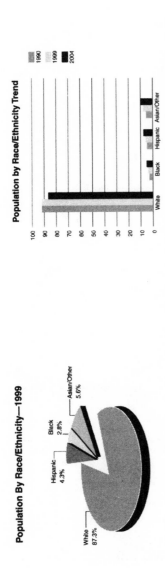

Population By Race/Ethnicity—1999

Asian/Other 5.6%

Black 2.8%

Hispanic 4.3%

White 87.3%

Population by Race/Ethnicity Trend

1990 1999 2004

White Black Hispanic Asian/Other

Between 1999 and 2004, the White population is projected to decrease by 4252 persons and to decrease from 87.3% to 84.7% of the total population. The Black population is projected to increase by 850 persons and to increase from 2.8% to 3.3% of the total. The Hispanic/Latino population is projected to increase by 1151 persons and to increase from 4.3% to 4.9% of the total. The Asian/Other population is projected to increase by 2292 persons and to increase from 5.6% to 7.0% of the total population

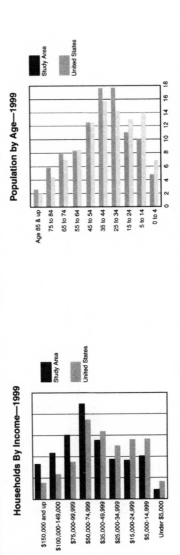

Households By Income—1999

Study Area
United States

$150,000 and up
$100,000-149,000
$75,000-99,999
$50,000-74,999
$35,000-49,999
$25,000-34,999
$15,000-24,999
$5,000-14,999
Under $5,000

Population by Age—1999

Study Area
United States

Age 85 & up
75 to 84
65 to 74
55 to 64
45 to 54
35 to 44
25 to 34
15 to 24
5 to 14
0 to 4

0 2 4 6 8 10 12 14 16 18

The average household income in the study area is $69965 a year compared to the U.S average of $53198. The average age in the study area is 39.9 and is projected to increase to 40.8 by 2004. The average age in the U.S. is 36.5 and is projected to increase to 37.3 by 2004.

(800) 442-5277

© 1998-99 Percept Group, Inc.

Sources: Percept, National Decision Systems, U.S. Census Bureau

ID# 20338:6-543

Worksheet for Studying Ministry Area Profile

ANALYSIS OF MAJOR POPULATION GROUPS (LIFESTYLE SEGMENTS)

name of group	% of pop.	characteristics	est. % of cong.	likely life concerns	likely program preferences	church strengths that might appeal to this group	what we might add or change to reach this group

The Abilene Paradox Goes to Church

Jerald L. Kirkpatrick

Excerpted from *Congregations* (May-June 2002). Used by permission.

The letter was crystal clear: "You have precipitously dismissed the most valuable member of the church staff. And now you will pay the price."

So it seemed. After 40 years of employment, the choir director at Sunnyvale Church was being let go. When the pastor and the personnel committee chair asked her to retire, she left the meeting in a huff: "I don't know what you're talking about."

Reaction was swift. One-third of the choir left for another church. The organist resigned in solidarity with the director. Word got around town that after years of faithful service, Sunnyvale was cutting Louise loose. What a shame. And what a surprise!

Prolonged Indecision

Well, not so great a surprise as one might think. Investigation disclosed that a sizable group of church members had had serious reservations about Louise for years—her choice of music, her manner of dealing with people, even her musical ability. Those people had repeatedly registered complaints to the liturgy and personnel committees, but no action was taken.

The committees themselves often discussed Louise's job performance, going so far as to warn her, "Things have got to change." For more than 20 years, it seemed, the committees were constantly preoccupied with changing Louise and the music program.

Nothing changed. Louise continued to do as she had always done. She bullied the pastor, ignored the critics, and verbally abused the choir. Her manner became more brusque. Finally, when the pastor and personnel committee could stand it no longer, they acted. But the reaction hurt the church. Members blamed one another for the debacle, even changing sides in the debate. Before the dust settled, the pastor had left; the personnel chair had resigned; the church was divided.

Why hadn't things changed? Why didn't the people do what they wanted to do 30 years earlier? The answer is easy. The "Abilene Paradox" had come to church.

Feelings Concealed

The Abilene Paradox is a management concept introduced more than 25 years ago by Jerry B. Harvey.[1] Harvey asks why organizations don't do what their members agree should be done. His concept is based on an ill-fated outing he and his family made from Coleman to Abilene, Texas, on a hot summer night to eat mediocre cafeteria food. No one really wanted to go, but each agreed to make the trip, thinking everyone else favored the idea. Harvey contends that had family members disclosed their true desire to stay at home, no conflict would have surfaced later about having gone.

Old First Church had weathered many storms in its downtown location, including attempts to move the congregation to the suburbs. In recent years, however, a new generation had become active, and plans were under way to build a new sanctuary and office complex at the present site. The board appointed a building committee and the committee hired an architect. After extensive listening sessions, the architect took what he had learned and produced a preliminary plan.

When the architectural model was shown to members, nothing seemed right. The bell tower was the wrong size. The sanctuary was not oriented properly. The traffic pattern in the office complex was unsatisfactory. The architect countered every complaint with survey results: "When we asked you about this, you said, . . ."

During this phase, First Church called a new senior pastor. In the first meeting after his arrival, he summed up what committee members already knew. No one believed the church needed new buildings. Redecorating and minor remodeling would suffice. The committee paid the architect and thanked him for his time. The plans disappeared into a file cabinet, never to be seen again.

What had happened? The committee—and by extension, the whole congregation—had taken action contrary to the data it had for dealing with problems. As a result, problems were compounded rather than solved.[2] That, in a nutshell, is the Abilene Paradox. No one wanted to be the "odd one out" who disagreed with the other committee members. Although countless parking-lot discussions may have centered on the idea's wrong-headedness, individual members could not bring themselves to do what they privately agreed must be done. No one wanted to be exposed to humiliation, ostracism, or criticism, so each person concealed his or her feelings from the group. I am reminded of Adam, who said, "I heard the sound of you in the garden, and I was afraid, because I was naked; and I hid myself" (Gen. 3:12).

Resisting a Firm Decision

Some years ago, when I served a congregation in southwestern Oklahoma, we decided we needed an associate pastor. The moderator appointed a committee and it went to work. We asked the judicatory for names of prospective ministers and began the search. Oddly, no potential candidate seemed to have the right qualifications. As we winnowed the portfolios, we discovered that virtually every one had some deficiency; some were unqualified for any position. Finding no candidate who met our expectations, we asked the judicatory for more names. Even with two subsequent lists, we couldn't agree on anyone. Finally, someone in the judicatory office said, "I'm not sure this person is available, but you might try her."

We were elated. Here was a live one. We telephoned her; she was interested. We did a phone interview and liked what we heard. She agreed to visit us.

After the visit, at which we had met her and her family, we sat down to see if we wanted to negotiate with her. Here was the moment of truth. As the discussion went back and forth, I first thought we were ready to call her. Then reservations began to surface about her family. I pointed out that we were calling her, not hiring her family. More discussion followed. People wondered if she would stay with us only long enough to get a church of her own. I countered that two or three years were better than none.

Finally, it became clear that no one wanted to call an associate. Each had held this opinion for some time, but no one had expressed reservations in the committee. I understood then why it had been so difficult to reach this stage. We didn't want to get there. We were desperately looking for a reason not to call an associate. It was too painful to admit that we had neither the money nor the size to support another full-time pastor.

Although it was difficult to tell the candidate, the committee chair confessed our predicament. She graciously accepted our decision, but did point out that we had strung her along for quite a while.

A few months later, we hired a part-time youth director through a local employment agency. We all agreed that we had done the right thing.

Phony Conflict

Why did we focus on the candidate's family or her career plans while hiding our agreement not to hire anyone at all? Harvey calls this behavior "phony conflict."

Phony conflict occurs in the Abilene Paradox because people agree on the actions they want to take and then do the opposite. The resulting anger, frustration, and scapegoating—generally termed *conflict*— are not based on real differences. Rather they stem from the protective reactions that occur when a decision that no one believed in or was committed to in the first place goes sour. In fact, as a paradox within a paradox, such conflict is symptomatic of agreement.[3]

I believe that my own strong advocacy for calling an associate made the committee's job harder. Since no one wanted to disagree with the pastor, each person went through the motions, assuming everyone else was on board. In fact, my response to questions about the candidate's family or motivations could be seen as bullying. Had the committee failed to discover that the congregation could not afford another professional staff person, we might have gone down the rocky road to Abilene, blaming each other when things did not turn out well.

Blame Game

That, in fact, did happen in a church served by one of my old classmates. The senior pastor lobbied for an associate; the committee found one and recommended him to the congregation. All sorts of reservations were evident, but no one spoke up. Finally, after two or three years of difficulty, in which the associate was judged a "wrong fit" and the senior pastor was characterized as a martinet, members resorted to expressing their frustration and anger in the offering plate. Both senior and associate pastors had to leave. Both were damaged, spiritually and professionally.

What is the alternative to "going to Abilene"? What can leaders and pastors do to avoid this potential disaster? Harvey thinks organizations can do many things; by extension, so can congregations. People must break the cycle of silence and blame that accompany the Abilene Paradox.

Speaking Truth in Love

The best way is open confrontation—preferably in a group setting.[4] The accuser must tell the truth—speak the truth in love, we church people are disposed to say. The accuser must own up to his or her position and prepare to take the consequences. This approach lets the group know that the accuser fears the committee is about to make a decision contrary to the church's best interests.

One might say something like this:

> I know I may have said things before that made you think I was supportive of what we are about to do, but I have had other thoughts. I don't think we will succeed in doing this. In fact, I believe we will be acting against the church's interests if we do it. I wonder if anyone else thinks as I do. Actually, I'm pretty sure most of you do. If we don't do something now, we will recommend a project to the church that is bound to fail, and hurt us in the process. I need to know where you stand.

The accuser can expect two kinds of results—technical and existential. For the accuser, the existential experience seems more important.

At my Oklahoma church, we experienced a technical result. We stopped negotiations with our candidate, regrouped, and hired a part-time youth director. Everyone agreed that our change of direction was warranted, and the passage of time confirmed that.

On the other hand, Sunnyvale Church suffered existentially. Many people felt hurt by the forced retirement of the music director. A sense of failure pervaded the congregation, and people looked for a scapegoat.

The church did not resolve anything until members admitted their own complicity.

How does the Abilene Paradox come to church? It comes just as it comes to any other organization. All organizations are made up of human beings, and, as prophets have told us, humanity is prone to act against its own best interests. How is the Abilene Paradox prevented? One does that by recognizing the symptoms, confronting them, and being forthright with each other. Or, as we say in church, by speaking the truth in love.

Notes

1. Jerry B. Harvey, "The Abilene Paradox: The Management of Agreement," *Organizational Dynamics* (Summer, 1974). Harvey is professor of management science at George Washington University, Washington, D.C.
2. Ibid., 20.
3. Ibid., 28f.
4. Ibid., 32f.

A Short Guide to *Lectio Divina*

From *Discover Your Spiritual Type: A Guide to Individual and Congregational Growth* by Corinne Ware (Bethesda, Md.: Alban Institute, 1995). Used by permission.

Select a scripture passage.

Lectio: Read the passage carefully, getting the sequence and detail without thinking too much about the meaning. Imagine the time of day, season of the year, smells of the land, sounds of the countryside, the human touches—all the elements that would make this scene real to you. Transport yourself into the setting using your imagination.

Meditatio: Read the scripture again. Why is there a record of this particular event or saying? What is the significance of this passage in the large scheme of things? What does this piece mean? How does that affect an understanding of God? Of conduct? Do you see yourself in any of the characters in the passage?

Oratio: Allow your feelings to surface as you read the passage again. Do you feel happy, sad, angry, or guilty? Silently or verbally talk this through with God; tell God what you feel about what you have read. Comment in your prayer on anything in the passage to which you respond.

Contemplatio: Sit quietly, breathe deeply and regularly, and let your mind go blank. As you quiet your inner self, simply listen in your heart. If you receive some impression or thought, quietly notice it; then focus your attention on remaining open. If you have no thoughts or impressions, return your mind to the scripture passage. After a while, open your eyes, rested and refreshed, expressing gratitude for your experience.

An Oral Tradition
Approach to Bible Study

From *In Dialogue with Scripture: An Episcopal Guide to Studying the Bible,* Linda L. Grenz, ed., Adult Education and Leadership Development (New York: Episcopal Church Center, 1993), pp.88–89. Used by permission, courtesy of The Domestic and Foreign Missionary Society of the Protestant Episcopal Church USA.

This method and variations on it have been used throughout many parts of the world. It is a variation on the base Christian communities methods of South America.*

STEP 1.   Each person shares his or her experience in the areas of prayer from the session before. If this is a first session, begin with STEP 2.

STEP 2.   Read the passage slowly. (One person reads out loud.)

STEP 3.   Recall the word or phrase that catches your attention.

STEP 4.   Each person shares the word or phrase within the group.

STEP 5.   Read the passage again (opposite sex of the first reader).

STEP 6.   Think out/write: "Where does this passage touch my life, my community, our nation, our world today?" Think about all the people you encounter, not just those in your own "circle of friends." (three to five minutes)

STEP 7.   Each person shares the above: "I . . . ."

STEP 8.   Read the passage out loud again.

STEP 9.   Think out/write: "From what I have heard and shared, what does God want me to do or be this week? How does God invite me to change?" (three to five minutes)

---

*This method was published in E-Share (Office of Evangelism Ministries) under the name "The African Method." Since its origins are not agreed upon (some say African; others, South American or USA), and the name reinformces the concept of Africa as a single country (rather than a huge continent with many countries and cultures), the Adult Education and Evangelism staff officers have decided to change the name.

STEP 10.   Each person shares the above: "I . . . ."

STEP 11.   Each person prays for the person on their right, naming what was shared in STEP 10, and repeats that prayer daily until the group meets again.

NOTE: In steps 3, 7, and 10, be brief. Do not elaborate, explain, or teach. That which is said is offered to the center of the group. Others do not respond to or build on what is said as if they were in a discussion group.

A Time of Centering
at the Start of a Meeting

From *Discerning Your Congregation's Future: A Strategic and Spiritual Approach* by Roy M. Oswald and Robert E. Friedrich, Jr. (Bethesda, Md.: Alban Institute, 1996).

The practice of centering at the beginning of a gathering allows people to let go of all the baggage they brought with them to a session. Centering allows people to focus on themselves for a few minutes. Here's the general outline:

Ask people to close their eyes and look at the interior landscape of their lives. Encourage them to take deep breaths to help them relax physically. Explain that we relax best when the chest, neck, and head are in a straight line, our feet are flat on the floor, and our hands and arms fall loosely on the lap.

Encourage participants to loosen areas of tension in their bodies, and invite them to become aware of the predominant feelings rumbling around inside them. They need not do anything with those feelings but should just note that the feelings are there and affect their participation. Ask them to become aware of their self-image at the moment. Once again, do not ask them to change that self-image but simply to become aware of it.

After encouraging this heightened awareness of their bodies, feelings, and self-image, invite participants to become aware of any baggage they have brought with them to the session, such as concerns heavy on their hearts or responsibilities left uncompleted. Because they can do nothing about these concerns at the moment, invite participants to package them up and send them to God. Suggest they take a few seconds to offer a silent prayer, unburdening themselves for the duration of the session. Invite them to give themselves the gift of being totally present and open to fellow participants and the content of the session.

Finally, invite them to try to view themselves through the eyes of God—with eyes of grace. Remind them that regardless of what feelings they have had rumbling about inside or their self-image, at this very moment God absolutely delights in their being. They are unique in the universe, and God holds their specialness close to God's heart. In God's omnipresence, God has eyes only for them. Through their baptisms, they are connected to this God for eternity; there is absolutely nothing that can separate them from the love of God. Invite them to sit for a few moments and become aware of how good it feels to do absolutely nothing except enjoy the peace of God.

After a few minutes of silence, ask participants to become aware of where the group needs to be particularly open, in a listening stance, as you move to the agenda of the evening. Because the purpose of each meeting will be different, try to outline where you need to enter a discernment process, seeking the Spirit's guidance on the matters at hand.

Often it is helpful to offer meditations on sections of appropriate biblical passages, sometimes with opportunity for group discussion. Discussion should be kept brief and to the point. Some passages for meditation will come from the Hebrew scriptures, others from the Christian scriptures. The passages are meant to lend a broader, theological connection to the work being done.

In any event, do not give way to the temptation to skip over this time for personal spiritual growth in order to "get down to business." These times help people make the transition from their daily activities to the spiritual business of the session, and they pay rich dividends in the increased ability of participants to focus on the job at hand.